For Donald
with fond memories

[barcode: D0630151]

Secular Revelations

Secular Revelations

❧ THE CONSTITUTION OF THE UNITED STATES
AND CLASSIC AMERICAN LITERATURE

MITCHELL MELTZER

HARVARD UNIVERSITY PRESS
Cambridge, Massachusetts, and London, England   2005

Library of Congress Cataloging-in-Publication Data

Meltzer, Mitchell.
    Secular revelations : the Constitution of the United States and classic
American literature / Mitchell Meltzer.
        p. cm.
    Includes index.
    ISBN 0-674-01912-1 (alk. paper)
    1. American literature—19th century—History and criticism.
2. Nationalism and literature—United States—History—19th
century. 3. Literature and state—United States—History—19th
century. 4. National characteristics, American, in literature.
5. Constitutional history—United States. 6. United States.
Constitution. 7. Secularism in literature. 8. Revelation in literature.
I. Title.

PS217.N38M45 2005
810.9'358—dc22   2005046491

To my beloved L.R.B.
אשת חיל

Contents

Acknowledgments

Writing may be a solitary activity, but making a book is a social act, and there are a number of people whose help it is my pleasure to acknowledge. In working on *Secular Revelations* I have incurred the greatest debt to, and derived the greatest pleasure from, my friendship with Professor Angus Fletcher. Like many before me, I have stolen freely from his fecund, subtle, and altogether extraordinary imaginative intelligence and learning. For his generosity and his unflagging support I am permanently grateful.

I want as well to record my appreciation to Lindsay Waters of Harvard University Press who exhibited unfailing kindness and consideration through some difficult moments along the path of publication.

Professors Joan Richardson and Jacqueline Di Salvo of the Graduate Center of the City University of New York provided crucial support at an early stage of this project and made useful suggestions for revision of a first draft of this manuscript. Marc Kaminsky and Derek Miller were early on, and throughout, sources of needful encouragement and wisdom. I am especially grateful to Professor Steven Goldberg and Alan Rosner, not only for the time they took for critically reading the entire manuscript but also for the great pleasure of their company and their conversation. I must also mention the late Carol Saltus, a great inspiration in many respects, and a model of literary passion.

Thanks also to Sarah Weber of Rare Books and Special Collections of Notre Dame University for her helpfulness in procuring the illustrations of the fugio cent from the Robert H. Gore Jr. Numismatic Collection.

I will have difficulty ever repaying the loving encouragement and the tireless editorial commitment of my wife, Laurie Binder, but I am determined to keep trying. And what I owe our two almost perfect children, Benjamin and Rebekah, is beyond what I can articulate, and more than they will ever fully comprehend.

Secular Revelations

The Constitution
and American Literature

We have it in our power to begin the world over
again. A situation similar to the present, hath not
happened since the days of Noah until now.

Tom Paine, *Common Sense*, 1776

What has the Constitution to do with American literature? This argument of this book is that, in fact, both the formation and the distinctive qualities of American literature in its classic period, known also
as the American Renaissance, derive from the United States Constitution. The attempt to explain how so rhetorically listless a legal and
political document as the Constitution, rarely alluded to in the literature itself, can in any way account for such original, often outrageous,
literary masterpieces as Herman Melville's *Moby-Dick*, Walt Whitman's *Leaves of Grass*, and the *Essays* of Ralph Waldo Emerson requires a retelling of the story of the nation's peculiar founding, issuing
in the Constitution as a secular revelation.

The otherwise familiar narrative of the Constitution's framing will
here take as its focus the problem most clearly articulated by Hannah
Arendt in her study *Of Revolution* as "the most elementary predicament" confronting modern political life, namely the need to overcome
the "profound instability" that results from the "the emancipation of
the secular realm from the tutelage of the Church."[1] In other words,
how can human beings, absent the sanction of some transcendent or
mythical realm, lay a secure and durable foundation for political life?

A higher, more-than-human sanction—whether the source of such
authority derives from the sanctified traditions of time immemorial, or
a theory like the divinity long said to hedge a king—has always seemed
a necessary condition for the creation of a lasting polity. The solution
of the American Founders to this quintessentially modern dilemma re-

sulted in what this book calls a secular revelation. The idea is self-contradictory, for the secular can be defined as precisely that which is not revealed, just as a revelation is what we would not know by secular means alone. What I will argue is that a secular revelation is indeed self-contradictory, but only in the sense that any paradox involves a self-contradiction, for that is what the Constitution is—a profound, living paradox. It is a strange hybrid. On the surface the Constitution is an entirely secular text, without so much as a mention of the divine, and yet just beneath this godless surface flows the force of a pure revelation. It is by means of this very paradox that the Constitution both exercises and evades the uncanniness of its authority.

A moment's reflection will reveal that America's founding document exercises a most peculiar kind of status in American life. It is not merely that few, if any, texts of the modern world have begot an interpretive practice denser, more diverse, or methodologically more self-conscious—and this for a people notoriously scornful of history and tradition. Engrossed on antique parchment, this product of the late eighteenth century is felt by Americans to emanate so profound an aura that the world's most powerful, and arguably one of its most aggressive and skeptical, nation-states continues to submit to the Constitution as the ultimate source of its political authority. There is not, and never has been, a politically potent national voice that questions the document's status, that decries the Constitution as an old and burdensome inheritance. On the contrary, the very epithet, "unconstitutional," continues to bespeak an unquestioned and absolute standard of judgment. Conflicts engaging citizens' deepest convictions are channeled into disputes not over the legitimacy of the Constitution but only over its proper interpretation.

Even now, at the outset of the twenty-first century, and notwithstanding the recent, decades-long resurgence of fundamentalist Christianity in American political life, it is striking that there has been no widespread public movement to insist that the Constitution submit itself to a higher authority. Rather, there has been a continued assumption of absolute consistency between Scripture and the eighteenth-century "bundle of compromises."[2] In the case, for instance, of the bitterly disputed *Roe v. Wade* over which some have been willing either to spill blood themselves or to apologize for those who do, there has been no argument that the 1787 text, if it allows such interpretive findings, must itself be illegitimate, only that certain judges and justices had in fact violated that Constitution. It may well be that the Christian

Right in its currently emboldened incarnation does aim for a theocratic polity in which their interpretations of ancient Hebrew and Greek texts determine the contours of American political life, but it is notable that they themselves seem sincerely to believe—however preposterously— that such an outcome is not merely consistent with, but actually re- quired, by the 1787 Constitution of the United States.

One could perhaps argue that this is an overstatement of the Con- stitution's authority for all spectrums of American political opinion, mistaking the Constitution of We the People for the People themselves, and that the ultimate authority in the United States resides not in the letter of the text but in the sovereign People themselves. The People, after all, are free to amend the Constitution; indeed, they are free even to replace it. Although it is true that the Constitution provides for a clear and occasionally exercised right of amendment (though in fact seriously limited by Article V of the body of the Constitution), the very procedure of amendment, as well as that for the convening of a new Constitutional Convention, follows clear constitutional provisions. It is therefore dubious that any authority, the People included, can be said to subsume that of the text itself.[3]

For the Constitution is not merely a legal or a political document. In regard to the world of American culture, it is as much cosmogonical as it is governmental: the question it attempts to answer is not only who shall rule and by what means—the question raised by the victory of the Revolution—but how to begin from a blankness, how to estab- lish a new identity, how to consciously found a civilizational life without an inhibiting arbitrariness.[4] In the ordinary course of events, peoples appear and nations arise over many long years, across ages, and their past is consequently lost in a primeval mist, stretching back to so-called time immemorial. Historians can study the remaining ev- idence—and DNA now permits increasing, and increasingly disturbing, exactitude and accuracy—to reconstruct the movement of the peoples who would form a so-called People (the Russians, for instance, or the French, or the Chinese) and trace the suppression of some peoples along with the dominance of others in that long forgotten formation. But history is not memory, and it is memory by which people order their identities, whether or not the memory bears any relation to his- tory.[5] The Russians, the French, and the Chinese are as-if eternal. But in the new nation of the United States, history and memory become close to identical, at least in the crucial realm of national origin. It was, as they called it, the New World. America's founding racist violence—

the extirpation of the native population and the enslavement of Africans—thus occurred in the unforgiving light of history. But it is just this nakedness of American origins that ironically makes the construction of an American beginning both possible and desirable.

But one might object from the start that it is not the Constitution that gave birth to the United States, but rather the *Declaration of Independence*. Is not that document of the Revolution most often thought of as the touchstone of American political inception? It was on the anniversary of the Declaration, after all, that both Nat Turner and John Brown planned their radical attacks on slavery, that Walt Whitman chose as the date on which to publish his first edition of *Leaves of Grass*, that Thoreau set out for his experiment in living on Walden Pond. With its ringing affirmations that "all men are created equal," and their "unnalienable right to Life, Liberty and the pursuit of Happiness," the Declaration of Independence amounts to something like the very conscience of American political identity. But of course for all its eloquence, the document did not in itself accomplish the colonies' independence—that required nine long years of war's bloodshed and cruelty. Nor did the independence that came from the 1783 victory in that war itself transform the former colonists, now no longer British but citizens of new states, into a single people or one nation. And yet, within not much more than a decade, they assumed precisely that status: the American people of the United States; and both the peoplehood and the united nation were creations of the federal Constitution.

However much the Declaration of Independence may rightly be considered America's conscience, it is the Constitution of the United States that gave birth to the nation's consciousness. Indeed, its very first words, "We the People"—notably not We the New Yorkers and the Virginians and the Georgians, et cetera; nor We the People of the sovereign states—these words do not merely invoke the People, they very nearly create it.[6] It is only mildly polemical to insist that the very notion of the United States is, first and foremost, a sheer verbal invention, analogous to the World in the first chapter of Genesis, created by words alone. Written—or to use the traditional term, "framed"—in 1787, and ratified in 1789, the Constitution originated a polity, transformed a voluntary confederation of indisputably sovereign states into a single Nation, and the inhabitants of those new states into one People.

Thus it would seem only a reasonable assumption that the relation between the United States Constitution and American literature has been extensively examined. This assumption is only strengthened by the trend of literary criticism in recent decades to interrogate any text that promises even the remotest relation to literature—particularly any text susceptible to political interpretation—and to make it part of the increasingly capacious canon created by and for the academic discipline of English. Given this often extraordinary extension of the domain deemed appropriate to literary—or as it is just as often now referred to, cultural—studies, what turns out to be a striking paucity of literary critical reference to America's founding document must come as something of a puzzling surprise.[7]

And yet it seems as if the relative meagerness of comment about the larger cultural force of the Constitution is not, in fact, limited to the realm of literary study; the puzzle is a more general one.[8] Consider the testimony of two scholars who undertook major studies of the Constitution for the underwhelming celebration of its bicentennial in 1989. Michael Kammen begins his historical survey, *A Machine That Would Go of Itself: The Constitution in American Culture,* by noting that, notwithstanding the enormous accumulation of scholarship on and about the Constitution, his own work would be the first attempt in two centuries "to describe the place of the Constitution in the public consciousness and symbolic life of the American people."[9] Indeed, "the most revealing cluster of pertinent source material"—the papers from the Centennial Commission of 1887 and from the Sesquicentennial of 1937—had remained unexamined through all the intervening years. Similarly, the political scientist George Anastaplo, in the introduction to *The Constitution of 1787: A Commentary,* notes his own surprise in finding that prior to his own attempt, the Constitution had attracted in its first two hundred years not a single commentator who cared to consider the document independently of its accompanying "judicial and other official interpretations and applications." In fact, as Anastaplo observes, there had till then not yet been written "any other book-length, section-by-section commentary of the United States Constitution proceeding primarily from the original text itself."[10]

I will argue that in fact the Constitution became in time the very spring of American literary imagination, and that there exists an unstated constitutional poetics. This constitutional poetics provides the dynamic framework, conscious or not, for the nation's classic literature, and the so-called American Renaissance is best understood as a renaissance indeed of the founding mode of secular revelation. Aside from commentary on an important early speech of Abraham Lincoln's, and some rather brief remarks on Nathaniel Hawthorne and some few others, I will focus on three writers working in representative genres: Emerson as an essayist, Whitman as a poet, and Melville as a novelist. I am not thereby implying that these are the three "greatest," "most important," or even "most representative" writers, only that they are prime instances of a new American literature, different in important respects from the English literature before them, and in themselves of undoubted significance.

Given my ambitious claim to demonstrate a link between the Constitution and classic American literature, it is wise to remember the old saw that there is nothing new under the sun. I do not purport to be overturning the decades of thought and comment on the literature of the United States. On the contrary, this sequence of essayistic arguments is meant to establish one single new perspective—in a word, the constitutional—as a way of understanding many of the most familiar and venerable insights into this now long-studied subject.

I use three terms throughout this work that require brief preliminary clarification. "Founders," a name often used to refer strictly to the men who served at the Constitutional Convention of 1787, is used here more generally to describe the major participants of the movement from Independence through the first few national administrations, the generation including men like Thomas Jefferson and John Adams, who were in Europe during the Convention, and women as well, such as Mercy Warren and Abigail Adams whose gender barred them from formal positions of influence.

The second term, "America" and "American," can refer, of course, to two continents and a host of nations, but in this context they refer exclusively to the population of the former British colonies—though by no means were all of their inhabitants British—of the North American mainland.

The third term that may raise questions is the use of the word "distinctive" to apply to a national literature. What would require a sustained argument to establish is here merely assumed—since the argument is an old and familiar one—that whatever the considerable merits of writers such as Edward Taylor and Anne Bradstreet, or Washington Irving and James Fenimore Cooper, and however clearly American in their subject matter and some of their thematic concerns, none of these writers so abandoned British literary forms as to offer what the next century would call the shock of the new. So it seemed to their contemporaries, and so it has seemed since. Distinctive does not, of course, mean utterly different. Differences and similarities are matters of degree only; but it is precisely that degree which is of interest.

PART ONE

The Constitution as a Secular Revelation

CHAPTER ONE

At the Beginning

In the beginning all the world was America.

JOHN LOCKE, *Second Treatise of Government*, 1690

There is certainly nothing new about the newness of the New World. As a dream it is millennia older than what Europe named the New World of the Americas.[1] Finding access to a pristine realm, a land fresh from Creation, whether named Arcadia or the Garden of the Hesperides, cherubim-guarded Eden or the lost continent of Atlantis, is among the most ancient of human desires. When the hyperactive curiosity and enflamed acquisitiveness of the European Renaissance sent men ranging across oceans where by accident they found the new lands of America, it seemed as if they had transported this timeless mythic wish into the unadorned light of history. What had always been unreachable fantasy had suddenly become a real place that could be mapped, accessible to exploration. So incredible did this seem that two decades after Columbus's first voyage, the pious Humanist Thomas More, in imagining such a New World, named it, as if still in a half-playful disbelief, *Utopia* (1516), Latin for *No Place*. Two centuries later, John Locke in his *Treatises on Government* (1690) could write with neither skepticism nor irony that "In the beginning all the world was America."[2]

But for those who came not merely to explore the New World but to inhabit it—to make ordinary, quotidian lives within its deeply unfamiliar environment—this unprecedented merging of the mythic and the historical resulted in some very odd effects. As late as the second half of the eighteenth century the French settler St. John de Crèvecoeur was still asking, "What then, is the American, this new man?" The modern art critic Harold Rosenberg offered a helpful commentary to

Crèvecoeur's famous question: "To be a new man is not a condition but an effort—an effort that follows a revelation in behalf of which existing forms are discarded as irrelevant or are radically revised."[3] Surprisingly enough, the developing societies formed by these New World settlers—at least those who inhabited what would become the mainland British colonies—began to experience some of the peculiar aspects of that unhoused condition and effort we call modernity. The historian Jon Butler, surveying the colonies from 1680 to the verge of the American Revolution, has gone so far as to describe these mainland colonies as, in fact, "distinctively modern":

> They became ethnically and nationally diverse, not homogenous. They developed transatlantic and international economies that supported a vigorous domestic trade and production. Their politics looked ahead to the large-scale participatory politics of modern societies. They exhibited the modern penchant for power, control and authority over both humanity and nature that brooked few limitations or questions about their propriety. And they displayed a religious pluralism that dwarfed the mild religious diversity found in any early modern European nation.[4]

Notwithstanding the Europeans' Edenic fantasies, the settlers had not, of course, returned to their origins but had instead become as strangers in a strange land. Most unlike the long-settled humanity they found in the New World whose mythic security we endorse by referring to them as "native" peoples, the European settlers had no deep roots to which they could cling, no complex connectedness to the places they seized as their own.

The religious historian, Mircea Eliade, called such a sense of rootedness, of a people's possessing a mythically coherent attachment to their land, an *illud tempus*, a *that time*. The *illud tempus* is a nonarbitrary point of beginning, a ground of absolute origin, when the really real for them as a people had its inception. Edward Said, in his early literary criticism, had such an origin in mind as a contrast to what he explicitly called a beginning, for a beginning is all that an origin is not: precisely dateable, a matter of the here-and-now. An origin, he explains, is by its nature passive, something that is as possessing as it is possessed, and so distant as to be clouded by innumerable layers of history.[5] Thomas Mann in the Prologue to his great biblical epic *Joseph and His Brothers* refers to such an origin as "the well of the past." "Very deep," he describes it, and adds, "Should we not call it bottomless?"[6] Whereas origins are given, ahistorical, and partaking of the eternal, beginnings are the very mark of contingency, available at any moment, a possibility whenever and wherever there's a mind and a will to make it so.

However much the early settlers felt themselves "in the beginning," they were not thereby relieved of the deeper need to establish some ground of primal legitimacy. We can see this on the very surface of colonial affairs, in what Michael Kammen has described as "the early American obsession with land titles and with surveying" and the veritable "quest for accurate boundaries," which he attributes to the need "for social and cultural norms and for stable political institutions."[7] More fundamentally still, this hunger for an *illud tempus,* a solid, incontestable ground from which to build is apparent in the settlers' repeated attempts at foundational constructions. From the earliest settlements the colonists swore Agreements and Oaths, entered into Covenants, devised Compacts and Constitutions, composed Fundamentals and Charters, penned Orders and Frames of Government. A "Catalogue of American Founding Documents" assembled by the political scientist Donald S. Lutz lists close to one hundred and fifty such foundations, all but the last eighteen from well before the era of the American Revolution.[8]

The most important thing to notice about these foundations is the most obvious—that they are all verbal. The settlers did, of course, engage in profound works of physical habitation, often transforming their new environment. Within a half century of their settling the northern reaches of Cape Cod, for instance, the thick forests they discovered upon landing were utterly consumed, the black earth itself eroded away to the sand dunes that still stand today; and everywhere the native peoples, where they impeded the settlers' appetite for land, were cleared with a similar decisiveness and ruin. But for the settlers' attempts at constructing origins they did not mark the earth, set up pillars, or make sacrifice at a particular spot: they clung to the use of language. This peculiar status language possessed for the mainland colonists has been long recognized and in recent decades has in fact been given an ever-increasing emphasis. To some critics like Christopher Looby in his *Voicing America* and Jay Fliegelman in *Declaring Independence,* it was the orality of speeches, sermons, and publicly declaimed documents that gave language its special generative potency in the minds of the settlers. To other critics—of recent note Michael Warner in *The Letters of the Republic* and Larzer Ziff in his survey of *Writing in the New Nation*—it was specifically the printed word in which the crucial initiating force of language inhered.[9] In either case, as if in compensation

both for the stark absence of those physical monuments and immemorial cultural landmarks that give order to both inner and outer landscape, for these settlers it was their very words they carried with them,
their language itself, that had become invested with a vast, inherent
New World authority.

In part, of course, all the compacts and frames of government owed
much to the legacy of Puritan covenant theology, a reflection in turn
of ancient Hebraic text-centeredness, itself derived from the Greek ide-
alization of study.[10] The accompanying attitude toward language has
often been traced to those same Bible-obsessed New Englanders, who
had, after all, devoted themselves to an almost rabbinic textual engagement, seeking to construct their daily social and political lives upon
the Word of God.[11] Benjamin Franklin, a child of Boston, well represents this emphatic linguistic orientation, as he well represents so many
aspects of colonial American culture. As a young man of 23 and in
perfect health, he had composed his now celebrated epitaph:

> The Body of
> B. Franklin,
> Printer;
> Like the Cover of an old Book,
> Its Contents torn out,
> And stript of its Lettering and gilding,
> Lies here, Food for Worms.
> But the Work shall not be wholly lost:
> For it will, as he believe'd, appear once more,
> In a new & more perfect Edition, Corrected and amended
> By the Author.[12]

Almost like a metaphysical poet of a century earlier, the young
Franklin so straddles the line between inherited piety and the wit of
new learning that it is difficult to know whether what he is evincing
here is his devotion to traditional religious categories or to the new
world of letters and learning. So consistent is his imagined relation to
language that fully half a century later, addressing his son with the first
part of his *Autobiography*, Franklin remarks upon the blessedness of
his life by making use of the same image: "That Felicity, when I reflected on it, has induc'd me sometimes to say, there were it offer'd to
my Choice, I should have no Objection to a Repetition of the same
Life from its Beginning, only asking the Advantage Authors have in a
second Edition to correct some Faults of the first."[13] He begins his
Autobiography with an account of "this obscure Family of ours," by

highlighting two sets of facts for each of his forbearers: their religious affiliations and, otherwise inexplicably, the quality and quantity of their literary productions, in prose or verse, such as they were, for not a one of them could be described as a writer or even a practitioner of Franklin's own profession of printing. It seems as though the work in language they had left behind them gave these distant Old World relations whatever New World substantiality Franklin could imagine for them.

But it should be remembered that this investment in the word cannot be understood as an exclusively New England inclination. Along with the Puritan biblical and covenantal background, there must also be acknowledged the effects of Enlightenment learning with its commitments to reasoned objectivity as opposed to inherited superstition and the hearsay of tradition. The discourse of rational argument seemed to hold sway through what now seems a surprisingly broad spectrum of the population. Indeed, it has often been claimed that the final decisive impulse to independence had begun not with the shot at Concord which Emerson a half century later would describe as "heard round the world," nor on the heels of any particular outrage by the British king or his troops, but by the reading from one end of the colonies to the other of Tom Paine's pamphlet, *Common Sense*. George Trevelyan in his *History of the American Revolution* went so far as to insist that "it would be difficult to name any human composition which has had an effect at once so instant, so extended and so lasting. . . . It worked nothing short of miracles and turned Tories into Whigs."[14] Even compensating for Trevelyan's Whig sympathies, *Common Sense* has often been described as the single most successful political pamphlet in Western history. Certainly many of Paine's contemporaries maintained a similar conviction. General Washington credited its "sound doctrine and unanswerable reasoning" for persuading many "to decide upon the propriety of separation." Washington's fellow Virginian Edmund Randolph described its effect more plainly still: "the public sentiments which a few weeks before [the publication of *Common Sense*] had shuddered at the tremendous obstacles, with which independence was environed, overleaped every barrier."[15] Yet it is no diminishment of Paine's great stylistic achievement—relying, as Gordon Wood has pointed out, on his readers knowing nothing more than the Bible and the Book of Common Prayer—to insist that its extraordinary impact depended upon a population unusually susceptible to verbal articulation and argument.[16]

The young Washington Irving was thus drawing on a long American heritage when three decades after Independence, he made comic satire of a language-mad new nation, having his fictional visitor from the East, Mustapha Rub-A-Dub Keli Khan, write home about this strange logomanical world:

> To let thee at once into a secret, which is unknown to these people themselves, their government is a pure unadulterated LOGOCRACY or *government of words*. . . . Every offensive or defensive measure is enforced by *wordy battle;* and *paper war;* he who has the longest tongue, or readiest quips, is sure to gain the victory—will carry horror, abuse and *ink-shed* into the very trenches of the enemy, and without mercy or remorse, put men, women, and children, to the point of the—pen![17]

Similarly, two years later, in *The History of New York,* Irving's Dutch historian Dietrich Knickerbocker introduces the British settlers by explaining to his readers just what kind of freedom had motivated their setting out from the Old World:

> [T]heir liberty of conscience likewise implied *liberty of speech* . . . so that rather than submit to such horrible tyranny they one and all embarked for the wildernesses of America, where they might enjoy unmolested, the inestimable luxury of talking. . . . [18]

What, then, could be more natural than to see the Revolution's central linguistic act in the Declaration of Independence from Britain, and to understand that act as the mark of beginning for the new nation? The Frenchman Jacques Derrida, from his deconstructing perspective, sees it this way in a brief talk he entitled "Declarations of Independence." Concerned with a subject that will arise in a later chapter, namely, who it is that can sign such a linguistic act, Derrida describes the Declaration as a kind of "declarative act which founds an institution."[19] Jefferson wrote in that document in the name "of the Representatives of the united States of America," those scattered "inhabitants of America" whom Paine addressed in *Common Sense,* "that these United Colonies are, and of Right ought to be Free and Independent States; that they are Absolved from all Allegiance to the British Crown, and that all political connection between them and the State of Great Britain, is and ought to be totally dissolved."

Moreover, it is Jefferson's eloquent phrase-making that is regularly cited as representing most powerfully the Founding era's expressive achievement. His words seem to capture the very moment of the People's inspired self-discovery. It is, however, a matter of historical fact that the Declaration served no such function. Kenneth Silverman in his compendious survey of American culture during the Revolution, published in 1987, noted that though "scores of engravings song, skits, plays, and ringing odes had cheered or bewailed the events leading up to Jefferson's document . . . no one in 1776 bothered to paint, engrave, or dramatize its creation, or to celebrate its meaning in a broadside poem or a piece of music."[20] Moreover, Pauline Maier in her illuminating study of the Declaration's reception has demonstrated that for its contemporaries the document itself possessed comparatively little significance.[21]

Freed from our present mythic assumptions about the document, this is not in itself difficult to understand. The Declaration of Independence officially marked the end rather than the beginning of anything new. The old regime had now come formally to a close.[22] Maier describes how every sign and symbol of the monarchy, from taverns to churches, suffered a thorough destruction amid the celebratory glee that greeted Congress's announcement of independence. In New York City the rebels made use of a gilded equestrian statue of George III in the manufacture of lead bullets for the coming war to oppose him. But it was not Jefferson's document that ignited these crowds: the Philadelphia papers had published the news of independence on July 2, while Jefferson's draft was still being debated, and the news had traveled quickly to the other colonies. The words of the Declaration of Independence merely confirmed the deed. Only in retrospect—decades after the fact— did Jefferson's universalizing eloquence appear to exert what the linguistic philosopher J. L. Austin would call a performative force, enacting what it articulated. Pauline Maier sums up the evidence, and her own surprise, thus:

> What were the Americans celebrating with their processions, their ceremonial bonfires, their "illumination," the firing of guns and ringing of bells, the printed pages that they "fixed up" on the walls of their homes? The news, not the vehicle that brought it; Independence, the end of monarchy, and the assumption of self-government, not the document that announced congress's decision to break with Britain. Considering how revered a position the Declaration of Independence later won in the hearts and minds of the American people, their disregard for it in the earliest years of the new nation verges on the incredible.[23]

The colonies had declared what they were not: they were no longer British. But now what were they, and what were they to be? There was neither the time nor the inclination to address such questions when independence itself had still to be earned on the battlefield. When they did act to establish their legitimacy, it took the form of constituting their former colonies as states. The vast diversity of the North American continent's landscape and climate had done to the European settlers just what it had done to the native settlers thousands of years earlier, fractured them into different and distinct societies.[24] Spread along a narrow band of the eastern seaboard, the new settlers formed separate and distinct societies, their distinctiveness arising both from the local conditions and from the regional folkways they brought with them.[25] Virginians did not imagine themselves sharing an identity with the inhabitants of Massachusetts, nor did either people conceive of themselves as constituting one nation with Pennsylvanians, nor Pennsylvanians with New Yorkers.[26] It had been a mere three years since the very first meeting of the Continental Congress, of which more members had been to London than had ever set foot in Philadelphia, the largest city of North America, where the Congress convened. Indeed, amid the business of declaring independence in Pennsylvania, Jefferson had written to friends in Virginia how very difficult it was at just such a time to be so far from "my country."[27]

When the colonists declared their independence, they possessed no grand scheme of union and certainly none of nationhood. Independence in and of itself possessed great value and was the reigning practice in many New World lives. Every European man and woman who arrived at the continent's shore, whether driven there by hope or desperation, or as often as not by some combination of the two, had, for the most part, voluntarily left behind all that was familiar, all that bound each to homes and villages, indeed to everything then recognized as the humanly civilized world. The sailing itself—months across the open ocean—was more than likely to be difficult, with the passenger in even the best circumstance running a considerable risk of serious illness or death. These were people who had not merely departed for the New World: they had all but abandoned themselves to it.

Jay Fliegelman in *Prodigals and Pilgrims: The American Revolution Against Patriarchal Authority* has explained how this abandonment had not generally been shadowed by traditional shame and guilt, but instead had come to be associated with a strong sense of initiating independence and innocence. To choose to leave home had in the eighteenth century gradually come to be seen as a source of self-respect. A new conception of the family, with a reconfigured understanding of the child's and parents' responsibilities to each other, had become established. Fliegelman's wide-ranging study is in part about this strong current of change in the realms of education, in the theories of child development, and in what we would now call family politics. Fliegelman is concerned with the high tide of these developments in the latter half of the eighteenth century, and in this context what he describes, through the use of a great variety of sources—from educational treatises and textbooks to the severely abridged and widely read colonial versions of *Robinson Crusoe* and *Clarissa*—is how the passage from the Old World to the New had come to be analogized to the development of an individual from childhood to maturity.[28] Leaving home came to be seen not as a betrayal of the family, an attack upon the Father, but instead as a healthy and necessary journey out from the safe, protected harbor of parental care, into the full and open independence of adult life. This developmental view was further intensified, if also complicated, by the Protestant insistence on the individual's relation to his Father in heaven, over and above his father at home.

As a representative instance of this change, the parable of the Prodigal Son came to be powerfully reimagined and reevaluated. Fliegelman describes Crusoe's refusal to return to "parent and prescriptive Christianity" after the "conversion [attending] his island isolation": "The circle of the prodigal's return has snapped; it has become again the straight line of the pilgrim's progress." To the colonists in North America, Crusoe came to represent a reinterpretation of what had been a recursive return to the origin of father and home. What had been an eternal return, divinely sponsored, became an act of spiritual freedom, the taking on of an adult's burden of open-ended departure, a new beginning. In a similar way, Richardson's Clarissa, by resisting the tyrannous authority of her father—tyrannous because it extended beyond its rightful limits—could become a type of the revolutionary.[29] Tom Paine's impatient argument for an end to colonial dependence—he had himself arrived in America just two years before—made use of just such reasoning: "We may as well assert," he wrote, "that because a child has thrived upon milk, that it is never to have meat; or that the first twenty years of our lives is to become a precedent for the next twenty."[30]

Fliegelman himself cites Ben Franklin, and it would be almost impossible for the sage of Philadelphia not to come to mind once again. The first and most memorable section of his *Autobiography*, written in 1770 before anyone had seriously contemplated independence, is a literary invention that so successfully articulated aspects of this common white male experience of setting out, as to have seemed for centuries now as much an allegory for the pursuit of an American life as a personal account. Ben departs from Boston, escaping, in fact, from an apprenticeship to his older brother—an Old World hierarchy—and arrives in Philadelphia to create his inimitable self. Beginning with nothing more than his penny loaf of bread, he cuts a new trail to honor and renown. Franklin does not return to his family in Boston, just as the colonists will not return to their dependence upon the Crown. In each case it is not merely a freedom that is being exercised—though it is that—but a self-imposed demand that has been imposed, a demand that the future be chosen rather than inherited or fated.

European visitors have often noted how harsh this demand for personal independence can be. D. H. Lawrence at the beginning of this past century, in his brilliant *Studies in Classic American Literature,* stated it with powerful simplicity:

> They came [to America] largely to get *away*—that most simple of motives. To get away. Away from what? In the long run, away from themselves. Away from everything. That's why most people have come to America, and still do come. To get away from everything they are and have been.[31]

Given so deep an investment in an ideal of personal independence, it is no surprise that historically the colonists had never evinced much interest in a common perspective. It was not until 1754, preparing for war against the French and their Indian allies, and facing the practical need of a common defense, that anyone had so much as proposed any serious plan for a colonial "union."[32] None other than Benjamin Franklin had then put forward the "Albany Plan of Union." Written earlier in the year, itself a response to rising conflict with the Indians, Franklin had published the plan accompanied by America's first political cartoon—a snake separated into segments with the motto "Join or Die." The delegates to that colonial conference did in fact unanimously approve a version of the Albany Plan, but it met an equally unanimous rejection by the separate colonies, at least by those that paid any attention to it at all. Thus, even in the face of military emergency, the colonists did not have a sufficient sense of themselves as a collective, sharing a common identity, to permit them to unite. Their one shared identity resided in their relation to the Crown, in where they had come from far less than in where they were.

Indeed, the Crown and the Parliament in the face of initial complaints rising from the colonies in the 1770s responded with such complacency precisely because they believed that no unified action, least of all a workable union, could be expected from the colonists. As late as 1765, John Dickinson of Delaware, who would go on to sign the Declaration of Independence, had confidently assured William Pitt, the secretary of state, that any attempt at an American independence from the Mother Country would be a disaster:

> What, sir, must be the Consequences of that Success? A Multitude of Commonwealths, Crimes and Calamities of mutual Jealousies, Hatreds, Wars and Devastations; till at last exhausted Provinces shall sink into Slavery under the yoke of some fortunate Conqueror.[33]

When Boston responded to the "Tea Act of 1773" with its December Tea Party, and the British in turn imposed a series of so-called Coercive Acts—soon known throughout the colonies as the Intolerable Acts—the colonists did manage to organize a Continental Congress to be held in Philadelphia in 1775. This left the king's ministers, as Pauline Maier describes them, "dumbfounded."[34] Unified colonial action had seemed inconceivable, and without the boycotting support of the other colonies, Massachusetts would likely have been unable to sustain its resistance to British demands. Yet still a year later, in March of 1776, John Adams was possessed by the reasonable fear that independence would remain unacceptable to the People because the different colonies simply lacked any sufficiently common political perspective. Just two months before, at the January convening of the Second Continental Congress, no more than a third of the delegates had looked favorably upon the possibility of independence.[35] Only after the publication of Paine's pamphlet and a series of British blunders, such as the royal governor of Virginia inciting slaves to revolt against their rebellious masters, did all the colonies unite in a bid for independence.

The formal aspect of this agreement issued in the Articles of Confederation, adopted by the Continental Congress in 1777, though not formally ratified by all of the sovereign states—a necessary precondition—until 1781. These articles amounted to a makeshift arrangement for coordinating unanimously reached decisions and served the needs—though not very effectively—of prosecuting the war. There has, of course, been a long-running historical debate over how the Articles compare to the Constitution of 1787 in their fealty to the spirit and purposes of the Revolution; but there is little dispute that the Articles were never, in their own time or since, of any national symbolic importance.

The war came and went, leaving a distinctly communal independence to contend with. The Red Coats surrendered at Yorktown, and among the customary mournful tunes played by the defeated British band was a setting of a nursery rhyme, "The World Turned Upside Down":

> If mammas sold their babies
> to gypsies for half a crown;
> If summer were spring
> and the other way round
> Then all the world would be upside down.[36]

The world had certainly turned upside down, and not merely for the British. The independence that had been declared a half decade earlier had brought with it not merely the tentative and provisional cooperation of wartime, but a newly felt need for a measure of more ordered coordination. Such order could only come at the expense of some degree of independence, now no longer from Britain but from one another. Yet how can independence, experienced as a personal value, be shared across so vast a physical and cultural space without losing anything worthy of the name? Having made good on their declaration, the states had to grapple with the conundrum of any initially successful revolution: having destroyed the old order, how were they now to order things anew? The power that had been so successfully wrested from the perceived tyranny had now to be reformulated. Having become independent from Britain, they now needed to arrange a dependence upon one another.

What they required was something like that *illud tempus,* a collective origin, from which they could develop a new collective identity. The war had succeeded only in transforming separate colonies into separate states, that jealously guarded their sovereign independence, willing to maintain their Confederation precisely because it demanded so little of their hard-won independence.

CHAPTER TWO

The Path to Union

What could Norton mean in saying that the only
great men of the American past were Franklin &
Edwards? We have had Adams . . . Washington & the
prophetic authors of the Federalist, Madison &
Hamilton.

EMERSON, *Journals*, 1841

If we are to inquire into the formation of a collective identity for the
people of these newly independent states, it is the *Constitution of the
United States* that we must approach. Here is a document tacitly bespeaking a quite extraordinary commitment to the generative power of
language, and yet with the arguable exception of the somber purpose-
fulness of its brief Preamble, the Constitution is utterly devoid of anything resembling eloquence.[1] To the Declaration's soaring rhetoric it
offers colorless rules and definitions, its prose intended, as a recent
historian has described it, "not for inspiration but for instruction."[2]
But it is from this governing instrument that the former colonists derived what became for them an almost proper name: "We the People."
The fact is, however, that the Union was a highly unlikely outcome of
the process set in motion by the War for Independence.

After the Declaration of Independence and until the Articles of Confederation were ratified in 1781, the Continental Congress remained,
aside from the army, the only national institution, and it pursued the
ensuing war by a system of administration only gradually, and never
very successfully, developed. Aware of its uniquely national function,
Congress did act with a great consciousness and concern for its prestige
and prerogatives, yet it never freed itself from a reliance upon the individual states. Even in regard to its most crucial task of provisioning
the army, the Congress could do nothing without the states, no matter
how ineffectually the states in fact fulfilled their responsibilities.

Ironically, after the Articles of Confederation were formally ratified by all the states, there was a further ebbing of the power of the Confederation Congress. By 1783, two years into government under the Articles, and after victory in the war, Congress's authority had been so diminished that the elected representatives lost interest in attending; the mere calling of a quorum became a regular challenge. Yet there remained no other unified authority: it was the Confederation Congress or nothing. Consequently, even such elementary matters as the continuing, and sometimes bitter, border disputes between individual states remained unsettled.

But it was first and foremost in the economic realm that this relative absence of a central authority caused the most acute difficulties. Britain, along with the rebels' former allies France and Spain, had begun restricting trade with the new nation, already hampered by the separate states that were themselves erecting barriers, such as tariffs, against one another and thus still further limiting trade. The Confederation Congress had insufficient power to contest either of these developments. Most crucially, and of the greatest long-term significance, the Confederation Congress could never find an acceptable mechanism by which it could reliably raise revenue, the *sine qua non* of any governing authority: a national 5 percent tax on imports had been twice proposed, and twice defeated. Even in the one area where the Confederation Congress possessed theoretically exclusive authority, that of the relations between any of the states and foreign powers, it had great difficulty making use of its power. Western expansion depended to a considerable degree upon the national government's capacity to negotiate with the European powers and to offer protection to whose who would migrate. But the Articles of Confederation had weakened the central authority almost to the point of paralysis.

Yet those who wished for reform feared that any move to create an overarching authority over the states would be interpreted by the now independent citizens as nothing less than the self-aggrandizement of a corrupt Congress. Had not the colonists, after all, overthrown their king precisely to protect themselves against such a central authority, one that could exercise its power at a distance from those it governed? This revolutionary perspective did not simply vanish when the war with Britain had come to an end. Indeed, their newly established schemes of representation reflected a deep suspicion of political power. Representatives to the state legislatures were generally considered little more than messengers of their constituency's views. Elections were consequently held annually, and those who were elected were often subject to recall. Moreover, in many of the state legislatures, as well as in the Confederation Congress, there were strict term limits. Article Five of the Confederation stipulated that no delegate could serve in the Congress for more than three years out of every six.

All attempts to reform the Articles in the direction of increasing Congress's authority had failed, doomed in advance by the Confederation's Thirteenth Article requiring unanimous ratification by the states for any proposed alteration or amendment. Reformers counseled each other to remain patient. Many of them hoped that the British themselves, by acting as imprudently as they had before the war and by trying to impose onerous impediments to trade, might encourage a unity among the new states.

One of the most active reformers, James Madison, himself forced by term limits from the Confederation Congress, continued to work for reform from within the Virginia Legislature. In a position to observe up close the behavior of the state legislators, he came to attribute the paralysis of the national political system as much to their crude parochialism as to the Articles themselves:

> Is it to be imagined that an ordinary citizen or even an assemblyman of Rhode Island in estimating the policy of paper money, ever considered or cared in what light the measure would be viewed in France or Holland; or even in Massachusetts or Connecticut? It was a sufficient temptation to both that it was for their interest.[3]

Nor was this Madison's view alone. The crisis experienced by the political elite, and fretted over in their private correspondence, derived not from an unfunded and powerless Congress alone, but from what to them seemed clear democratic abuses—most especially in the area of paper money, credit, and debt. It seemed as if the revolutionary commitments to disinterestedness and virtue upon which they believed the Republic depended were rapidly eroding under the pressures of the small-minded and the self-serving.[4]

Madison, in concert with his colleague George Washington, arranged a meeting between Virginia and Maryland to work out disagreements between the states about navigation of shared waterways. In 1785 they signed the "Mount Vernon Compact," settling all outstanding issues regarding the Chesapeake and its tributaries, after which the commissioners resolved to propose another meeting, this time for a larger number of states. The next year, Madison passed through the Virginia legislature an invitation to all the states to meet at Annapolis in order to consider matters of commercial interest within the Confederation.

It was on this Annapolis Conference that Madison settled his hopes for reform. Of the thirteen states invited to the Conference, only eight even bothered to name representatives, and of these eight, only five state delegations attended. Two of the delegates—Madison himself and the New Yorker Alexander Hamilton—are often credited with quickly transforming this dismal result into a call for a second convention to be held the following May, this time in Philadelphia, "to devise such further provisions as shall appear to them necessary to render the constitution of the federal government adequate to the exigencies of the Union."

The course of 1786 offered little comfort to those concerned with reform of the Articles of Confederation. The problems only intensified. New Jersey had refused to honor any new congressional requisitions; New York had effectively vetoed the impost. In Massachusetts Daniel Shays and his fellow farmers had raised the cry of rebellion. Fears of disunion, or worse, were very real. Madison acknowledged in his private correspondence that whereas the notion of new, separate confederacies among the states had been held in "long confinement to individual speculations & private circles," it was now "beginning to shew itself in the Newspapers."[5] And should that happen, it would seem inevitable that the great European powers would begin to swoop in and form competing alliances among the states.

Again the Virginia Legislature took the lead, appointing seven delegates to this second convention, any three of whom were authorized to represent the state. Virginia was followed by New Jersey, Pennsylvania, North Carolina, and Maryland. Only then, in February of 1787, did the still reluctant Congress itself endorse the idea:

> Whereas there is provision in the Articles of Confederation and perpetual Union, for making alterations therein. . . . And whereas experience hath evinced, that there are defects in the present Confederation, as a mean to remedy which, several of the States . . . have suggested a convention for the purposes expressed in the following Resolution. . . .
>
> Resolved, That in the opinion of Congress, it is expedient, that. . . . a Convention of Delegates, who shall have been appointed by the several States, be held at Philadelphia, for the sole and express purpose of revising the Articles of Confederation . . . [to] render the federal Constitution adequate to the exigencies of Government, and the preservation of the Union.[6]

The quality of the resulting state delegations varied considerably. The two most renowned participants were unquestionably the hero of the

Revolution, the retired General George Washington, by all accounts the most popular and respected man in North America, and Benjamin Franklin, then an ailing 81 years old. Of the others there was a considerable range of ability and distinction. Most had played some important role in the Revolution, and fully three-fourths had one time or another served in the Congress. If they were not all men of wealth, they were nearly all, not surprisingly, of an elite social standing. Some of the most famous men of the Revolution, however, were not present. Thomas Jefferson and John Adams were both serving as ambassadors abroad; Patrick Henry and Richard Henry Lee refused appointment to the Convention. In all, twelve states appointed seventy-four delegates, of whom fifty-five participated in the convention, although some for only a small fraction of its four and a half months duration. At the completion of the Convention's work there were a mere forty-two delegates in attendance.

The Convention that gathered in Philadelphia from May to September of 1787 had seemed to its supporters to be a last chance for empowering a national authority. Not that Madison, or any of the other delegates who straggled into Philadelphia between its appointed opening of May fourteenth and the ten days it took for the seven states required for a quorum to arrive held out any great hopes for solving the nation's difficulties. As Madison wrote to Edmund Pendleton: "In general I find men of reflections much less sanguine as to a new than despondent as to the present System."[7] If, after all, they had been unable over four years to effect the most modest and gradual reforms, how likely were they to tackle the difficulties in this one grand effort?

They met in the State House, built in 1732 and by colonial standards a grand public building. The paving stones about the building were covered with earth to quiet the passing traffic, and a guard was placed both outside and inside the Hall where the delegates met, for the Convention proceeded under a rule of strictest secrecy—a matter to which this account must return. Sessions were held every day but Sunday, almost always from ten in the morning until three in the afternoon.[8] Voting was by state, with each state present entitled to one vote. A simple majority of the states present, given the quorum of seven states, sufficed for all matters considered.

Aside from his active participation in every phase of the deliberations, as well as in the delegates' evening socializing, Madison returned every night to his rooms, and at the risk of sheer exhaustion composed from his thorough notes a full account of all that had transpired in the

Convention, recording who had spoken when and precisely what each had said. It is primarily to these notes that we owe most of what we know about the proceedings. Through them we can follow the various plans and compromises that issued in the Philadelphia Convention's improbable success.

To begin with, and most strikingly, the delegates gave short shrift to the Articles of Confederation, the revision of which was the sole task the Congress had authorized: they went to work almost at once upon an entirely new foundation of government. To offer the briefest summary of their proceedings: Madison diligently prepared a plan that he had submitted to the Convention by his Virginia colleague Edmund Randolph, which has since become known as the Virginia Plan. They commenced to debate its various provisions, engaging in extended discussion before the Committee of the Whole. Among other matters discussed, and most crucially, were the size and scope of the executive, and the means and apportionment of representation in the proposed national legislature. It is this latter issue that brought the Convention to a standstill. Madison's plan had envisioned a unicameral legislature with the number of representatives elected from the several states strictly in proportion to their population. The small states balked at what they feared would be their inevitable domination by the large states. An alternative plan was then introduced, this one proposed by William Paterson and since known as the New Jersey Plan. As opposed to the Virginia Plan's proportional representation, the New Jersey Plan called for equal representation accorded to each state. But now the large states dissented. What followed came to be called the Great Compromise, otherwise known as the Connecticut Compromise, because it was drafted by, among others, Oliver Ellsworth and Roger Sherman, both of Connecticut. This plan provided for proportional representation in a lower House of Representatives and equal representation from each state in an upper body, the Senate. It was this compromise that ultimately passed.

Just as the delegates were eager in the end to reach a compromise on this primary conflict between the small and the large states, so did they quickly bury any possible conflict regarding the status of slavery. But in marked contrast to the South's unembarrassed defense of slavery a few short decades later, it was at this time still clear to the men of all sections that the institution cast so dark and shameful a shadow upon the republican experiment as to dictate an evasion of its very name. There were therefore no "slaves" as far as the Constitution was concerned, only persons and percentages thereof—that fateful enormity of the three-fifths formula utilized to account for the enslaved.

On the last day of the Convention, September 17, the Constitution was read, signed, and immediately made public. That the Convention was meeting, and where, had been matters of public knowledge, as was its express purpose to improve upon the national government; but no one knew what, if anything, to expect, and this kept public speculation and interest to a minimum. There were no crowds in the streets outside the Philadelphia State House. Although we know from Madison's notes that the delegates in the Convention regularly reminded themselves that public opinion set limits to the options they could consider, they nevertheless took quite extraordinary and astonishingly successful measures to keep their proceedings secret. This was not merely the conventional privacy practiced by deliberative bodies in the eighteenth century—a practice that only gradually gave way with the First Congress—but every word spoken in the Convention, every entry in its journals, indeed any and all discussion of the Convention's concerns or deliberations, all were held in the strictest secrecy. This secrecy applied not merely to the public at large but extended even to close friends of the delegates, their relations, indeed their political associates. The ban on information was absolute. Nor was there anything *pro forma* about this ban. Guards were posted around the State House to discourage the curious, and not a stray scrap of paper was permitted to leave the room.

There is a revealing anecdote about the seriousness of this policy, its all but sanctified quality, highlighting as well the role played by the otherwise silent George Washington who presided as the officer of the Convention on a raised platform. Max Farrand tells the story in his long-standard account of the framing:

> One of the members dropped a copy of the propositions which were before the convention for consideration, and it was picked up by another of the delegates and handed to General Washington. After the debates of the day were over, just before putting the question of adjournment, Washington arose from his seat and reprimanded the member for his carelessness. "I must entreat Gentlemen to be more careful, least our transactions get into the News Papers and stir the public repose by premature speculations. I know not whose Paper it is, but there it is (throwing it down on the table), let him who owns it take it." At the same time he picked up his Hat, and quitted the room with a dignity so severe that every Person seemed alarmed. . . . It is something remarkable that no Person ever owned that paper." (p. 65)

One effect of this secrecy was that when the Convention finished its work, the Constitution was presented not as a mere political document, one that had been hammered out, phrase by phrase, through four long and contentious months of compromise, but as if it were suddenly all at once revealed. "We the People" the text begins, for who else could possess such authority to start anew? In the Convention itself, this conclusion had come to seem inevitable. But as Max Farrand describes it: "such a phrase would have been impossible at the beginning of the convention; it was accepted without question at the end" (p. 191).

But then what of the status of those delegates, locked away in their Philadelphia chamber, whose signatures in fact form the conclusion to the document? According to the Constitution's final paragraph, they were something between "the States"—or what we must conclude were representatives of the states—and mere witnesses:

> Done in Convention by the Unanimous Consent of the States present the Seventeenth Day of September in the Year of our Lord one thousand seven hundred and Eighty seven of the Independence of the United States of America the Twelfth in Witness whereof We have hereunto subscribed our Names.[9]

There is something more than a little indirect about this formulation. Madison himself referred to it in his notes as "this ambiguous form." Add to this the unprecedented secrecy practiced by the delegates and the result is an almost hopelessly complex calculus of the source of authority. The historian Edward Countryman in his summation of the Convention and Ratification describes the whole process of the People's sovereignty and the Constitution with a realistically casual acceptance: "There was an element of myth making and fakery involved, of course," but it is this very "of course" which covers much that is essential in understanding the background conditions of constitutional authority, and with it the broader conditions for the future development of American literary imagination.[10]

Just where did the authority of this Constitution originate?

The People,
Having Spoken, Speak

I have the highest veneration for those Gentlemen,—
but, Sir, give me leave to demand, what right had they
to say, *We, the People?*

PATRICK HENRY AT THE VIRGINIA RATIFYING CONVEN-
TION, JUNE 1788

It will be helpful to pause here in order to consider, however briefly, the various political motives of the Convention, and thus the Constitution's relation both to the legacy of the Revolution in general and more specifically to the prior governing arrangements under the Articles of Confederation. The account given so far has focused on the perceived need for a more powerful unifying authority. Needless to say, this is a vast historical subject, and one in which political vision, allegiances, and commitments are bound to play a substantial part. Since at least the late nineteenth century, and most emphatically since the publication of Charles Beard's vastly influential work *An Economic History of the Constitution of the United States* (1913), historians have questioned the motives of the Founders and have attempted to reopen the debate begun by the defeated opponents of the Convention and the Constitution it produced. To Beard, the delegates had in fact conjured up a crisis of governance under the Confederation as a mere pretext. Their real intentions were reactionary and were guided by their deep investments in financial speculation.

Beard's claim that such speculators dominated the Philadelphia Convention has long been decisively disproved, but that is not to say that the interests of property were not important, or even predominant, in the motives of those who sought a reform of the Articles. Indeed, something like a consensus has formed among historians that the men behind the Constitutional Convention—beginning with Hamilton and Madison—were in fact pursuing a conservative, even in part an antidemocratic agenda. What remains largely open to debate is precisely how, in the context of the late-eighteenth-century British world, such terms as "conservative" and "democratic" are to be understood.[1]

Hannah Arendt in her philosophical study *On Revolution* helpfully recalls that the very term *conservative* refers to "a political creed" that as "an ideology owes existence to a reaction to the French Revolution and is meaningful only for the history of the nineteenth and twentieth centuries." Similarly in regard to the idea of "democracy" and the "People," she crucially distinguishes between the experience of the American Revolution and the later revolution in France, which has become the model of revolution now automatically assumed. Her point is sufficiently subtle and significant to warrant an extended quotation:

> The word "people" retained for [the Founders] the meaning of manyness, of the endless variety of a multitude whose majesty resided in its very plurality. Opposition to public opinion, namely to the potential unanimity of all, was therefore one of the many things upon which the men of the American Revolution were in complete agreement; they knew that the public realm in a republic was constituted by an exchange of opinion between equals, and that this realm would simply disappear the very moment an exchange became superfluous because all equals happened to be of the same opinion. They never referred to public opinion in their argument, as Robespierre and the men of the French Revolution invariably did to add force to their own opinions; in their eyes, the rule of public opinion was a form of tyranny. To such an extent indeed was the American concept of people identified with a multitude of voices and interests that Jefferson could establish it as a principle "to make us one nation as to foreign concerns, and to keep us distinct in domestic ones."[2]

The most influential recent view is that of Gordon Wood, for whom the struggle was one of the "worthy against the licentious," that is, a reaction of those members of the elite, like Madison and Hamilton, who with an aristocratic conception of political leadership feared the licentious excesses of democracy. These "worthy," however, used the arguments and the language of radical democracy to defeat the more radical democrats. Thus, they significantly increased the authority of both the Senate and the Executive, while emphasizing the representational aspect of all the governing bodies, and consequently, according to Wood, they "helped to foreclose the development of an American intellectual tradition in which differing ideas of politics would be intimately and genuinely related to differing social interests . . . thereby contributing to the creation of that encompassing liberal tradition which has mitigated and often obscured the real social antagonisms of American politics."[3] In other words, to put the matter in the simplest terms, the Federalists were in fact nationalists, supporters of a strong central government, and their opponents, named by them the anti-Federalists, were actually federalists proper, those, that is, who were interested in maintaining the most power at the level of the states.

Did the Constitution favor the interests of those who possessed property? Yes. Did it favor established elites? Yes. Was it antidemocratic? Yes, to the extent that it assured that politics would be primarily the business of prominent men, with each state possessing only two senators and each House member representing some 30,000 people, with long terms—six and two years, respectively—and the Senate, along with the presidency, elected only indirectly by the People. But it was certainly a republican government, democratic in the sense that ultimately the governors could rule only with the consent of the governed.

Yet in crude Marxist terms, in addition to favoring the elites and the property holders, the Constitution also favored those who dreamed of an increase in status or property—in other words, it favored the progressive forces of economic development and modernization. If it represented a defeat for the most radical aspects of democracy generated by the Revolution, in which citizen–legislators would be kept on a very short leash held firmly in hand by the voters—the Massachusetts Assembly was fully four times the size of the First Congress—the Constitution also represented a victory for the "revolution of the bourgeoisie."[4] Its success in encouraging capitalist development seems clear enough.

Why, then, has the focus in this brief account of the Convention been on the need for union and a constituting authority? Not because this focus is any more the "real" reason behind the Constitution than the others—although it was real enough and by no means negated by conflicting considerations—but because the interest here is not in the political development of the United States, nor in its economic development, not even in what one might call its ideology. Nor is there any claim that such obvious political, economic, and ideological conditions as America's massive degree of slave labor and its peculiarly racist context, or the now increasingly obvious ramifications of the country's gender hierarchies, had no discernible effect on American literature. But what is here under investigation is the United States Constitution's unusual identity-generating force in the nation's life, and the quasi-invisible aspect of this governing document as a crucial factor in the development of a national literature.

Whether the Founders fulfilled the "revolutionary spirit of the country"—to use Hannah Arendt's terms—by converting the otherwise "futile rebellion and liberation" into a "constitution of the newly won freedom," or whether they in fact represented a kind of Thermidorean reaction to the democratic spirit of 1776, is of far less significance, from this perspective, than the question of how the Constitution managed to achieve so exalted a degree of authority. Those who planned and participated in creating the Constitution were acutely aware of this need for authority—thus, the great significance they attached to the recruitment of George Washington as a delegate. Madison, along with Hamilton and Jay, had urged Washington's involvement with the knowledge that the trust he inspired, in addition to his enormous popularity, would go far toward establishing national credentials for the entire effort. But in itself this was by no means sufficient. Throughout the process of Ratification, to a review of which we now proceed, this concern for legitimacy became central to both sides in the hard-fought campaign.

The success of the Convention, the fact that it resulted in a proposed instrument, did not in the least assure the reformers' desired object. The Confederation Congress had first to consider the document and, if it approved it, send it on to the several states where deliberative bodies expressly elected for the purpose would assemble to consider its ratification. When nine of the thirteen states agreed, the constitutional regime would begin. But the reaction in the states was an open question, and its defeat in any of the four largest states—Virginia, Pennsylvania, New York, or Massachusetts—would have made any union impracticable.

Aside from all these hurdles, no one, least of all the men of the Convention themselves, had any very clear idea, when it came to it, how the Constitution would pragmatically function. Repeatedly, in speeches to the Convention, the delegates would remind one another of how vigilant they must be not to inadvertently tie the hands of those who would in future be building what they, the delegates themselves, had only framed. Thus Edmund Randolph, in the second month of the convention, reminded the Committee of Detail that "in the draught of a fundamental constitution" their labor must be "to insert essential principles only; lest the operations of government should be clogged by rendering those provisions permanent and unalterable, which ought to be accommodated to times and events."[5]

The Confederation Congress, after three days of an intense and often angry debate, did allow the process begun at Philadelphia to continue, though they sent the Constitution on to the states pointedly without comment. Writing to Richard Henry Lee of "the *new* Constitution as it is already called," Samuel Adams used the omnipresent image of architecture to describe his first reading: "as I enter the Building I stumble at the Threshold. I meet with a National Government, instead of a foederal Union of Sovereign States."[6] Elbridge Gerry spoke of the proposed Constitution in even more dire terms as "a many headed monster; of such motley mixture, that its enemies cannot trace a feature of Democratic or Republican extract."[7] George Mason claimed it was "at present impossible to foresee whether it will, in its operation, produce a monarchy or a corrupt oppressive aristocracy."[8] And Patrick Henry, the most mesmerizing of revolutionary orators, who had opposed the Convention from the start—"I smelt a rat," he said, when turning down appointment to the Virginia delegation—opened the Virginia Ratifying Convention by declaring the Republic "in extreme danger." Rhetorically insisting upon his respect for those who had convened in Philadelphia—"I have the highest veneration for those Gentlemen [of the Convention]"—he immediately challenged them on the proposed governing instrument they had produced, "but Sir, give me leave to demand, what right had they to say, *We, the People.* My political curiosity, exclusive of my anxious solicitude for the public welfare, leads me to ask, who authorized them to speak the language of *We, the People,* instead of *We, the States?*"[9]

Every state, with the exception of Rhode Island, held elections for ratifying conventions, and each of those state ratifying conventions, aside from North Carolina's, saw its part of the process to completion. The first five states to ratify the new Constitution—Delaware, Pennsylvania, New Jersey, Georgia, and Connecticut—did so expeditiously, between September and the following January of 1788, but the crucial large states had yet to be heard from.

The reformers did more than wait for a response. They organized a sustained and aggressive campaign to convince the ratifying conventions, and the people at large, of the wisdom and necessity of the Philadelphia Convention's work. In what amounted to the first national political campaign in the country's history, hundreds of pamphlets were published, of which the most famous, and afterwards most influential, were the *Federalist Papers.* As with almost all of the other pamphlets written during the controversy, the *Federalist Papers,* hurriedly penned by Alexander Hamilton with crucial contributions by Madison and a few written by John Jay, were published under a pseudonym associated with Republicanism, in their case the ancient Publius. Although Washington and Franklin had both lent their estimable names to the campaign, what bore the weight of persuasion was the mass of these pseudonymous pamphlets, largely written with a logic and cogency, and at an intellectual level, that a consensus of readers—historians and political philosophers—have long judged a high-water mark for democratic discourse.

The *Federalist Papers* themselves, though published in newspapers, were written primarily as a handbook of arguments meant to arm the Federalists in the crucial New York and Virginia conventions. The opposition to the new Constitution possessed sufficient force by the time of the Massachusetts Convention in February to threaten the very course of ratification. Their strongest objection, and the one that stalled the Massachusetts Convention, was the lack of a bill of rights. Consistent with the secrecy of the Convention's proceedings, which permitted only the final document itself to be revealed, the Federalists in Massachusetts refused to consider any changes to the proposed Constitution. They did promise, however, the addition of amendments amounting to a bill of rights as one of the new government's first actions. This not merely persuaded the Massachusetts Convention, but also provided a model for ratification in the two remaining large states. Given a similar assurance, both managed to ratify the Constitution, though neither did so by impressive margins: Virginia by a vote of 89 to 79 and New York by a mere 30 to 27.

But the question posed by the most articulate and principled anti-Federalists, namely, by what authority delegates were to speak not merely for the states but for the very People themselves, remained the largest theoretical stumbling block to the Constitution's legitimacy. The men of the Convention had used the formula of "We the People" as a proleptic response to this very question. The very process of ratification, providing for the election of separate conventions in each state to vote on the Constitution, had been borrowed from Massachusetts, which itself had developed the innovation in 1780 as a way of establishing popular legitimacy for its state constitution. It was felt that in the case of so fundamental a political instrument they needed at least the appearance of popular sovereignty; but then how, in the end, is anything like a People's sovereignty possible?

There is, to begin with, Paine's common-sense distinction between a society in which there can exist what could be called a perfect popular sovereignty, and a government in which the sheer numbers of individuals necessitates some scheme of representation. The larger the society forming a government, the greater the weakness of representation, since there must, for practical purposes, be some upper limit to the number of representatives. This was one of the chief concerns of critics of the Constitution in regard to the national government it invented. Indeed, on the very last day of the Philadelphia Convention the proportion of persons to representatives in the lower house was adjusted downward. As Madison records it:

> Mr. Gorham [delegate from Massachusetts] said if it was not too late he could wish, for the purpose of lessening objections to the Constitution, that the clause declaring "the number of Representative shall not exceed on for every forty thousand," which had produced so much discussion, might not yet be reconsidered.[10]

Washington himself urged this immediate readjustment, and the figure was lowered to 30,000 by a unanimous vote.

During the debates for ratification, Madison would come to argue in *Federalist No. 10*, the most celebrated of the papers, that it was precisely the large scale of the national legislature that would save the new Republic from factions with "the instability, injustice, and confusion introduced into public councils [that] have, in truth, been the mortal diseases under which popular governments have everywhere perished." The size of the population represented would create so many factions, so many interests, that no single faction could achieve a majority status that could subvert the very notion of popular sovereignty.[11]

But even if there were no objection to the fact of representation itself, the question of the People's sovereignty still entailed inherent paradoxes. Stanley Elkins and Eric McKitrick in their exhaustive survey of the *Age of Federalism* explain how vexed the very notion of sovereignty was in the period. It was something of a platitude that sovereignty was, theoretically at least, indivisible. In terms of the British constitutional tradition, it was Parliament, meaning "king-in-Parliament," that was sovereign: "There was no province of government from which Parliament's authority could be excluded; and sharing any portion of it with any other body would be *imperium in imperio,* a solecism, a logical absurdity."[12] Nevertheless, the Founders developed a conception of the People's sovereignty that managed that very logically absurd feat. They argued that sovereignty did not, as the anti-Federalists assume, reside in the states; that it could reside only in the whole of the People. And though the People could not logically give any of it away, they were still free to delegate it as they saw fit—precisely what they had done by ratifying the Constitution.

By this argument it was the very defenders of the sovereignty of the states who were actually opposing the legitimate rights of the People to assert the highest and final authority. As in all such political struggles neither this single argument nor arguments alone were responsible for the ultimate victory; but by the summer of 1788 the states had become a constitutional Union.

CHAPTER FOUR

Almost a Miracle

I do not believe that the constitution was the offspring
of inspiration, but I am as perfectly satisfied that the
Union of the States, in its *form* and *adoption,* is as
much the work of a Divine Providence as any of the
miracles recorded in the Old and New Testament were
the effects of a divine power.

BENJAMIN RUSH, 1788

On the eve of the Revolution, Tom Paine had exulted over the messi-
anic possibility "to begin the world anew." John Adams in his
"Thoughts on Government," written at about the same time, put the
matter with barely less enthusiasm: "How few of the human race have
ever enjoyed an opportunity of making an election of government more
than of air, soil, or climate for themselves or their children."[1] If not
always at this ecstatic pitch, some at the Constitutional Convention
seemed convinced that their work promised something similar. Madison and Hamilton both asserted in the Convention that they "were
now to decide for ever the fate of Republican Government"; Gouverneur Morris claimed "the whole human race will be affected by the
proceedings of this Convention." James Wilson, after the Convention,
made, if possible, a still bolder claim:

After the lapse of six thousand years since the creation of the world,
America now presents the first instance of a people assembled to weigh
deliberately and calmly, and to decide leisurely and peaceably, upon the
reform of government by which they will bind themselves and their posterity.[2]

The critic Robert Ferguson cites Bacon's essay "Of Honor and Reputation" to underline the exalted role these men imagined themselves
having been given to play.[3] Bacon lists four "degrees of sovereign honor"
of which "in the first place are *conditores imperiorum,* founders of states
and commonwealths" and "in the second . . . *legislatores,* lawgivers."[4]

It is not then quite as surprising perhaps that this legal assembly, subject to all the ordinary historical conflicts of ideas and material interests, could yield so thorough and pervasive a mythology as that surrounding the "miracle" at Philadelphia. And if the invocation of "miracle" seems to restrict the investigation to only popular and un-critical accounts, consider the famous description the Deist Thomas Jefferson gave, from his post as ambassador in Paris, of the men who had gathered at Independence Hall in Philadelphia—nothing less than "an assembly of demigods." James Madison, writing to his friend and confidante Thomas Jefferson a month after the Convention adjourned, summarized his amazement at the work it achieved:

> The great objects which presented themselves were 1. to unite a proper energy in the Executive and proper stability in the Legislative departments, with the essential characters of a Republican Government. 2. to draw a line of demarkation which would give to the General Government every power requisite for general purposes, and leave to the States every power which might be most beneficially administered by them. 3. to provide for the different interests of different parts of the Union. 4. to adjust the clashing pretensions of the large and small States. Each of these objects was pregnant with difficulties. The whole of them together formed a task more difficult than can be well conceived by those who were not con-cerned with the execution of it. Adding to these considerations the natural diversity of human opinions on all new and complicated subjects, it is impossible to consider the degree of concord which ultimately prevailed as less than a miracle.[5]

This acknowledgment of the "this-worldly" political origin of the Constitution, only to be followed by an almost-assertion of its mirac-ulous quality is a surprisingly typical response. Benjamin Rush, after viewing what was called the Federal Procession, a parade in Philadel-phia on July 4, 1788, celebrating the Constitution's ratification, com-mented:

> I do not believe that the Constitution was the offspring of inspiration, but I am as perfectly satisfied that the Union of the States, in its *form* and *adoption,* is as much the work of a Divine Providence as any of the mir-acles recorded in the Old and New Testament were the effects of a divine power.[6]

Even a simple assertion of the secularity of the Constitution's framing often feels the need to begin with an explicit denial of a divine inspi-ration, as Robert Morris does in concluding with what seems the ob-vious: "While some have boasted it is a work from Heaven . . . I have many reasons to believe that it is the work of plain, honest men, and such, I think, it will appear."[7]

John Murrin attributes the Constitution's early apotheosis to its very fragility, to the fact that it "became a substitute for any deeper kind of national identity:"

> Hovering there over a divided people, it aroused wonder and awe, even ecstasy. Early historians rewrote the past to make the Constitution the culminating event of their story. Some of the Republic's most brilliant legal minds wrote interminable multivolume commentaries on its manifold virtues and unmatched wisdom. Orators plundered the language in search of fitting praise. Some may even have put the document to music. This spirit of amazement, this frenzy of self-congratulation, owed its intensity to the terrible fear that the roof could come crashing at almost any time. Indeed, the national walls have taken much longer to build.[8]

But what nevertheless remains surprising is how this mythic aura seemed after ratification to overcome even the opponents of the Constitution—by most estimates nearly half the nation. After all, had the Convention failed to arrive at a compromise—and any reading of Madison's notes from the Convention makes it clear that this was a distinct possibility—or had the several states balked at its ratification, all these remarks would join the untold number of other enthusiastic and subsequently disappointed hopes to which the American Revolution, like every revolution since, has given birth. It is one of the greatest challenges facing any attempt at historical imagination to maintain a lively sense of contingency: the more you know about how everything hangs together, the more difficult it is to embrace the knowledge that few if any events of the past warrant the word "inevitable"; that any number of factors—from the sublime to the ridiculous—may have altered what can afterwards appear to be an iron chain of causality. If this is true of such grand themes as the rise of great powers, or the gradual development of technologies, then all the more so is it the case in regard to such a local and contingent phenomenon as the framing and ratification of the American Constitution. History always threatens to become mythic almost as a natural consequence of its merely having happened. When the history involves so primal a realm as a people or a state's foundation, the lure of the mythic becomes almost irresistible.

Since the rediscovery in the late nineteenth century that the people of the states had in fact been divided almost evenly between supporters and opponents of the new Constitution, historians have engaged in the necessary business of demythologizing and have long asked how and why this "apotheosis of the Constitution" had occurred.[9] For however vigorously some historians have adopted a perspective critical of the Constitution as a fulfillment of the promises of the Revolution, no organized political force after the ratification ever did. As Lance Banning summarized the political conditions of the new Union's first decade:

> As early as the spring of 1791 the Constitution was accepted on all sides as the starting point for further debates. Within four years of ratification the Republican opponents of the new administration—a party which probably included a majority of the old Anti-Federalists—insisted that they stood together to defend the Constitution against a threat that originated within the government itself. While interest in fundamental amendments persisted for years, determined opposition to the new plan of government disappeared almost as quickly as it arose. . . . The quick apotheosis of the American Constitution was a phenomenon without parallel in the western world. Nowhere have so many fierce opponents of a constitutional revision been so quickly transformed into an opposition that claimed to be more loyal than the government itself.[10]

Elkins and McKitrick offer a similar description and describe the result as "one of the minor marvels of American history."[11] As an explanation for this sudden shift in allegiance, Banning adduces the prevailing republican ideology with its absolute need for a constitution as a standard against which to hold the government. But from the point of view of this account, the question becomes the more general one—namely, What is it about the Constitution that allowed it to achieve and maintain sufficient authority to form a People? For what Hamilton famously called "a bundle of compromises" this is rather extraordinary treatment.

Clearly, the motive was to prevent the kind of tampering that could unravel such a potentially fragile construction: any change in one compromise would likely put pressures on many others. To pursue this question further, it is necessary to return once again to the framing itself. To what degree did those in the Convention consider the question of the mythic or the religious or sacred aspect of their work?

The first thing to notice about the delegates' religious concerns is that notwithstanding the place of religion in colonial American society and the active participation of ministers in the Revolution, there was, aside from one former Baptist preacher, not a single clergymen among the delegates. Still more notable, in all the four and a half months of deliberations, only one delegate so much as mentioned any idea of the Divine, or noted the relevance or importance of religious life. And who was that delegate? None other than Benjamin Franklin.

Aside from Washington, no other American possessed Franklin's eminence, either at home or in the larger world.[12] A man whom Edmund Burke addressed as the Friend of Humanity, Franklin had just returned to America from France after almost a decade delighting Paris and being delighted by it, as the Confederation's minister plenipotentiary. Now 81 years old and in ill health, on the first day of the Convention he was carried through the streets of Philadelphia in a litter manned by four prisoners from the city's jails. Although, as in the case of Washington, his presence was highly valued for the aura of legitimacy it gave to the convention, Franklin rarely spoke. Never much of an orator even in his prime, in the debates of the Convention Franklin would write out what little he had to say, and his colleague James Wilson would speak the words as the great sage sat and listened. In some respects, he seemed like a figure from another era. His first speech advocated unpaid government offices as a sound principle for disinterestedness. But not one of the delegates would seriously consider the proposal, since unlike Franklin, who had retired with financial security forty years earlier to pursue a life of public service, the delegates were young men with no intention of choosing between abjuring office or renouncing material advancement.

The next time Franklin spoke at any length came only after a month of close argument among the delegates had failed to find any substantial agreement on the all-important question of proportional representation. Gouverneur Morris claimed afterwards that "the fate of America was hanging by a hair."[13] This time Franklin read the speech himself, according to Carl Van Doren, "in his low, soft, hesitant voice, addressing his words directly to Washington in the Chair, almost as if this matter were between the two."[14] It was in this short speech that Franklin made the single substantive reference to the Divine in the whole of the Convention's deliberations. The enlightened philosopher and scientist decried the little progress the Convention had made as "a melancholy proof of the imperfection of Human Understanding," and continued:

> In this situation of this Assembly, groping as it were in the dark to find the political truth, and scarce able to distinguish it when presented to us, how has it happened, Sir, that we have not hitherto once thought of humbly applying to the Father of lights to illuminate our understandings. . . .
>
> I therefore beg leave to move—that henceforth prayer imploring the assistance of Heaven, and its blessing on our deliberations be held in this Assembly every morning before we proceed to business.[15]

It is certainly worth emphasizing that it was Franklin, a man famous for almost everything but his piety, who should have made this proposal. Writing over half a century later, the pioneering American historian, biographer, and editor, Jared Sparks, was still defending Franklin against charges of hostility to religion in general and Christianity in particular. He quotes from Franklin's epistolary answer late in his life to Yale College president Ezra Stiles who had inquired about his religious sentiments. Although Sparks acknowledges that Franklin's response was "not very precise," he insists that it has none of the "cold and heartless fidelity, which some writers have ascribed to him, and for which charge there is certainly no just foundation."[16]

Franklin's seemingly benign request for prayer elicited an almost complete lack of interest. Some raised objections that the measure would perhaps reveal a dangerous desperation in the proceedings; others that the Convention had no funds to hire a minister. According to Madison, there were several unsuccessful attempts "for silently postponing the matter by adjournment," and when the adjournment ultimately carried, that ended the matter. It was not put to a vote, at that time, or afterwards.[17]

The reason why now seems impossible to recover. To Stephen Botein, addressing explicitly the "religious dimensions of the early American state," the incident is easy to characterize: "old Benjamin Franklin made a rather embarrassing show of piety."[18] Other conjectures have been raised to explain the lack of response. Was there a problem involved because of the different Protestant denominations represented and the Catholics? Was it deemed improper in Philadelphia where the Quakers did not offer prayers at political assemblies? Did Hamilton speak up, as some tradition has it, and renounce any need for "foreign aid"? Or did Franklin himself merely make the gesture to impress upon the divided delegates the seriousness of the undertaking, and their need for cool heads and compromise? In reading over Madison's notes, one certainly develops a sense of the intensely demanding, practical business at hand, with new proposals, rejections, and counterproposals coming at the delegates nearly every day. Perhaps, notwithstanding their respect for Franklin, they simply had no patience for ceremony, however pious. It was left for Franklin to note on his manuscript: "The Convention, except three or four persons, thought prayers unnecessary." Does this note register astonishment? sarcasm? implied criticism of the body of delegates? The entire brief episode reveals how much remains unrecoverable about the inner sense of the Convention's proceedings.

Yet perhaps there is another explanation for both Franklin's prayerful speech and the delegates' silence, an explanation that points toward a deeper understanding of the Constitution's difficult-to-account-for authority. Franklin was a man utterly at home with secularity and at the same time was possessed of a placid, minimally doctrinal acceptance of the Divine, as he was likewise persuaded of a necessary place for religion in the life of a community. Thus, he supported all the churches of Philadelphia, regardless of their denomination. Franklin had no compunctions about associating God with the new Constitution, even if only by the intercession of prayer, because the quasireligious nature of the Convention's business must have seemed obvious to him. This is all the more striking when we return to his concluding speech at the Convention, not because the speech makes use of religious language or motifs. Quite the contrary. Just as Franklin alone alluded to God during the Convention, so at its end it is he who emphasizes the profoundly secular grounds on which they were forced to take their vote.

And in fact Franklin begins this last speech with good-natured mockery of religious sects and their certitudes, quoting the essayist Sir Richard Steele's dedication to the Pope: "the only difference between our Churches in their opinions of the certainty of their doctrines is, the Church of Rome is infallible and the Church of England is never in the wrong." And generalizing further still, from religion to human nature itself, Franklin quotes "a certain French lady" who arguing with her sister confesses that she meets "with no body but myself, that's always in the right—*Il n'y a que moi qui a toujours raison.*" All this is appended to Franklin's opening statement: "I confess that there are several parts of this constitution which I do not at present approve, but I am not sure I shall never approve them," which he afterwards takes up again:

> In these sentiments, Sir, I agree to this Constitution with all its faults, if they are such; because I think a general Government necessary for us, and there is no form of Government but what may be a blessing to the people if well administered. . . .
>
> For when you assemble a number of men to have the advantage of their joint wisdom, you inevitably assemble with those men, all their prejudices, their passions, their errors of opinion, their local interests, and their selfish views. From such an assembly can a perfect production be expected? It therefore astonishes me, Sir, to find this system approaching so near to perfection as it does. . . .
>
> Thus I consent, Sir, to this Constitution because I expect no better, and because I am not sure, that it is not the best.

Franklin's final speech is, in its way, a miniature masterpiece of what Arthur O. Lovejoy calls the "method of counterpoise." To Lovejoy "the group of extraordinarily able men" who made the Constitution "had few illusions about the rationality of the generality of mankind." They "held, in the main" a highly negative appraisal of human nature and human motivations, namely, that it "was actuated always by non rational motives—by 'passions,' or arbitrary and unexamined prejudices, or vanity, or the quest of private advantage—and yet as always inwards and incorrigibly assured that [a person's] motives *were* rational." Thus, the Founders turned quite naturally to counterpoise: "accomplishing desirable results by balancing harmful things against one another." The model for this was Newton's celestial mechanics, in which the planets' centrifugal force is precisely balanced against their centripetal force, "these two otherwise mischievous forces cause these bodies to behave as they should." To Lovejoy, the men of the Convention realized that their "problem was not chiefly one of political ethics but of practical psychology, a need not so much to preach to Americans about what they *ought* to do, as to predict successfully what they *would* do" and thus the applicability of the Newtonian model.[19]

Franklin's conclusion itself is a perfect application of this general method, a positive statement arising from a combination of negations: "I consent . . . to this Constitution because I expect *no* better, and because I am *not* sure, that it is *not* the best." And thus he concludes:

> On the whole, Sir, I can not help expressing a wish that every member of the Convention who may still have objections to it, would with me, on this occasion doubt a little of his own infallibility, and to make manifest our unanimity, put his name to this instrument.

Note that Franklin's words do not bind the signatories to a formal endorsement of the document, but merely ask that as members of state delegations, they all agree to sign as witnesses. When Charles Cotesworth Pinckney, a delegate from South Carolina, thought to reach beyond this ambiguity and pledge himself to the Constitution's ratification, Franklin responded: "It is too soon to pledge ourselves before Congress and our Constituents shall have approved the plan." The anticipatory character of *We the People* was not lost on Franklin. As it happened, even after last-minute changes were accepted, there remained three delegates still present (Elbridge Gerry, Edmund Randolph, and George Mason) who could not bring themselves to sign. Franklin's speech, alone not bound by the secrecy of the proceedings, was sent to a number of his correspondents and in less than six months had been reprinted over thirty-six times, and in nearly every state.[20]

It was Franklin alone who made reference to religion, as it was Franklin who insisted that anything like the certainty of the religious realm was out of the question. Is this not another application of counterpoise, or what might be called more generally a positive acceptance of tension, or balance, though certainly of a much subtler and tacit sort?

But perhaps it was not all that tacit. Consider Franklin's contribution to the ratification debate. He does not merely hint at myth or miracle: in his newspaper essay, entitled "A Comparison of the Conduct of the Ancient Jews and of the Anti-Federalists in the United States of America," he aims directly at the very model of divine revelation. Employing his characteristically fictionalizing wit, he relays the speech of a "zealous Advocate for the propos'd Federal Constitution:"

> On the whole, it appears, that the Israelites were a People jealous of their newly-acquired Liberty, which Jealousy was in itself no Fault; but, when they suffer'd it to be work'd upon by artful Men, pretending Public Good, with nothing really in view but private Interest, they were led to oppose the Establishment of the *New Constitution* [Franklin's italics], whereby they brought upon themselves much Inconvenience and Misfortune.[21]

And to be certain that the full implication of this argument is clear, Franklin proceeds paradoxically—another kind of tension—to disclaim the very analogy between the Constitution and the Holy Book, precisely by way of affirming it:

> To conclude, I beg I may not be understood to infer, that our General Convention was divinely inspired, when it form'd the new federal Constitution, merely because that Constitution has been unreasonably and vehemently opposed; yet I must own I have so much Faith in the general Government of the world by Providence, that I can hardly conceive a Transaction of such momentous Importance to the Welfare of the Millions now existing, and to exit in the Posterity of a great Nation, should be suffered to pass without being in some degree influenc'd, guided and governed by that omnipotent, omnipresent and beneficent Ruler, in whom all inferior Spirits live, and move, and have their Being.

Perhaps it was Franklin alone who could allow the secular and revealed aspects of the Founders' undertaking to flicker without alarm.[22] When the conditions of its framing are considered together, along with the function that it exercises, the Constitution seems a peculiarly hybrid kind of phenomenon, a paradox, secular and revelational at once.

Why, for instance, is God absent not only from the proceedings of the Convention but from the document itself?[23] This absence did not go unremarked, ultimately leading to a failed attempt at an amended preamble ("Recognizing Almighty God as the source of power in civil government, and acknowledging the Lord Jesus Christ as the governor among nations").[24] The religious scholar Martin Marty, having read in their entirety the two Library of America volumes on *The Debates of the Constitution,* making note of "all references that could be construed as religious" through the 2,387 pages of documents, finds what he calls "terribly slim pickings," and concludes that "the two volumes confirm the idea that the founders' practical politics displaced and left little room for sustained discussion of the metaphysical, metaethical and theological backdrop to constitutionalism." Specifically in regard to the ordinary matters of religious life, "one would hardly know from these collected documents that Americans were churchgoers." The clergy are "all but invisible." References to the Bible specifically as a source of authority are "extremely rare." In one of them Dickinson "uses I Corinthians 12 on the body of Christ as an analogy for 'the benefits of union' in the republic."[25] To this account might be added the fact that in the whole of the *Federalist Papers* there is not a single reference to God.

There is no question in all this that the Founders, like the vast majority of their fellow Americans, knew their Bible, but as Jon Butler in his recent history of American religion, *Awash in a Sea of Faith,* says of the Revolution, constituting the nation was "a profoundly secular event." When after the Revolution the ministry was able to "sacralize" it, it was strictly by virtue of the fact that so many of the clergy had, as it happened, supported the Revolution.

CHAPTER FIVE

The Paradox of Secular Revelation

"We are One"
"Mind Your Business"

<small>LEGENDS FROM THE TWO SIDES OF THE FRANKLIN OR
"FUGIO" CENT, 1787</small>

For the Constitution to work, it must be a wholly secular document
and it must be a revelation. It must be fully secular, yet fully revealed.
But if it were a revelation, it would have to meet the criteria established
by the biblical model, and for Protestants most especially Old Testament criteria. When God comes down upon Sinai, a thick cloud of
smoke hides the mountaintop. The people assemble at the foot of the
mountain, warned not to proceed further. Only Moses ascends. The
revelation sets out a scheme of government—how the People are to live
among themselves—along with some particular laws. And the People
accept it, vowing to Moses, "All that the Lord had spoken, we will
do."[1] The Constitutional Convention, along with the Ratification,
seems to accord squarely with this Sinaitic model. Four clear indices of
revelation in the Sinai account have their parallels in 1787—that only
a representative of the people actually receives it; that the reception is
veiled in absolute secrecy; that the revelation itself declares something
like a scheme of government along with some particular laws; and that
the People give to it their voluntary acquiescence. And both biblical
revelation and Constitution are, of course, verbal artifacts.

Yet the most striking parallel of the constitutional founding to the
Sinaitic revelation is that in both cases a group of separate, if related,
social entities became a People. The biblical Hebrews had similarly
come from elsewhere to their land and thus faced the conundrum of a
beginning without an origin, and both the biblical revelation and the
Constitutional Convention converted that beginning into something

that was also an origin. The tribes of Israel became a nation and the Chosen People, so the states of the former colonies became a nation and a People.

Analogies of this general sort were a commonplace of the typology that obsessed early New England, and it is difficult to believe that that heritage did not play some part in the American founding. But it must be stressed that neither those who framed the Constitution nor those who ratified it consciously subscribed to any such typological understanding. And the Constitution was as much the work of the South, and indeed of the Middle Colonies—perhaps more so—than of New England. Moreover, typology is a form of analogical interpretation that is anything but a matter of secrecy and evasion. It is all the more interesting, therefore, as we examined in the last chapter, how very muted, tactful, and as-if the typological suggestions were. It is all in the realm of Lincoln's famous reference to the Americans as "an almost Chosen People," an assertion accompanied by a denial. Paradoxy has replaced orthodoxy.

On the face of it, conceiving the blueprint-like Constitution as a revelation is a rather far-fetched notion. There is certainly little reason to believe that the Constitution was consciously modeled on biblical, or Sinaitic, revelation. But on what was it modeled? The Founders believed that they had more or less invented the form themselves, with hints from the State Constitutional Convention of Massachusetts of a few years earlier. Subsequent historians have largely agreed.

And yet, the ambiguity of the representative status of the delegates, together with the secrecy of their proceedings is, at the least, an interesting parallel. Rakove claims that "the most remarkable aspect of the Convention's four-month inquiry was that it was conducted in virtually absolute secrecy, uninfluenced by external pressures of any kind."[2] Secrecy itself casts something of a mystery about the proceedings, just as things secret have a kind of natural association with things sacred.[3] That this extreme secrecy continued even after ratification makes it perhaps that much more striking. Not only did the surviving delegates keep a remarkable fealty to the Convention's rule, but Madison, notwithstanding the urging of others, refused to publish his Notes, the only thing amounting to a full record of the course of the Constitution's creation, until after his death. And he was the last of the delegates to die, just one year short of a half century after the Convention completed its work.

As for the people's voluntary acceptance of the Constitution, Madison himself in a speech on the floor of the House of Representatives in 1796, addressed its high significance when discussing his personal knowledge of the Convention's "intention," and whether that intention could serve as a guide for understanding the Constitution:

> After all, whatever veneration might be entertained for the body of men who formed our constitution, the sense of that body could never be regarded as the oracular guide in the expounding the constitution. As the instrument came from them, it was nothing more than the draught of a plan, nothing but a dead letter, until life and validity were breathed into it, by the voice of the people, speaking through the several state conventions.[4]

What of the content of the Constitution and any analogy to revelation? The United States Constitution is often described, along with its precursor state constitutions, as the first written constitution. It is now agreed, however, that its great innovation was instead in the very nature of its content, the radical aspect of its supremacy. It is not merely the "supreme law," as it says itself, in regard to the laws of the separate states; it is superior to any laws whatever: it is the law of the laws. Moreover, the Americans themselves knew very well that their greatest achievement was the creation of this high, overarching authority. When they looked at England, they saw a sovereign Parliament that obeyed no law but that of its own devising; in 1713 it passed the Septennial Act which went so far as to extend its own duration. It is precisely because Britain lacked not a written constitution per se, but a government-framing constitution, a law by which the law itself must operate, that Paine could say with conviction that "there is no constitution in England."

How to explain the complete and indeed the surprising absence of any religious reference in the Constitution itself, and the rarity of such reference in the ratification debates? Is it because it would introduce a frame of reference precisely in conflict with the underpinnings of the very process of constituting the new nation? In order for the sacred aspect of the Constitution to function, at least two conditions had to be met. It could not be made explicit, and the Bible itself, *the* historical revelation, had to be kept out of sight. There was nothing irreligious about the Convention and nothing hostile to religion in the Constitution. But it is as if the Bible and all its accompanying myths—and the word is used neutrally here, not as a token of unbelief—had to remain off stage if the Constitution were to assume the role assigned it, of constituting a people, *e pluribus unum,* a One from the Many.[5]

Yet the Constitution has been so often imagined as a machine, the very essence of secularity. A machine is a most unlikely image to come to mind when considering a revealed text. Kammen in *The Machine that Would Go of Itself* explains that the metaphor behind his title remained dominant from the ratification debates until at least a hundred years afterward.[6] In 1981 Gary Wills, examining the *Federalist Papers*, still comfortably uses the figure: "A constitution," he writes, "is precisely, an *ordering,* a proper articulation into parts; a machine for living."[7]

What keeps general reflection on the Constitution in American culture a strangely subdued, even occluded, affair is, perhaps, just this paradox of its secular and revealed character. It is not a *secularized* revelation. In its formation and its function, it is simply secular from one perspective, as it is revealed from another. Not that these aspects or faces of the Constitution actually work together. In an ordinary way, the combination makes no sense. It violates logic. It is *para doxos,* beyond belief. But then John Dickinson had famously insisted that logic could play no part in the Constitution's construction: "Experience must be our only guide," he told his fellow delegates. "Reason may mislead us."[8] And Max Farrand concludes his account of the Constitution's framing by acknowledging that

> it was not a logical piece of work. No document originating as this had and developed as this had been developed could be logical or even consistent. That is why every attempted analysis of the constitution has been doomed to failure. From the very nature of its construction the constitution defies analysis upon a logical basis.[9]

It is as a secular revelation that the Constitution met the challenge that Hannah Arendt described as confronting all modern political life, namely, its "most elementary predicament" of needing to overcome the "profound instability" that results from "the emancipation of the secular realm from the tutelage of the Church."[10] The United States Constitution established authority for an American national life from a paradoxically middle position, now assuming a transcendent authority, now insisting on an uncompromising secularity.

The practice of constitutional interpretation, from the first Congresses to the present, reflects this paradoxical quality. The belief in original meaning, the idea that the meaning of the text was somehow fixed by the Founders, or the ratifiers, coexists with what could be described as a tension, or a contradiction, namely, the idea of an or-

The Franklin, also known as the "Fugio," cent was authorized by Congress in 1787 and thus, strictly speaking, predates the constitutional regime, although its two contrary legends—*We Are One* and *Mind Your Business*—perfectly express a minted conflict between the two national impulses, toward a transcendent oneness and toward a materialistic dispersion. (Courtesy of the Hesburgh Library, University of Notre Dame.)

ganic constitution whose meaning changes with the changing times. Is it a revelation, handed down to us to live by and preserve, or is it a machine of our own making, one we can revise and rework and reinterpret as it suits us? Joseph Ellis, in his recent popular book on the Founders, describes the debate between these two irreconcilable conceptions as historically unresolved, and then comments: "If that means the United States is founded on a contradiction, then so be it. With that one bloody exception, we have been living with it successfully for over two hundred years."[11]

Framed in strictest secrecy, claimed proleptically as of the whole People's authorship, obscuring the very existence of the nation's religious life while it assumes a transcendent, overarching authority, a beginning that was also an origin, and replete with Sinaitic analogies, the Constitution of the United States befits a nation conceived in paradox, in which independence brought mutual dependence, and sovereign states remained intact within a sovereign Union.

The first national coin minted by the government of the United States, in the same year as the Constitutional Convention, provides an apt metaphor for the Union's paradoxical foundation. On one side, thirteen interlocking rings, themselves together forming a larger ring surrounding the almost mystical motto, "We Are One." On the obverse side, below the sun and a sundial, are the doggedly secular, hortatory words: "Mind Your Business."[12] It is as if the Constitution functions within the optically illusory sphere created by flipping this coin into the air. The two sides, "We Are One—Mind Your Business," cannot by their very nature be seen at one and the same time, except through this continuous oscillation.

PART TWO

An American Literary Renaissance

CHAPTER SIX

Declarations of American Literary Independence

Glorious our fall, since in a noble cause.
The bold attempt alone demands applause.

ROYALL TYLER, PROLOGUE TO *The Contrast*, 1787

In 1788, the year of the Constitution's ratification, Philip Freneau, the acknowledged "poet of the Revolution," published in the name of an imaginary sometime weaver and writer, the late Robert Slender, an "Advice to Authors" which begins with what would become an often repeated sentiment in the new nation: "There are few writers of books in this new world, and amongst these very few that deal in works of imagination, and, I am sorry to say, fewer still that have any success attending their lucubrations." A little further on, he defensively explains that "a political and a literary independence . . . being two very different things—the first was accomplished in seven years, the latter will not be completely effected, perhaps, in as many centuries." He offers ten numbered pieces of advice to the "genuine author," starting with a warning against dedicatory epistles "first invented by slaves, and . . . continued by fools and sycophants," and concluding with this stoical recommendation:

> 10. If fortune seems absolutely determined to starve you and you can by no means whatever make your works sell; to keep up as much as in you lies, the expiring dignity of authorship, do not take to drinking, gambling or bridge-building [Paine's would-be means of earning a living] as some have done, thereby bringing the trade of authorship into disrepute; but retire to some uninhabited island or desert, and there, at your leisure, end your life with decency.[1]

It has long been recognized how quickly, and impatiently, Americans proceeded from political independence and nation-building to a campaign for a new and independent American literature, a campaign that often amounted to a simultaneous demand and disappointment, and that was to continue for nearly half a century.[2] Not surprisingly, these declarations of American literary independence were diverse and changed with the changing conditions in the Union.

The dominant literary task demanded in the first decades of national life was the defense of the new republican government. It must be remembered that during the earlier Federalist period, most especially before Jefferson's election in 1800, though lingering on until after the war with the British in 1812, the survival of the newly constituted Union was by no means assured. There was, therefore, a general agreement about the urgency of literature coming to its defense. In part, this is a reflection of the larger denotative range of the contemporary notion of "literature," one still in keeping with Samuel Johnson's definition of "learning; skill in letters." Works of philosophy and scholarship were valued as highly for their literary skill as for the soundness of their factual presentations or their arguments. But literature in our now more usual sense of poems and novels was likewise dominated in the early years of the Union by a peculiarly communal and didactic purpose. As Michael Warner has pointed out in *The Letters of the Republic*, the American writers of these years considered all of their "engagements with print activities," even when primarily aesthetic in aim, as participating in "the republican public sphere [and] subject to its norms."[3]

In practice, this often meant didactic (and doggedly imitative) verse. Thus Timothy Dwight, in the introduction to his consciously derivative "Greenfield Hill" of 1794, offers an unembarrassed didactic defense of his work: "Poetry appears to be as advantageous an instrument of making useful impressions as can easily be conceived. It will be read by many persons who would scarcely look at a logical discussion."[4] Poetry, by this view, is an instrument, one designed for its therapeutic qualities, with the weaknesses of its readers in mind. There is nothing meant to be condescending in this, anymore than there is anything indecorous when Royall Tyler has the Prologue in his play, *The Contrast*, apologize for its dramatic shortcomings with an assertion of its communal, republican intentions:

> Should rigid critics reprobate our play,
> At least the patriotic heart will say,
> "Glorious our fall, since in a noble cause.
> "The bold attempt alone demands applause."[5]

Ralph Waldo Emerson, looking back from the perspective of 1852 on these early attempts at a national literature, evinces nothing but scorn, contending that "from 1790 to 1820 there was not a book, a speech, a conversation, or a thought in the state."[6] In the case of imaginative literature, at least, Emerson's judgment has long seemed, however uncharitable, not altogether inaccurate. Their historical interest has always been substantial, but the works, even when executed with intelligence and passion, were overwhelmingly imitative of far more engaging English, specifically neo-classical, precursors.

Even in recent decades, when reversionary rescue of previously denigrated literary works has become an academic industry, it has been difficult to alter radically history's judgment of the new nation's first writers. What effort there has been to revise the critical consensus regarding these writers has required a parallel revision of the very criteria for literary critical judgment.

Michael Gilmore in the most recent *Cambridge History of American Literature* exemplifies what might be called the current historicist orthodoxy when he insists that the earlier consensus "takes for granted the existence of an ahistorical notion of what constitutes literary achievement, one that gives absolute primacy to aesthetic value."[7] Without quite falling prey to this shell game of literary valuation, Michael Warner in his thoughtful, aforementioned study devotes himself to an examination of the early American novel while explicitly denying any attempt "to redeem these novels as triumphs of artistic intention." He goes so far as needing to justify his engagement in what he describes as a "proto-literary field," the study of which could amount to "mere antiquarianism," by the opportunity it provides for "rethinking the relation of cultural goods to the public sphere."[8] For he, too, shares in the notion that these early novels must be understood as "features of a public sphere rather than a liberal aesthetic." And since he describes the novel form as "by nature divorced from the public sphere, designed as an occasion for a specially private kind of subjectivity" he concludes, not surprisingly given these assumptions, that these "novels could only narrate their anxieties about the hazard to the republic that they themselves posed."[9]

Far and away the most penetrating recent critic of this republican literature, in its didactic aim of union as well as in its authentic "aesthetics of order and control," is Robert Ferguson, who in his crucial book, *Law and Letters in American Culture*, reimagined the historical "configuration of law and letters" that dominated the period, and thus addressed with insight the genuine, if modest, literary achievements of the new nation's earliest writers. While he shares with other revisionist critics a desire not to sacrifice "the creative context of early national writings to the success story of a later literature" and to acknowledge "the original meaning and strength of the republic's first books," when he cites the collected correspondence between John Adams and Thomas Jefferson as "the central literary accomplishment of the period," he makes no move to obfuscate the notion of the literary, adducing as confirmation the opinion of one of modernism's high priests of aesthetic value, Ezra Pound.[10]

As Ferguson explains, the Federalists, who politically dominated the Union until the election of Jefferson in 1800, and continued to dominate culturally until at least as late as the War of 1812, conceived of republicanism as a polity precariously balanced between the oppression of tyranny and the licentiousness of democracy. Their Revolution had focused on the tyranny of the king; their fears of democracy became lodged in the image of the later events in France, and most especially as those Revolutionary events became interpreted by their ideological enemies, beginning with the formidable Edmund Burke. Thus, Ferguson shows how the didacticism of the literature of this period of Federalist domination had a strongly conservative cast and aimed at fostering a stable communal unity. It found its most appropriate aim in addressing an assembly of auditors: "In the early republic the unity of a listening audience was simultaneously a type for and a step toward a unified country." Ferguson cites the definition of eloquence offered by Hugh Swinton Legaré—"poetry subdued to the business of civic life"—to describe both the purposes and the prevailing pressures with which the earliest American poets, dramatists, and novelists of the United States worked. Legaré was not only attorney general and then secretary of state under Tyler, but the South's dominant literary critic— itself a revealing combination and unlikely to occur at any later time in the nation's history.[11]

It is one of the great contributions of Ferguson's study that it explains what would otherwise be the very strange fact that so very many of the most significant early American writers were associated with the study or practice of law, among them Charles Brockden Brown, John Trumbull, Royall Tyler, Hugh Henry Brackenridge, Washington Irving, William Bryant, and James Fenimore Cooper (p. 66). All of these writers had trained as lawyers, and half had actively practiced the profession, at least for a time. Indeed, the study of law had largely replaced the earlier emphasis on education for the ministry. Higher education itself was a rare commodity. According to Ferguson, by the early years of the republic no more than one in five hundred adult males had any higher education, and of these it was the lawyers alone for which such education had become a distinctive mark of their profession. And it was the ancient forensic orator, Cicero—his marble bust notably presiding over the idealistic debates in Charles Brockden Brown's novel, *Wieland* (1799)—who served as the model for the early American lawyer. Circuit-riding lawyers traveled throughout the country and, in courts that served then as now a quasitheatrical function, held forth with all their eloquence before the local population and one another. They thus became quite naturally the spokesmen for the new legal, and with it the political, order. Ferguson helpfully quotes Alexis de Tocqueville in explaining why lawyers assumed so central a literary position to the effect that "the government of the Union depends almost entirely upon legal fictions; the Union is an ideal nation, which exists, so to speak, only in the mind, and whose limitations and extent can only be discerned by the understanding."[12]

In the alliance formed between the law and letters, between the legal profession and the aims of the literary, it was unquestionably the law that held the dominant position. In part this was a simple, practical matter: it was impossible to earn a living in America by writing alone. Brockden Brown, for example, the first American to declare himself a professional writer, left his law career in Philadelphia for a literary career in New York with only the greatest trepidation, and after two years of prodigious literary production, writing his five strongest novels, retired from literature to enter business. More to the point, such exclusive literary activity was not seen as in itself desirable and would amount almost to an abandonment of the cause of Union. As a pointed instance of this attitude, Ferguson cites a letter addressed to the young Henry Longfellow by the editor of the *United States Literary Gazette*, Theophilus Parson Jr., to show how long literature's subordinate status lingered. Longfellow had written of his longing to abandon his father's law office for literary work at the *Gazette*, to which Parson replied:

> There is a stage in the progress of a bright mind, when the boy has thrown away his toys and marbles, but the young man is still so far a child as to value things more by their elegance and power of amusing than by their usefulness. He plays with his books and thinks he is working when he is

only playing hard. . . . Get through your present delusion as soon as you can; and then you will see how wise it will be for you to devote yourself to the law.[13]

Beginning with the War of 1812, with the Union's increasing commercialism, the law itself began to be transformed. There came to be a rapidly expanding accumulation of case law, and the world of the refined and eloquent man of letters began to give way to the rising tide of democracy based on universal white male suffrage. Where once a lawyer needed to be a highly educated man, versed in the classics and in the literary past, what he now increasingly came to need was a mastery of the ever-increasing number of law textbooks. In keeping with this development, all the state bar associations dropped the requirement of a college education. Daniel Webster, the very paradigm of the lawyer as a generalist orator of the early republic, found in his later years that he could function professionally only with the assistance of friends who had mastered the new technical legal competence. However magnificent his grasp of the larger notion of the "Law" in the singular, Webster grew increasingly ignorant of the plural "laws."[14]

It had been "Law," the grand, abstract singular—not the laws, the gradual accumulation of statutes and precedents—with which these men of letters had been preoccupied. Their education prepared and encouraged them to generalize with informed eloquence about history, society, and politics and bring well-honed literary resources to their aid. Their literature engaged similar concerns. Brockden Brown's powerfully fascinating novels, for instance, tend to elaborate wildly burgeoning allegories in which abstract principles of law and social order often occupy a prominent position. The most effective of them, *Wieland* (1798), confronts the reader with a frightening case of confused sources of authority and fraudulently ventriloquized voices. Jay Fliegelman in a masterful introduction to the novel contends that "Brown's master trope of ventriloquism is . . . a metaphor not only for secularization—man speaking in lieu of God—but for the absent presence of an anonymous author"—raising just the kind of large questions of society and order that these lawyer-writers felt themselves educated to consider.[15] Brackenridge's *Modern Chivalry* (1792; 1815) is similarly concerned with the principle of law, with the fate of the Founders' high valuation of law when confronted by the democratic reality of frontier life. Likewise for Washington Irving, the law as a system of order is an obsessive object of his humor and his satire.

With the increasing complexity of the law, and the movement from generalists to specialists, the legal profession drifted away from its association with both humane learning and literature. Higher education became increasingly unnecessary, replaced by more technical education in the law. Along with this transformation of the profession, the political conditions became less amenable to the lawyers' eloquent rhetoric. As long as the primary national task seemed to be the justification of the republic, such rhetoric had its place; but as the question of slavery and its place in the nation came to the fore, rhetoric began to divide rather than unite. What became necessary was increasingly difficult compromise, and skills required to foster compromise—often as not the product of crabbed negotiations and purposeful ambiguity—are altogether different. One does not rouse a people into compromise.

As the intimate alliance between law and letters lost its motive force, declarations of American literary independence developed an increasingly nationalist fervor, and with such declarations came a demand for some startling kind of newness commensurate with the startling newness of the nation. We can hear the echo of such declarations midway into the century and beyond, in sentiments like that expressed by Melville in his encomium to Hawthorne of 1850: "Believe me, my friends, that men are not very much inferior to Shakespeare are this day being born on the banks of the Ohio. And the day will come when you shall say, Who reads a book by an Englishman that is a modern?"[16]

An often quoted passage from Longfellow's *Kavanaugh, A Tale*, his brief autobiographical fiction of 1849, a dialogue between a schoolteacher, Mr. Churchill, and a brash entrepreneurial would-be magazine editor, well captures both the common noisiness of these declarations and the lingering dissent they aroused:

> "I think, Mr. Churchill," said he, "that we want a national literature commensurate with our mountains and rivers,—commensurate with Niagara, and the Alleghenies, and the Great Lakes."
>
> "Oh!"
>
> "We want a national epic that shall correspond to the size of the country; that shall be to all other epics what Banvard's Panorama of the Mississippi is to all other paintings,—the largest in the world!"
>
> "Ah!"
>
> "We want a national drama in which scope enough shall be given to our gigantic ideas, and to the unparalleled activity and progress of our people!"
>
> "Of course."

"In a word, we want a national literature altogether shaggy and un-shorn, that shall shake the earth, like a herd of buffaloes thundering over the prairies!"

"Precisely," interrupted Mr. Churchill; "but excuse me!—are you not confounding things that have no analogy? Great has a very different meaning when applied to a river and when applied to a literature. . . . A man will not necessarily be a great poet because he lives near a great mountain. Nor being a poet, will he necessarily write better poems than another, because he lives nearer Niagara."

"And as for having it so savage and wild as you want it, I have only to say, that all literature as well as all art, is the result of culture and intellectual refinement."

"Ah, we do not want art and refinement; we want genius—untutored, wild, original, free."[17]

When an American literature did arise that to some degree met this hyperbolic demand, it was only after the configuration of law and letters had largely failed and the realm of law had ceased its struggle to harness and thereby control literary imagination. Only then did the Constitution itself become imaginatively potent. Although as the primary legal instrument the Constitution had occupied an important place as a symbol of law's conservative check on tyranny from above and anarchy from below, the fact of self-constituting itself, of the People's giving themselves the law, did not reach deeply into any American poetic practice. Ironically, only after literary expression began to lose interest in what could be called an explicit republican ideology of the legally constituted Union is it possible to trace the effect of the Constitution's *paradoxical* form on the aspiration for an independent American literature. It is almost fair to say that the less the Constitution served as a manifest theme for the nation's literature, the more profoundly it developed as a latent, formative influence.

In part, no doubt, such a consequence of the Constitution's central place in the nation's life needed to await some sense of the document's survival, its working "success." And for the lawyers, their professional familiarity with the legal business of the constitutional regime could only have obscured the very peculiarities of that regime. Their interest in justifying the new order's legitimacy and assuring its stability would not have been well served by considering more deeply the paradox of its very authority. What these writers were busy defending they would have hardly had the time or the inclination to meditate and wonder about. The very change from Law to laws, and with it the transformation of lawyers' education from generalized humanistic learning and eloquence to detailed study of accumulating statutes and case law, allowed the phenomenon of the Constitution itself to settle into what we call the background. It needed to recede into the past, out of immediate danger, in order to become available for more formal, less merely thematic, inspiration.

Ferguson concludes his account of the configuration of law and letters with an eloquent description of Abraham Lincoln as its anachronistic epilogue, describing him as in many respects a throwback to the forensic orators who were the literary representatives of the young republic. But from the perspective of this investigation the most striking feature of Lincoln's rhetorical practice is the way in which it represents a new relation to the Constitution. The Founders have died; the revelation is decisively in the past. What does it mean to follow them? What is the Constitution to these new generations? It is in answering this question that the Constitution comes to permeate more deeply into the American imagination and to generate the nation's peculiar literary renaissance.

CHAPTER SEVEN

Preserving the Revelation

And, in short, let it become the political religion of
the nation; and let the old and the young, the rich
and the poor, the grave and the gay, of all sexes and
tongues, and colors and conditions, sacrifice unceasingly upon its altars.

ABRAHAM LINCOLN, ADDRESS TO THE YOUNG MEN'S
LYCEUM IN SPRINGFIELD, 1838

The most important of Abraham Lincoln's early speeches, his 1838
Address to the Young Men's Lyceum in Springfield, would seem retrospectively to be the culmination of the Constitution's ratification in
American political life.[1] In his speech Lincoln articulated a view of the
Constitution, largely in accord with the Whig rhetoric of his time, that
would remain consistent throughout the remainder of his life and that
would guide him through the long, complex, and ultimately successful
struggle of the Civil War.

It is helpful first to take note of some of the radical changes that
had occurred between the early republic and the late 1830s when Lincoln delivered his Springfield Address. With the second victory over
England in 1815 and the passing of the revolutionary generation, a
new spirit arose, not only of rising democracy (however, to our way
of thinking, severely limited by gender and race) but also, and not in-
cidentally, of increasing political divisiveness. Even before the dominance of the era-naming figure of Andrew Jackson, the fact of party
conflict—not merely the division into factions, however bitter, which
Jefferson had still hoped to transcend, but the entrenched and established opposition forces we now associate with mass democracy itself—had become an accepted aspect of American political life. The
course of Jackson's presidency merely intensified these national divi-
sions. Upon "King Andrew's" retirement, his handpicked successor,
Martin Van Buren, a veritable party boss, neither imagined nor desired any end to this division. The issue of tariffs—demanded by the

North for the protection of burgeoning industry and dreaded by the South—and most significantly, of course, the issue of slavery, increasingly a strictly Southern institution, had together threatened the very Union that the Constitution had established. A series of compromises, hard-fought and acrimonious, failed to bring the country back to a secure sense of a shared republican experiment. Just as the South vigorously defended slavery, and its right to extend the institution to new lands in the West, an increasingly radicalized abolitionism demanded an immediate end to enslavement. The Missouri Compromise of 1820, intended to settle the issue of slavery in the vast area of the Louisiana Purchase and to ensure a balance between slave states and free states, had maintained at best an uneasy peace between many in the South who resented any federal law limiting slavery and those in the North who considered the compromise a shameful acquiescence in slavery's expansion.

Nor were these the only changes. With the development of early industry came the beginnings of a market economy. Immigration dramatically increased, as did the movement of people westward, encouraged by the vast program of internal improvements, many of them in transportation—another issue of sustained political contention—of which Lincoln himself was a strong supporter. Amid such steady and dramatic transformations, it is not surprising that the subject of Lincoln's Address to the Young Men's Lyceum, "The Perpetuation of Our Political Institutions," had become an increasingly common topic upon which to wax eloquent.

Addressing these young men in 1838, Lincoln was not much more than a young man himself. At 29, still single, having just two years earlier received his license to practice law, he was in the middle of a successful career as an Illinois state legislator. Indeed, he had played a crucial role in winning for Springfield the seat of the state capital from Vandalia. In his Address, he posits two clear points of reference—a then and a now: then is the time of the Revolution when the founding of the government "was felt by all to be an undecided experiment," and now, a time when that experiment was "understood to be a successful one."[2] This, then, is the time to approach the urgent question of how best to preserve that governing "legacy bequeathed us, by a once hardy, brave, and patriotic, but now lamented and departed race of ancestors" (p. 29). Lincoln calls specific attention to a threat against this legacy of "our fathers," calling it "something of ill-omen amongst us":

I mean the increasing disregard for law which pervades the country; the growing disposition to substitute the wild and furious passions, in lieu of the sober judgment of Courts, and the worse than savage mobs, for the executive ministers of justice. This disposition is awfully fearful in any community; and that it now exists in ours, though grating to our feelings to admit, it would be a violation of truth, and an insult to our intelligence, to deny. (p. 29)

Lincoln cites two specific instances of this lawlessness. One was in Mississippi, where a vigilante campaign against gamblers continued "until first Negroes, then white men supposed in league with Negroes, then strangers present merely for business, till dead men were seen literally dangling from the boughs of trees upon every road side." The other instance was in St. Louis where a mulatto man who "within a single hour from the time he had been a freeman, attending to his own business, and at peace with the world" had been chained to a tree and burned to death (p. 30). Lincoln then anticipates the young men's' question, "But you are, perhaps, ready to ask, 'What has this to do with the perpetuation of our political institutions?' " With the spread of such lawlessness, he explains, the protection of people and of property will no longer be secure, and thus the crucial "attachment of People" to the government will weaken. It will then be only a matter of time before "men of sufficient talent and ambition will . . . seize the opportunity, strike the blow, and overturn that fair fabric, which for the last half century, has been the fondest hope, of the lovers of freedom, throughout the world" (p. 32).

With all the eloquence of a forensic preacher, Lincoln asserts that there is an answer to this threat of lawlessness:

As the patriots of seventy-six did to the support of the Declaration of Independence, so to the support of the Constitution and Laws, let every American pledge his life, his property, and his sacred honor;—let every man remember that to violate the law, is to trample on the blood of his father, and to tear the character of his own, and his children's liberty. Let reverence for the laws be breathed by every American mother, to the lisping babe, that prattles on her lap;—let it be taught in schools, in seminaries, and in colleges;—let it be written in Primers, spelling books, and in Almanacs;—let it be preached from the pulpit, proclaimed in legislative halls, and enforced in courts of justice. And, in short, let it become the political religion of the nation; and let the old and the young, the rich and the poor, the grave and the gay, of all sexes and tongues, and colors and conditions, sacrifice unceasingly upon its altars. (pp. 32–33)

Here, very explicitly, Lincoln takes on the task that Ferguson explains as the driving purpose of the early configuration of law and letters—a defense of the republican government. In and of itself, the outline of this solution was not original with Lincoln. But we need only read his most famous precursor for this rhetoric of constitutional preservation, Daniel Webster, to sense the new force that Lincoln brings to the argument. Here is Webster, commemorating the fiftieth anniversary of the Battle of Bunker Hill in 1825:

> And let the sacred obligation which have devolved on this generation, and on us, sink deep into our hearts. Those who established our liberty and our government are daily dropping from among us. The great trust now descends to new hands. Let us apply ourselves to that which is presented to us, as our appropriate object. We can win no laurels in a war for independence. Earlier and worthier hands have gathered them all. Nor are there places for us by the side of Solon, and Alfred, and other founders of states. Our fathers have filled them. But there remains to us a great duty of defence and preservation. . . . Let us cultivate a true spirit of union and harmony. In pursuing the great objects which our condition points out to us, let us act under a settled conviction, and a habitual feeling, that these twenty-four States are one country. Let our conception be enlarged to the circle of our duties. Let us extend our ideas over the whole of the vast field in which we are called to act. Let our object be, OUR COUNTRY, OUR WHOLE COUNTRY, and AND NOTHING BUT OUR COUNTRY.[3]

Literary effectiveness aside—and Webster's rhetoric sounds like pedestrian barrel-thumping in comparison to Lincoln's—what is immediately most striking is how much more somber and religiously resonant Lincoln's words are. It is in this sense that Ferguson describes Lincoln as both the culmination and a change in the relation between the law and the literary, combining "legal abstraction and religious feeling in different and powerful ways."[4] It is as if the revelational aspect of the Constitution's secular revelation receives an open, full-voiced assertion in the face of threatened lawlessness.

Lincoln's religion has long been a matter of discussion and debate—in his own time, and among scholars and historians since. He belonged to no church. Indeed, it is not clear that religion is at all the proper term for his somber and stoical fatalism. In his resistance to evangelicalism and to religious enthusiasm of every sort, he is again closer to the lawyer–writers who came before him than he is to his contemporaries who were increasingly given to ever new and yet more enthusiastic religious expression. Yet he maintained his very personal attitude toward religious matters with a kind of perfect balancing between the play of language and the assertion of belief. Typical is the response he offered to a newspaper editor's query about his habits of prayer: "I have been driven many times upon my knees," he explained to him, "by the overwhelming conviction that I had nowhere else to go." Lincoln kneels here as if on the very knife-edge of religion and secularity. Is this prayer in the sense that the editor meant? It is, and it is not.

Whatever one makes of Lincoln's religious convictions, there is no question that the Bible was the most important book in his life, as well as in the development of his prose. One can hear it very plainly echoing through his plea for preserving the Constitution. In a way that recalls the early Rabbinic teaching of the Mishnah to "make a hedge about the torah," Lincoln advocates an Old Testament commitment to sober and persistent mindfulness, akin to the passage in Deuteronomy known to Protestants as the "Great Commandment," and used for the central Rabbinic prayer, the "Schema": "And these words, which I command thee this day, shall be in thine heart: And thou shalt teach them diligently unto thy children, and shalt talk of them when thou sittest in thine house, and when thou walkest by the way, and when thou liest down, and when thou risest up."[5]

But Lincoln does not end his speech here, when, as David Herbert Donald in his recent Lincoln biography suggests, "most listeners must have thought he had nearly finished."[6] He continues, instead, with a second related threat against the achieved constitutional union, one that since Edmund Wilson's chapter on Lincoln in *Patriotic Gore* has frequently been interpreted as a warning against the likes of Lincoln himself—against men not merely of ambition but of "towering genius," those belonging to "the family of the lion, or the tribe of the eagle."[7] Such men, Lincoln warns, will not be content merely to preserve the legacy of the revolution:

> Towering genius disdains a beaten path. It seeks regions hitherto unexplored. It sees no distinction in adding story to story, upon the monuments of fame, erected to the memory of others. It denies that it is glory enough to serve under any chief. It scorns to tread in the footsteps of any predecessor, however illustrious. It thirsts and burns for distinction; and, if possible, it will have it, whether at the expense of emancipating slaves, or enslaving freemen.[8]

Lincoln warns that what had till then maintained the institutions of government could no longer do so:

I mean the powerful influence which the interesting scenes of the revolution had upon the passions of the people as distinguished from their judgment. By this influence, the jealousy, envy, and avarice, incident to our nature, and so common to a state of peace, prosperity, and conscious strength, were, for the time, in a great measure smothered and rendered inactive. (p. 35)

And again, Lincoln contrasts the Fathers' actions with what he understands this new time now demands:

They [i.e. the Fathers] were the pillars of the temple of liberty; and now, that they have crumbled away, that temple must fall, unless we, their descendants, supply their places with other pillars, hewn from the solid quarry of sober reason. Passion has helped us; but can do so no more. It will in future be our enemy. Reason, cold, unimpassioned reason, must furnish all the materials for our future support and defense. Let those materials be moulded in to general intelligence, sound morality, and, in particular, a reverence for the constitution and laws. (p. 36)

Lincoln here argues with a paradoxically fiery passion for a "cold, unimpassioned" reason, advocating a deeply conservative, and logical defense to preserve a thoroughly Romantic and inspired vision of a heroically self-constituted, self-governing people.

Thomas Jefferson, the founder most closely associated with Lincoln if only because, as we shall soon see, of the importance to Lincoln of the Declaration of Independence, nevertheless provides a striking contrast to this view of the Constitution. Jefferson had, at the outset, expressed great enthusiasm about the Constitutional Convention, as has been mentioned, referring to its participants as "an assembly of demigods." By the year of its ratification, he declared the Constitution itself to be "unquestionably the wisest ever yet presented to men."[9] Yet throughout his life, Jefferson harbored what was the most profound objection to the Constitution, more radical and far-reaching than anything suggested by the anti-Federalists. In contrast to the early Federalist writers, who as we have seen concerned themselves with the Constitution as a mechanism of social order and worried about the freedom of its interpretation, what disturbed Jefferson about the Constitution was the very thought of its stable perpetuity. Although he expressed this view during the campaign for ratification, he did so only in a private letter to James Madison, one that would not reach publication until 1829, three years after his death.

Jefferson and Madison, as colleagues and mutual confidants, shared a continuously probing political dialogue. On September 6, 1789, from his post as foreign minister to France, Jefferson explicitly raised a difficulty about the Constitution—indeed, about any Constitution—that had been on his mind but that, as he put it, in "the moment of making up general dispatches," he had not yet time to address. Now he begins at once with the crux of his concern:

> The question whether one generation of men has a right to bind another, seems never to have been stated either on this or our side of the water. Yet it is a question of such consequences as not only to merit decision, but placed also, among the fundamental principles of every government. The course of reflection in which we are immersed here on the elementary principles of society has presented this question to my mind; and that no such obligation can be transmitted I think very capable of proof. I set out on this ground which I suppose to be self-evident: *"that the earth belongs in usufruct to the living;"* that the dead have neither powers nor rights over it.[10]

The text here is characteristic of Jefferson both in the largeness of its claim and in its accompanying assertion of indisputable clarity; for many students of Jefferson, it has assumed a central place in the Jefferson canon.[11] Hannah Arendt, in her ruminations *On Revolution,* cites Jefferson as unique among the Founders in discerning the central "flaw in the structure of the revolution"—a flaw as characteristic of the French as of the American Revolution—namely, "that the principle of public freedom and public happiness without which no revolution would ever come to pass should remain the privilege of the generation of the founders."[12] Jefferson alone considered how to maintain what Arendt calls the "lost treasure" of the Revolution, namely, the possibility for fully engaged, individual participation in public affairs. This treasure, the plastic moment of revolution and its enlivening effects on those who live through it, becomes lost precisely in the attempt to settle the Revolution's achievement.

For a sense of this lost treasure of a revolutionary moment, consider a most unlikely witness, William Wordsworth, who testified to the happiness and freedom which he himself felt, though "untaught by thinking or by books / To reason well of polity or law," while residing in France during its Revolution.[13] In reading the following lines it should be remembered that by the time Wordsworth wrote them he had, in his political views, turned decisively against revolution:

> Bliss was it in that dawn to be alive,
> But to be young was very Heaven! O times,
> In which the meagre, stale, forbidding ways

Of custom, law, and statute, took at once
The attraction of a country in romance!
When Reason seemed the most to assert her rights
When most intent on making of herself
A prime enchantress—to assist the work
Which then was going forward in her name![14]

To begin the world anew, to participate in the vital creativity of the political realm, free to follow not the accumulated decisions and habits of the past, but only Reason itself—it is this loss that Jefferson feared would result from the very stability of any constitutional arrangement. That Jefferson continued to ponder the problem he expressed in the 1789 letter to Madison is evident from a letter some two decades later to Samuel Kercheval. Kercheval had written in 1816 to request Jefferson's views on the reform of the Virginia Constitution. Pleading his retirement, and his contentment to "ask but for rest, peace and good will," Jefferson nevertheless responded to Kercheval with an uncompromising reiteration of his views:

> Some men look to constitutions with sanctimonious reverence, and deem them like the Ark of the Covenant, too sacred to be touched. They ascribe to the men of the preceding age a wisdom more than human and suppose what they did to be beyond amendment. I knew that age well; I belonged to it, and labored with it. It deserved well of its country. It was very like the present, but without the experience of the present; and forty years of experience in government is worth a century of book reading; and this they would say themselves, were they to rise from the dead.[15]

Although he insisted that he was no "advocate for frequent and untried changes in laws and constitutions," Jefferson did offer at least two concrete suggestions of the means whereby, in his own terms, the dead might be prevented from governing the living. One was a proposal for periodically reconstituting the government, since "each generation is as independent as the one preceding . . . [and] it has then, like them, a right to choose for itself the form of government it believes most promotive of its own happiness."[16] This generational period, he suggested, could be established through the consultation of tables of mortality at nineteen years. Second, more realistically, perhaps, he proposed a system of wards, "little republics," like New England townships, "the wisest invention ever devised by the wit of man for the perfect exercise of self-government, and for its preservation," into which the country would be divided (p. 1339). Both of these innovations would keep open the opportunity for individual political action which a fixed constitution threatened to close down.

Nothing could be more opposed in spirit to Lincoln's attitude toward the founding document of the United States. Neither of Jefferson's suggested innovations was pragmatically workable, nor were they ever seriously attempted. His anxiety for the spirit of political freedom made possible by the Revolution and his concerns about the status of the 1787 Constitution, indeed about the potential status of any "perpetual" constitution, have played virtually no part in American political tradition, whereas the Lincoln we hear at Springfield represents the authentic voice of American constitutional tradition, for good or ill.[17] Lincoln's stance toward the Constitution is, moreover, the one he would hold to consistently through the rest of his life and by which he would prosecute the Civil War, an event that many historians view as the final settlement of the American Revolution.

Indeed, it is his commitment to a fixed and perpetual Constitution that determined Lincoln's particular response to the issue of slavery. Of the examples of lawlessness which Lincoln cites in his address, the one that would have been most obvious to his listeners had explicitly raised the issue of slavery, and yet he offers merely allusions to it, though the allusions to his contemporaries were unmistakable. In Alton, Illinois, not three months before Lincoln's address, a mob had murdered an abolitionist editor, Elijah P. Lovejoy, and thrown his press into the Mississippi. Whenever "bands of hundreds and thousands," Lincoln told the young men, "burn churches, ravage and rob provision stores, throw printing presses into rivers, shoot editors, and hang and burn obnoxious persons at pleasure, and with impunity; depend on it, this Government cannot last."[18] Neither a name, nor a place, nor so much as the dignity of its own sentence was granted to this attack which had in fact shocked Northern opinion.

But why? Aside from the political risk of any abolitionist advocacy, Lincoln disapproved of abolitionist agitation. Although unequivocally opposed to slavery, he objected to the abolitionists for the very reasons he articulated at Springfield: they stirred the passions, precisely the activity that would, in his mind, lead to the overthrow of government by the people. Mobs had twice previously tossed Lovejoy's press into the river, but they proceeded to burn down his warehouse and shoot the editor when he afterwards vowed to defend his third press with sixty armed abolitionists from surrounding towns.[19]

The year before Lincoln's address, he, along with fellow delegate Dan

Stone, had protested anti-abolitionist resolutions in the Illinois Legislature; but the terms of this protest were consistent with both his opposition to slavery and his equal opposition to emotional appeals for abolition. Where the resolutions had declared that "the right of property in slaves, is sacred to the slave-holding states by the Federal Constitution," the protest instead held that "the Congress of the United States has no power, under the constitution, to interfere with the institution of slavery in the different states." Similarly, although Lincoln and his fellow delegate declared that "the institution of slavery is founded on both injustice and bad policy," they also insisted that "promulgation of abolition doctrines tends rather to increase than to abate its evils."[20] This was the very position that Lincoln was to maintain repeatedly in the early years of the Civil War and in the face of the incomprehension of antislavery Unionists. That slavery "deprives our republican example of its just influence in the world" he had no doubt, but that the Union demanded a strict fealty to the Constitution, of this he was equally convinced. Only by means of the Constitution would the Union survive, and only the survival of the Union could guarantee a legal system of popular self-government.

When, in the midst of the Civil War, circumstances forced him, as he saw it, to emancipate the slaves of the rebelling states, Lincoln was to call upon the Declaration of Independence as though it were the passional basis for the Constitution. As he boldly asserted in his very brief statement at the dedication of the battlefield in Gettysburg, "our fathers brought forth on this continent, a new nation, conceived in Liberty, and dedicated to the proposition that all men are created equal." That the invocation of Jefferson's words from the Declaration of Independence as justification for the Civil War was a departure, both for Lincoln and for national policy, is evident from the response to the Gettysburg Address by the opposition press in the North. The Democratic *New York World* stated the case very plainly: "This United States," it vehemently protested, "[was] the result of the ratification of a compact known as the Constitution," that is, most assuredly not of the Declaration of Independence.[21] Gary Wills, in his literary and historical account of Lincoln at Gettysburg, dramatically attributed this innovation to Lincoln alone, as if in that speech alone he had transformed the relation between the Declaration and the Constitution:

[Lincoln at Gettysburg] not only put the Declaration in a new light as a matter of founding law, but put its central proposition, equality, in a newly favored position as a principle of the Constitution (which, as the Chicago Times noticed, never uses the word). What had been a mere theory of lawyers like James Wilson, Joseph Story, and Daniel Webster—that the nation preceded the states, in time and importance—now became a lived reality of the American tradition. The results of this were seen almost at once. Up to the Civil War, "the United States" was invariably a plural noun: "The United States are a free government." After Gettysburg, it became a singular: "The United States is a free government."[22]

Pauline Maier mildly dissents from Wills's account of *Lincoln at Gettysburg* pulling off the "giant (if benign) swindle" of injecting the Declaration into the Constitution. She insists, instead, that "virtually any [historical] subject is too complex for simple answers" and that in this case Lincoln's audience had been long prepared for the innovation.[23] However historians judge the precise degree of Lincoln's responsibility, we can see that in arguing in 1838 for the open sanctification of the text, even to the extent of advocating a civic cult based upon it, while at the same time expressing his hope that the struggle from which it issued "will be read of, and recounted, so long as the bible shall be read," Lincoln had attempted to answer not only the two threats he specifically cited—lawlessness and the inevitable rise of dangerously ambitious men—but the fundamental question raised by any fixed text used as a definitive guide not only for a People's present but for its future as well.

Again, in a Christian context, the Bible was the natural model for such a text. We can hear this with rather startling clarity when in 1854, at the dedication of Antioch College, the Reverend John Phillips stood before a table with "three costly bound Bibles" and said to the new College president, Horace Mann: "I speak in behalf of the donors of these Bibles. In the name of the Great God, I present them to you as the Constitution of the World."[24] It had by then already reached the point where the sanctification of the Constitution was so powerful that the secular text was offered as a very paradigm for the Holy Book itself.

In his view of the United States after the constitutional founding, Lincoln's biblical orientation—perhaps because of his very nondoctrinal devotion to scripture—marks a dramatic difference from Jefferson's enlightened rationalism. To Lincoln, cleaving to the letter of the Constitution, while at the same time infusing it with the principles of the Declaration, was the only assured means of preserving the institutions formed by the Revolution. The ancient rabbis in their way, as the Church Fathers had in theirs, found ways to seal off their revelations, thus to contain the destabilizing threat of unceasing scriptural expansion. Just as the rabbis valorized interpretation as the heir and guardian of prophetic inspiration, so Lincoln held up the law—itself the realm of endless interpretation—as the fulfillment and protection of America's governing Constitution. At the same time, and by the same means, Lincoln accomplished something the rabbis and the Church did not need to—namely, controlling the secularity of the nation's secular revelation. Where Jefferson argued—privately at least—that the ideals of the Revolution, as enunciated by the Declaration of Independence, were sufficient to guide new generations in entirely new acts of self-constituting, Lincoln, by having the Constitution absorb those principles of the Declaration, making, in M. L. Bradford's words, "a quasi religion of equality," preserved the Constitution against the very threat of secular instability. Lincoln reconfigured the paradox of a secular revelation into a mostly tacit dialectic between the fixed text of the Constitution—the letter—and the animating life within that text, the spirit of the Declaration.

Thus revelation ceases—as it must—; and it continues—as it must.[25]

CHAPTER EIGHT

Preserving the Paradox

What business have Washington or Jefferson in this
age. You must be a very dull or a very false man if
you have not a better & more advanced policy to
offer than they had. They lived in the greenness &
timidity of the political experiment. The kitten's eyes
were not yet opened. They shocked their contemporaries with their daring wisdom: have you not something which would have shocked them? If not, be
silent, for others have.

EMERSON, *Journals*, 1841

The American independence! that is a legend. Your
Independence! that is the question of all the Present.

EMERSON, *Journals*, 1854

Although neither a lawyer nor a politician, and not addressing himself
to the political public sphere per se, Ralph Waldo Emerson in speaking to the Phi Beta Kappa graduates at Harvard College was re-
sponding to much the same situation Lincoln faced in his Address at
the Springfield Lyceum. Emerson shared, with Lincoln and others, a
sense that the young republic now confronted not merely increasing
instability but a necessary reassessment of the legacy of the Revolution.
As we noted in considering Lincoln's speech, the Constitution itself had
begun to falter: its compromises—between the states' and the Union's
sovereignty, most pointedly on the issue of slavery—were crumbling
under the pressures of national expansion. The closed system of the
original states of 1787 was rapidly and radically opening, and with it
came a precipitous rise in political instability. Indeed, the very year
Emerson spoke at Harvard, 1837, the country was going through a
dramatic financial panic and depression; in his journal Emerson noted
that "what was, ever since my memory, solid continent, now yawns
apart and discloses its composition and genesis."[1]

While Lincoln tells the young men of the Lyceum that the world is
waiting upon them, the first generation after the passing of the last of

the Founding Fathers, to prove that popular self-government can persist and not fall prey to lawlessness, Emerson is encouraging the assembled young scholars to embrace the present as the time for America to fulfill "the postponed expectation of the world with something better than the exertions of mechanical skill."[2] For each speaker and his respective audience, the course of America's self-constituting had created opportunity for a new shared freedom, but this freedom needed to be encouraged and defended. The Revolution had offered them the future but had not guaranteed it.

In juxtaposing Emerson's Oration with Lincoln's Address, the very real distinction between the use of language in the realm of politics and its use in the realm of literature must be acknowledged. Acknowledging it, however, is a much easier matter than persuasively delineating it. When Oliver Wendell Holmes, a half century after Emerson's oration, known by then as "The American Scholar," called it America's "intellectual Declaration of Independence," it is clear enough that he did not mean that Emerson had needed, as the signers of Jefferson's Declaration had, to pledge his life, his fortune, or his sacred honor to anyone:[3]

> We . . . in the Name, and by Authority of the good People of these Colonies, solemnly publish and declare, That these United Colonies are, and of Right ought to be Free and Independent States; that they are Absolved from all Allegiance to the British Crown, and that all political connection between them and the State of Great Britain, is and ought to be totally dissolved.

Although, as has already been discussed, this legally binding Declaration did not have the identity-creating force later attributed to it, it did have political consequences. The signers, in fact, would have been hanged for treason. By comparison to this kind of language, really the formalization of an action, Emerson's Oration was mere words.

And yet Emerson's words did have consequences, albeit imaginative or symbolic consequences. Or as Emerson himself put it: "Words and deeds are quite indifferent modes of the divine energy. Words are also actions, and actions are a kind of words."[4] J. L. Austin, in introducing the idea of a speech act, makes a distinction between pragmatic, referential language, and literary language, describing the latter as parasitic upon the former. Referential language has real, pragmatic effects in a way literary language does not. He cites an American writer to make his point: "Walt Whitman" he explained, "does not seriously incite the eagle of liberty to soar."[5] According to Austin, nothing happens by means of this utterance. Yet this perspective needlessly diminishes the very real happenings of literary language. To use Austin's own example, we might well ask, where is one to encounter this "eagle of liberty," and how might one go about seriously inciting it to soar? We may be able to find the bird in a Bestiary or in some other text, but there is no such species in any of the Peterson Field Guides. Whitman does very much expect the Eagle of Liberty to soar, in the only sense that an Eagle of Liberty can do anything, in the only sense that there exists an Eagle of Liberty at all.

All that has been so far discussed about the United States Constitution and American literature has involved either explicitly political writers, or, in the case of those from the decades immediately following the creation of the United States, writers who aspired to act within the political or public realm, possessed by explicitly didactic purposes. Emerson is not an obviously political writer, nor is he obviously didactic. He does not address himself to the pragmatic difficulties of a people and a political entity founded upon a written Constitution, upon what we have referred to as a secular revelation. Yet the United States in which Emerson wrote and spoke was nevertheless dominated by these difficulties, and not merely in the obvious form of its daily politics. In any of the simplest and most immediate matters of communal identity and history, and of the often unarticulated but shared assumptions of social life, the fact of the Revolution, and the self-constituting self-government it gave birth to, was everywhere present.

It is difficult to recapture now how very new and tentative the Union of the states still was—not only as a political and economic unit but as a form of polity. It is well to remember that a reading of the diplomatic cables of the early 1860s reveals the shared European assumption that the rather bizarre experiment of popular government in the United States had, by then, reached its inevitable conclusion: disunity and dissolution. That the American Revolution and its constitutional regime was a central presence for the writers of what we now think of as classic American literature, composed from roughly the 1830s until the Civil War, should be no more surprising than that the French Revolution and the phenomenon of Napoleon were similarly central for the roughly contemporaneous writers of France.

When Oliver Wendell Holmes equated Emerson's "American Scholar" to the Declaration of Independence, he seems to have meant merely that Emerson, in speaking to the Phi Beta Kappa graduates, had decisively issued the call for a new American literature. Although

Holmes's casual assumption that the literary is so easily analogized to the political is worthy of note, his description as a summary account of the contents of Emerson's speech, which Holmes had in fact attended, is largely inaccurate. It is true that at the Oration's beginning and again at its end Emerson did—as if in a concession to what had become a tradition of the occasion—sound the familiar notes of this literary nationalism:

> Our day of dependence, our long apprenticeship to the learning of other lands, draws to a close. The millions, that around us are rushing into life, cannot always be fed on the sere remains of foreign harvests. Events, actions arise, that must be sung, that will sing themselves. Who can doubt, that poetry will revive and lead in a new age, as the star in the constellation Harp, which now flames in our zenith, astronomers announce, shall one day be the pole-star for a thousand years.[6]

And near the end:

> Mr. President and Gentlemen, this confidence in the unearthed might of man belongs, by all motives, by all prophecy, by all preparation, to the American Scholar. We have listened too long to the courtly muses of Europe. The sprit of the American freeman is already suspected to be timid, imitative, and tame. (p. 70)

But if the audience had expected any development of such patriotic sentiments, they must have been thoroughly disappointed. Instead, Emerson begins by citing a fable:

> that the gods, in the beginning, divided Man into men, that he might be more helpful to himself; just as the hand was divided into fingers, the better to answer its end . . . that there is One Man,—present to all particular men only partially, or through one faculty; and that you must take the whole society to find the whole man. (p. 53)

Both the form of this "old fable, which, out of an unknown antiquity, convey[s] an unlooked for wisdom," and the fable's explicit subject, point to the realm of origins. But these are not national origins, with their concomitant claim to historical truth; rather, these are origins of the human itself and are explicitly fabulous in character, or what we might call cosmic. Emerson tells the graduates that the fable "covers a doctrine ever new and sublime," so that it is not really a statement of origin in the sense of a putative history or genealogy but rather an insight. He illustrates this insight by describing a farmer as we meet him in society, or a soldier, or a professor, or an engineer, as merely fragments of men—"members [who] have suffered amputation from the trunk, and strut about so many walking monsters." This is caused, he explains, not merely by the specialization of labor but by a defect of individual vision:

> The planter, who is Man sent out into the field to gather food, is seldom cheered by any idea of the true dignity of his ministry. He sees his bushel and his cart, and nothing beyond, and sinks into the farmer, instead of Man on the farm. (p. 54)

Similarly, the scholar, who should be "Man Thinking," becomes a bookworm and a "mere thinker" (p. 54). By describing the doctrine as "ever new and sublime" Emerson means quite simply that it is true now, as he speaks; and that it is true not only for the young people he is addressing, but for everyone: "Is not, indeed, every man a student" he asks, "and do not all things exist for the student's behoove?" The specifically American scholar has become simply the student, and the student has become the human being: "And finally," he adds, "is not the true scholar the only true master?" (p. 54)

Emerson imagines a primal world, and insists that it is identical with this world, now. His famously optative mood is here, as often, leaning in the direction of the imperative. Addressing the young men of Phi Beta Kappa at 32 years of age, Emerson, like Lincoln at the Springfield Lyceum, is a young man himself, at the start of his own career. And just as Lincoln—speaking to himself, perhaps, as much as to them—makes a demand of his audience, namely, to worship the Constitution and its laws, so does Emerson. "The one thing in the world, of value," he tells them, "is the active soul. This every man is entitled to; this every man contains within him, although, in almost all men, obstructed, and as yet unborn." And this active soul is active in one way only, by the act of creation. Thus books, the form in which the mind of the past most impinges upon our consciousness, are of no value as such; in fact, misused they are a grave danger: "What is right use [of books]?" Emerson asks, and answers: "They are for nothing but to inspire. I had better never see a book, than to be warped by its attraction clean out of my own orbit, and made a satellite instead of a system."[7] What Emerson wants is that his young American auditors awaken and create—to Emerson these are all but synonymous verbs.

Lincoln had attempted to settle the political fate of the United States Constitution, at least in the basic outline of its status, and to a great degree he succeeded. The letter of that text did indeed become established as an absolute, but time-bound, embodiment of the truths of the Declaration. How does Emerson's invocation to the active soul relate to what Lincoln urges upon his audience? In the first place, Lincoln is interested—perhaps desperate is not too strong a term—to preserve the political institutions which, he believes, contain the promise of the American Revolution, whereas to Emerson "any institution," fixing any past achievement, is nothing less than the active soul's very enemy:

> The book, the college, the school of art, the institution of any kind, stop with some past utterance of genius. This is good, say they,—let us hold by this. They pin me down. They look backward and not forward. But genius looks forward: the eyes of man are set in his forehead, not in his hindhead: man hopes: genius creates. Whatever talents may be, if the man create not, the pure efflux of the Deity is not his. (pp. 57–58)

For Lincoln, the Revolution has passed, the primal time is over, and now the achievement of that time, the Constitution, must be given its proper sway, its authoritative status. Thus, he proposes acknowledging the Constitution's quasi-biblical status. Emerson insists, at least by implication, that from the perspective of the active soul, the Bible itself needs deauthorizing:

> The sacredness which attaches to the act of creation,—the act of thought,—is transferred to the record. The poet chanting, was felt to be a divine man: henceforth the chant is divine also. The writer was a just and wise spirit: henceforward it is settled, the book is perfect; as love of the hero corrupts into worship of his statue. (p. 57)

And what is here implied becomes explicit the next year in his Divinity School Address, condemning, as it does, "the assumption that the age of inspiration is past, that the Bible is closed." Such a view, he insists, in and of itself, indicates "with sufficient clearness the falsehood of our theology."[8]

Like Lincoln, Emerson is desperate to preserve the American legacy, but for him that legacy is not a fixed institution to be worshiped; it is not the historical achievement of the Constitution. For Emerson the American legacy is the paradox of the nation's self-constituting itself, and it is this capacity that he wants to preserve, not merely for the few and for the past but for the present moment and for everyone. Indeed, the acceptance of this paradox—that what is secular is what is revealed, what is out in the open is the deepest mystery—is what it means to live in the active soul.

And this, Emerson informs his audience, is directly related to the politics of the present. In his Oration he abandons "this abstraction of the scholar" to talk "of nearer reference to the time and to this country," and he points first to the rise of equality, "the movement which effected the elevation of what was called the lowest class in the state."[9] It is in keeping with this movement that what is most common and familiar is that to which the active soul is most drawn: "The meal in the firkin; the milk in the pan; the ballad in the street; the news of the boat; the glance of the eye; the form and the gait of the body." This is the very stuff of what we might call secular, everyday reality. It is here precisely where Emerson locates the spiritual realm:

> [S]how me the ultimate reason of these matters; show me the sublime presence of the highest spiritual cause lurking, as always it does lurk, in these suburbs and extremities of nature; let me see every trifle bristling with the polarity that ranges it instantly on an eternal law; and the shop, the plough, and the ledger, referred to the like cause by which light undulates and poets sing;—and the word lies no longer a dull miscellany and lumber room, but has form and order. (p. 69)

For Emerson it is in Nature at its most ordinary where the highest realm of the spirit is revealed. The secular is revelational; the two are one—the very basis for the paradox undergirding the Constitution.

And thus in his urging of the active soul Emerson comes to what he calls "another sign of our times, also marked by an analogous political movement . . . the new importance given to the single person" (p. 70). And here, too, it is the fact of paradox that is striking, this time itself explicitly political in its language, for it is this supreme individual who is the very source of union. "Every thing that tends to insulate the individual," he tells his audience, "—to surround him with barriers of natural respect, so that each man shall feel the world is his, and man shall treat with man as a sovereign state with a sovereign state;—tends to true union as well as greatness" (p. 70). Sovereignties tending to true union? One is tempted to ask whether any union could survive such an abundance of "sovereign states." Is this not akin to the very condition of lawlessness which Lincoln feared? What could be more lawless than the condition of each person a sovereign state?

But lawlessness is the last thing Emerson fears. For the scholar, for the individual mind, Emerson proposes only freedom. "Free even to the definition of freedom" is what he urges upon the individual. And he quotes the definition of freedom he has in mind: "without any hindrance that does not arise out of his own constitution" (p. 65). Even if we ignore the possibility of a punning allusion, conscious or not, to the nation's founding document, the contrast to Lincoln could hardly be more stark.[10] Again, it is not the Constitution in itself that Emerson is interested in preserving, but the very action of self-constituting. That this action necessitates inspiration—what Lincoln fears as passion—is to Emerson its very value and meaning. "It is a mischievous notion," he protests, "that we are come late into nature; that the world was finished a long time ago." And what this vision necessitates, above all else, is not worshipfulness, as Lincoln proposes, but "self-trust": "In self-trust," Emerson explains, "all the virtues are comprehended." He does not imagine such self-trust to be an easy matter. It demands that instead of "the ease and pleasure of treading the old road . . . he takes the cross of making his own, and, of course, the self-accusation, the faint heart, the frequent uncertainty and loss of time, which are the nettles and tangling vines in the way of the self-relying."[11]

It is as though the political idealism Jefferson espoused, but never found a practical way to implement, represented no more than the starting point for Emerson's vision. Jefferson proposed a union of little republics and the right of each generation to its own self-constituting. Emerson imagines not republics, but individuals, sovereign persons, and not merely the freedom to change generation to generation, but the freedom to cast off the truth of each moment in favor of the truth of the next.

To the overweening individual whose ambition Lincoln analyzes and fears, Emerson offers a response bespeaking a kind of pity:

> Men such as they are, very naturally seek money or power; and power because it is as good as money,—the "spoils," so called, "of office." And why not? for they aspire to the highest, and this, in their sleep-walking, they dream is highest. Wake them, and they shall quit the false good, and leap to the true, and leave governments to clerks and desks. The revolution is to be wrought by the gradual domestication of the idea of Culture. The main enterprise of the world for splendor, for extent, is the upbuilding of a man.[12]

This may well seem a desperate strategy and hope, a revolution strictly utopian. In part, this is no doubt a fair criticism of the political dangers of Emerson's championing of self-trust; but it is also in part merely a reflection of the inherent difficulty Emerson has in expressing the oscillation of a paradox with a static image of its imagined (and impossible) solution. To any objection of the sort Lincoln would make, Emerson offers a clear protest, one enunciated in the very first lines of his first published book, *Nature*:

Our age is retrospective. It builds the sepulchres of the fathers. It writes biographies, histories, and criticism. The foregoing generations beheld God and nature face to face; we, through their eyes. Why should not we also enjoy an original relation to the universe? Why should not we have a poetry and philosophy of insight, and not of tradition, and a religion by revelation to us, and not the history of theirs?[13]

It should be noted, lest he seem too airy in his aspirations to bear any comparison at all to the nuts and bolts of material life with which Lincoln is ultimately concerned, that Emerson was neither unaware of, nor indifferent to, the cost involved in such living with an active soul. He had in the very year of "The American Scholar" inherited from his first wife's estate a secure, if modest, income. In his journal he interrogated himself and to what degree this "accidental freedom by means of a permanent income" underwrote the life he urged upon others. He did himself acknowledge in his talk that his path leads "so often [to] poverty and solitude."[14] But no, he decided, "my direction of thought is so strong that I should do the same things,—should contrive to spend the best part of my time in the same way as now, rich or poor. If I did not think so, I should never dare to urge the doctrines of human culture on young men."[15] This does not, of course, necessarily settle the issue, but it demonstrates that Emerson was fully aware of it in its cold, hard material reality.

For Emerson, the beginning is not merely always available, it is always inescapable. He preserves the paradox of self-constituting, or the generation of secular revelations, by accepting completely the potential contradiction of this moment with the next. Even if, with Stanley Cavell, we dilate these moments and call them "moods," the radical destabilizing finds no firmer foundation.[16]

Lincoln wants to preserve the possibility of self-government, of political freedom, and thus he needs to control the very process that created such a government that it may not perish. Emerson wants to preserve the paradox of that creation that it may not cease.

CHAPTER NINE

The Literary Renaissance of Secular Revelation

> Above the atmosphere they live in, above the heads of
> all the American poets, and between them and the
> sky, floats the Constitution of the United States and
> the forms of English literature.
>
> JOHN JAY CHAPMAN, "WHITMAN"

Lincoln has been cast in this account as representing, as he himself had hoped, the capstone to the founding generation's great work. This is not to deny the immense political changes that took place between the late eighteenth and the middle decades of the nineteenth centuries in the United States, over the course of which the republic had begun to expand into something dramatically more democratic. But Lincoln pointed the way to completing the founding work of the People handing down the Law to themselves—the Law, not mere laws—in other words the very existential ground upon which the authority to create any such laws rested, what until the Constitution had always necessitated an explicitly religious sanction. The Americans had openly constituted themselves.

While Lincoln attempted to close the process of secular revelation for the sake of political stability, Emerson was opening it up to literary invention. Emerson's hopes for the success of the American experiment in self-government extended well beyond the realm of the political to something like the very possibility of an authentic, individual human selfhood itself. He ends his oration to the Harvard graduates with a vision of the future that approaches a kind of secular, individualized messianism:

> The study of letters shall be no longer a name for pity, for doubt, and for sensual indulgence. The dread of man and the love of man shall be a wall of defense and a wreath of joy around all. A nation of men will for the first time exist, because each believes himself inspired by the Divine Soul which also inspires all men.[1]

Emerson does not here insist that each will indeed *be* inspired by the Divine Soul; nor does he deny, or imply a denial, of the authenticity of such inspiration. He was not unaware of the moral danger attendant to his call for unconfirmed divine sanction, and in his central essay "Self Reliance" he pauses to bring a frontal attack against his own strategy:

> On my saying, What have I to do with the sacredness of traditions, if I live wholly from within? my friend suggested,—"But these impulses may be from below, not from above." I replied, "They do not seem to me to be such; but if I am the Devil's child, I will live then from the Devil." No law can be sacred to me but that of my nature. Good and bad are but names very readily transferable to that or this; the only right is what is after my constitution, the only wrong what is against it.[2]

From Lincoln's concern with obeying laws we have here an open embrace of philosophical anarchy—not *the* Constitution but "my constitution."

This is the very process of secular revelation that had been silently assumed by the Convention of 1787; only here it is made bracingly explicit. Where the Constitution occluded the aggressive circularity of its claim to ordain and establish its own ground, primarily by the mystification of We the People, as though a human collective of individuals could offer a transcendent, authorizing force, Emerson openly acknowledged it as a radically individual undertaking and accepted that there is nothing behind the Self but the Self, whose inner sense is the only recourse to the divine. By this Emerson is willing to live or die. His attempts to work this concept out will be discussed more fully in the following chapter; what is relevant here is that, as so many American readers and writers for the past century and a half have variously testified, Emerson is the signal figure who articulated the way to a distinct imaginative, and more specifically literary, culture for the United States by asking: "Why should not we also enjoy an original relation to the universe?" As opposed to Lincoln's political path, for Emerson neither the fixed Constitution nor any other institution would count as a settled achievement. Emerson came, in fact, to write one of his most brilliant essays on the figure of the circle, taking the Old World's very symbol for the perfect and eternal and subverting it into a figure of unceasing instability and newness, of the endless need, to quote a phrase of Gertrude Stein's, "to begin to begin again."

"Our life," Emerson wrote in "Circles," "is an apprenticeship to the truth, that around every circle another can be drawn; that there is no end in nature, but every end is a beginning, that there is always another dawn risen on mid-noon, and under every deep a lower deep opens."[3] Emerson refused any settled or fixed foundation, or rather he accepted that absolute newness was everything of value and that acts of self-constituting amid such unsettleable newness would be the American condition. It is this understanding applied to the inheritance of the United States Constitution that sets the terms for the new extraordinary American literature that F. O. Matthiessen would come in the next century rightly to call a renaissance.

Matthiessen focused on the first half-decade of the 1850s when this revival reached its peak of aesthetic daring and achievement, though he was hard put himself to justify the rightness of his label.[4] In his brief introduction, he offered only a curiously collapsing, awkward defense:

> It may not seem precisely accurate to refer to our mid-nineteenth century as a rebirth; but that was how the writers themselves judged it. Not as a rebirth of values that had existed previously in America, but as America's way of producing a renaissance, by coming to its first maturity and affirming its rightful heritage in the whole expanse of art and culture.[5]

From this context it is possible to see the source of Matthiessen's difficulty in the intractable paradox itself: this was a renaissance of beginnings, a rebirth that denies it is a rebirth because it insists on its being nothing but new birth, an endlessly first birth. There is a logic-denying self-contradiction in the very notion of a revival of the brand new.[6]

The most ambitious works of the American Renaissance aspire to be self-constituting, to offer themselves as forms of secular revelations. Indeed, a reader often feels compelled to ask of nearly all these writers' major works some such question as: Is this really an essay? Is this what a poem is? Can you call this a novel? Emerson writes prose, Whitman verse, and Melville narrative—as if each were forced to invent the activity, to constitute it afresh. When Melville described American writers as "isolatoes," he was referring not only to the social condition of their lives, but to the condition of their art as well. However we might evaluate works such as "Self Reliance," "Song of Myself," or *Moby-Dick*, they are not good examples of any generic literary procedure, and all have about them a kind of wildness long recognized even when not appreciated.

Of course, these are essayists, poets, novelists, what we rightly call secular writers and literary artists; they are not composers of constitutions or founders of states. But they all participated in what might be called a constituting or constitutional ideology. By ideology here is meant not a conscience doctrine or set of principles, but rather what the literary historian Andrew Delbanco has defined as "thought that is socially determined but unaware of its determination."[7] The peculiar circumstances of the European settlements that would become the United States had created conditions in which the idea of constructing a society, as if from scratch, upon a new, rationally ordered, consciously chosen foundation, seemed all but self-evident. How else to begin in a New World? The traditional answer that had always sufficed—let us proceed the way our forbearers proceeded—was neither wholly available nor for many desirable. Of course, there were traditions that were carried over from Europe and from other continents, such as Africa; the New World inhabitants did not somehow metamorphose into a new infancy when they touched the Atlantic coast. Nor did communication and commerce between the Old and the New World cease after the voyage. But there was no mistaking the raw world constructed within the North American wilderness for the "Time Immemorial" of European civilization. The mentality of that painfully young world, with its deepest roots still so shallow, made inventions that what would otherwise have seemed perhaps untenably artificial and utopian not merely reasonable, but necessary, even what we might call matters of second nature.

The contention here is that this constituting or constitutional ideology, cast into the very identity of the nation by the federal Constitution, is what accounts for the strange deformations of the literary traditions the Americans inherited from the English, for as John Jay Chapman once remarked, in an essay on Whitman, "Above the atmosphere they live in, above the heads of all the American poets, between them and the sky, float the Constitution of the United States and the traditions of English literature."[8]

By the most superficial comparison to their English or European contemporaries, there is a sense in which none of these American writers were altogether professional literary men; all were, in a significant sense, experimentalists. This is not merely because none of them could make much of a living from their works. This is no doubt a reflection of the immature American market for books, along with other factors such as the literary competition from Great Britain and the state of international copyright. The professional author was, after all, a relatively recent phenomenon in the English-speaking world. More to the point, in the case of these American writers, the relation between their authorial identities and the notion of gainful employment was an especially difficult and subtle matter, involving questions of poetics as much as of economics or sociology. It is not laid to rest by the simple fact that all of these writers, at different times and in different ways, eagerly hoped for sales and even did what they could to generate them. They were all experimental writers in the sense that the very status of literary activity remained for them very much an open question. All the arts, literature included, were, after all, historically associated with the elite, and these writers were every one of them thorough democrats, idealizing, or nearly, the labor of working men (and in the case of Whitman, at least, of women as well). Yet each seemed devoted to what the culture around them would refer to as different forms of idleness, in various modes of dissent from the ever-rising tide of the young nation's triumphant materialism.

"I lean and loaf at my ease," Walt Whitman proclaims in the first lines of *Leaves of Grass* in 1855.[9] And everywhere in that poem, ultimately entitled "Song of Myself," the poet is watching, describing, vicariously experiencing, and sympathizing with, not to mention sometimes erotically desiring other Americans at work; but he almost never depicts himself as engaging in anything resembling labor himself. Weighing over two hundred pounds and of a slow and ambling gait, Whitman had among his family, and his employers, a life-long reputation for laziness. Paul Zwieg in *Walt Whitman: The Making of a Poet* amusingly quotes "political adversaries" exploiting Whitman's reputation by describing him as "too indolent to kick a musketo."[10]

Melville, though a physically active man, able even in his sailor's retirement to scramble up the main mast rigging to delight fellow travelers at sea, was described by his brother Gansevoort as suffering not from "general laziness by any means—but that laziness which consists in an unwillingness to exert oneself in doing at a particular time. . . ."[11] Melville himself called his habit of procrastination—if that's what it was—"a sad failing."[12] That the figure of leisure and unprincipled inactivity appealed to him we can see plainly in a character like Long Ghost in *Omoo*. And there is throughout *Typee*, the first of his books of South Sea narrative, a delight in what from a nineteenth-century American point of view could only be described as sensual indolence coexisting with an anxiety about the profound lack of productivity among the island natives.

Indeed, a celebration of loafing, or an appreciation for laziness, is not the same thing as a disdain for work. What Newton Arvin notes of Melville—that "he came to the profession of letters as a kind of brilliant amateur, and he was never quite to take on, whether for better or for worse, the mentality of the professional"—is to some degree true of the other writers as well. There is some sense in which the amateur is committed to following desire and impulse in a way that substantially differs from a professional's relation to work.[13] In Chapter 62 of *Moby Dick,* "The Dart," Melville, however, offers an explicit justification for inactivity in the very seriousness and purpose of certain kinds of well-focused and determined work. Describing the heavy labor of rowing first required of the "harpooner or whale-fastener" before he throws his harpoon, and lamenting that therefore "taking the whole fleet of whalemen in a body . . . out of fifty fair chances for a dart, not five are successful," Melville (as he often does) suddenly lifts the chapter to the level of aphoristic generalization and concludes: "To ensure the greatest efficiency in the dart, the harpooners of this world must start to their feet from idleness, and not from toil."

Not surprisingly, it is the pontificating Emerson who most clearly articulates the value of inactivity and consequently its relation to the making of secular revelations. In a famous passage of *Self Reliance*, he vows to "write on the lintels of my door post, *Whim*" as if loafing and lazing were conditions next to holiness.[14] Stanley Cavell among others has pointed out that this vow is an explicit adaptation of the so-called Great Commandment of Deuteronomy:

> Hear, O Israel: The LORD our God is one LORD: and thou shalt love the LORD thy God with all thine heart, and with all thy soul, and with all thy might. And these words which I command thee this day shall be in thine heart. . . . And thou shalt write them upon the posts of thy house, and on thy gates.[15]

Emerson transforms this demand to be ever mindful of God's oneness into a demand to be ever mindful of one's own whim, the impulses of one's own mind. "Nothing," Emerson adds in the same passage, "is at last sacred but the integrity of your own mind."[16] Emerson had already claimed in *Nature* to be "part or particle of God," and once that is accepted what is the integrity of one's own mind but itself the oneness, the unity, of God? The commandment is not mocked by its link to whim; rather, whim is properly exalted; to pay heed to whim is nothing other than to pay heed to the oneness of God.

Idleness, laziness, devotion to whim—in the case of the writers of the American Renaissance, these are not merely instances of dissent from the material focus of American life but are themselves the very marks of revelation. The "whim" written upon Emerson's doorposts is the sign of a patient, if often difficult, receptivity, both inside the walls of his study and beyond them. As he notes one day in his *Journal*:

> A prophet waiting for the words of the Lord. It is the prophet's fault that he waits in vain? Yet how mysterious & painful these laws. Always in the precincts—never admitted; always preparing—vast machinery—plans of life—traveling—studies—the country—solitude—and suddenly in any place, in the street, in the chamber will the heaven open & the regions of boundless knowledge be revealed; as if to show you how thin the veil, how null the circumstances. The hours of true thought in a lifetime how few![17]

Whitman's loafing and leaning, like Melville's idleness in preparation for "the dart" and Emerson's painful patient waiting for those few hours of true thought, are all reflections of their engagement in revelation, in some version of prophecy.

But to prophesy is literally "to speak for." These authors, unlike the model of biblical prophets such as Isaiah and Ezekiel, do not punctuate their works with "Thus saith the Lord". Then for whom do these almost-prophets speak? Emerson again is always clearest on this point, for his constant message, that which he insists is both most true and most offensive to others, is nothing but "the infinitude of the private man." Here we have, expressed as a spiritual conviction, the simplest explanation for the basis of the American Constitution, what we describe by the term *self-authorized*, a profound paradox obscured by its casual familiarity.

However outrageous Emerson's claim is to speak from the depth of his own "infinitude," upon what more can the identity of "We the People" rest? The Constitution obscures this outrage through a mystification of the People, through the process of representation, the Convention's obfuscating manner of witnessing and signing its work, the procedures of ratification, and the very divided sovereignty established by the federal structure. Through these accumulated complexities and indirections, the Constitution as a secular revelation permitted an undefined, transcendent authority to be perceived and alluded to, though never with sufficient specificity to permit argument.[18]

Not all the writers of the American Renaissance equally shared Emerson's attitude toward this condition. More of that will be discussed later. The writers here considered did at the least share a psychic landscape of consciously self-constituted American life that Emerson had, first and most influentially, invoked for literary inspiration. In the discussion of individual writers that completes this book, I attempt to demonstrate the way in which the renaissance, or rebirth, of the mode of secular revelation first initiated by the United States Constitution was inflected through their own forms of expression. I will show that in each case the literary form inherited suffered a kind of deformation when filtered through the atmosphere of the Constitution into something rich and strange.

The primary evidence evinced for this constitutional poetics is the persistent presence of a cluster of qualities throughout these authors' vastly different kinds of literary works. These qualities have, for the most part, been long recognized; what has not been recognized is the way in which they correlate with the formal characteristics of the United States Constitution. This is the result, in part perhaps, of the strict segregation of the Constitution from the larger imaginative life of the nation, a condition that obtained even during the long decades of the Cold War with its celebratory enthusiasm of American distinctiveness. And perhaps, as well, it is the fact that the Constitution has been so much the Holy of Holies, the source of American cohesiveness and stability, that it has never been so profanely approached, but instead was left safely in the hands of its lawyer-priests. Moreover, as has so far been suggested, the Constitution itself, for perfectly clear pragmatic reasons, had no interest in elucidating its own paradoxical dynamic of the revealed and the secular, its vatic mechanics. Indeed, even for the writers who revived this dynamic with an interest in acknowledging that paradox, they found such elucidation anything but transparent.

It will be evident by now that this argument will not concern itself with the explicit constitutional views of any of these writers. Such a subject might certainly be of interest, and there is no such comparative study of their opinions about, or responses to, the Constitution available. There are, indeed, some well-known instances, primarily involving slavery, the central constitutional issue of their day. All these writers were, to one degree or another, opposed to slavery, and Emerson famously spoke out with rage against Daniel Webster's compromise with the South's peculiar institution and in admiration of the abolitionist terrorist John Brown.

No more than the constitutional views of these writers are their direct or symbolic references to the Constitution in their works necessarily of direct relevance to this study. Again, it is a subject of interest, and one could, merely by culling from the immense secondary literature addressed to these authors, compile a substantial catalogue of such allusions. Proof of influence based on allusions is often a misleading technique, at best. In the context of this argument, specifically it is not their responses, such as they were, to the Constitution per se that are relevant but their constitutional response to the life around them. The subject here is the poetics of these authors, their procedures of composition, the way in which they attempt to achieve aesthetic unities. In the case of Whitman, for instance, such constitutional allusions do seem to go quite consciously to the very heart of his poetic practice and are thus of immediate interest. But in other cases their interest in the Constitution, where it exists, is merely thematic rather than poetic, so that, for instance, Melville's allusions to the "ship of state," informing narratives as diverse as "Benito Cereno," *Moby-Dick*, and *The Confidence-Man*, are in many respects incidental to the primary concern here with the constitutional poetics of his formal procedures.

Still, one may feel compelled to ask, how does this relation between the late-eighteenth-century fundamental charter of government possibly exercise any kind of influence on the literary works of a half century and more later? What is the mechanism or mechanisms of the relation between the secular revelation of the United States Constitution and the later literature of the American Renaissance? Unfortunately, as is so often the case when attempting to find a nexus between complex social conditions and any activity—literary or otherwise—demonstrating such correlations and suggesting the likelihood of possible linkages is often the closest we can get to such a mechanism. We use words like "atmosphere," what the Germans call "Zeitgeist," retrospectively imagining the experiential texture of history as a way of skirting past the difficulty. We talk of an Enlightenment—though often now it has become "the Enlightenment project"—or of an "age of belief," recognizing the gross generalizations these pictures entail while being more or less helpless to think entirely without them. From a sufficiently distant perspective, it is both accurate and revealing to describe the Earth as a blue sphere, though that rather overlooks certain local features like the Sahara or the Himalayas. Similarly, to describe the early United States as a culture committed to the idea of beginning independently of and unassisted by the past—such a description no doubt overlooks all kinds of continuities and inherited pieties, but it likewise illuminates large-scale features that would otherwise be easily obscured.

Thus, the argument here is not merely that there are structural analogues between the founding document of the nation and the founding documents of the nation's literature. The Constitution is a vision of representation, more precisely of a controlled conflict of representations, which representations together allow for the construction of a totality that is politically called a Union. That is to say, the Constitution establishes a dynamic between what has here been named the secular and the revealed as a means of making a unified whole. This dynamic demands that certain processes, or properties, must be present for the bringing forth of new totalities—call them unions, or in the case of literature, compositions—that can participate in that constitutional vision. The point here is that that constitutional vision is the stuff of American identity, the foundation for a self-made people, and only participation in that vision could transform what would otherwise be merely a derivative branch of English literature into a new literary tradition.

The Fugio cent is a perfect image for such a whole composed by a paradox. The one side's sacred assertion of "We are One" does not translate, any more than it disputes or converts, the secular obverse of "Mind Your Business"; the one side is, and is not, a part of the other. There is simply no way to see both sides at once. In terms of a secular revelation, what is the nature of that liminal state that can bridge the secular and the revealed? What is it that exists between a coin's two faces? How is movement from one to the other possible? That darting moment of transition, that midair flip, is more a change in perspective than it is a motion, an othering that has the curious effect of reinforcing the oneness of the coin. It seems, in fact, to require something like a notion of quanta, of the possibility of discontinuous change, change absent any continuum: now this, now that, with nothing in between. The writers of the American Renaissance proceed by hovering about that nothing, and their compositions at their strongest—the subject of the last and final part of this book—attempt to keep both sides of that flipping coin in an artfully vertiginous view.

CHAPTER TEN

Essays in Time

Let who will ask, where is the fruit? I find a private
fruit sufficient. This is a fruit,—that I should not ask
for a rash effect from meditations, counsels and the
hiving of truths.

EMERSON, "EXPERIENCE," 1844

At the conclusion of a penetrating essay on Emerson, written as a book
review of James Eliot Cabot's memoir of the writer, Henry James am-
bivalently praised Emerson for "failing to strike us as having achieved
a style." And it is precisely style, James adds, that "is usually the bribe
or toll-money on the journey to posterity," a journey on which, James
assures us, Emerson is nevertheless on his way.[1] Of Emerson the essayist, James says simply that he "had never really mastered the art of
composition—of continuous expression." Indeed, James observed, "it
is hardly too much, or too little, to say of Emerson's writings that they
were not composed at all."[2]

Anyone who attempts reading through the two series of Emerson's
Essays understands precisely what James had in mind. There is eloquence enough to stun even those most resistant to their content, innumerable moments of memorable expression, unforgettable sentences.
But for a reader to remember afterward whether this or that stirring
articulation came from "Friendship" or "History," or perhaps "Nature," "Politics," or "Circles" is often exceedingly difficult. It is like
trying to recall amidst a lightning storm any one particularly striking
flash and thunderbolt. Here is a brief selection of Emersonian moments,
instances of his condensed eloquence; let any reader familiar with Emerson's *Essays* attempt to match each with its corresponding essay:

God offers to every mind its choice between truth and repose. Take
which you please;—you can never have both.[3]

Let the stoics say what they please, we do not eat for the good of living,
but because the meat is savory and the appetite is keen.[4]

I am always insincere, as always knowing there are other moods.[5]

Let a man keep the law,—any law,—and his way will be strown with satisfactions.[6]

We grizzle every day. I see no need of it.[7]

He that writes to himself writes to an eternal public.[8]

The dice of God are always loaded.[9]

Men descend to meet.[10]

Of any particular essay a reader can often discern a mood, an atmosphere; but as neither ordered expositions nor narrative sequences, lacking much of what makes for either argument or dramatic structure, the essays often defy summary. Emerson knew this as well as any of his critics. At work in 1838—the *Essays First Series* were published in 1841—he wrote to Carlyle: "Here I sit & read & write with very little system & as far as regards composition with the most fragmentary results: paragraphs incompressible each sentence an infinitely repellent particle."[11] To Margaret Fuller he explained how he was "inventing transitions like solder to meld irreconcilable metals."[12] Emerson lamented his "formidable tendency to the lapidary style," and upon completion of his first volume of *Essays* he conjured a number of images to convey his sense of the result: "I build my house of' boulders"; "[the essays are] only boards & logs tied together."[13] Nor was this characteristic of his *Essays* only. A decade later he would note in his journal: "I found when I had finished my new lecture that it was a very good house, only the architect had unfortunately omitted the stairs."[14]

Yet it would be false to describe Emerson as merely stringing together aphorisms. However extraordinary the effect of his superbly shaped sentences they do not feel as if they are merely planted in, but rather that they arise from, the surrounding discourse. Nor did he aim at any startling brilliance of effect: "I would have my book read as I have read my favorite books," he remarked in his journal, "not with explosion & astonishment, a marvel and a rocket, but a friendly & agreeable influence stealing like the scent of a flower or the sight of a new landscape on a traveler."[15] To what, then, can we attribute the pervasive discontinuity of his style?

All the biographies of Emerson agree on how long and arduous was the path to his own form and voice, his characteristic method. There was no blessed or fortuitous breakthrough, no clear way to literary achievement as there had been for Irving, or Cooper, or Emerson's contemporary, Longfellow. Beginning was a prolonged struggle, a kind of invention *ex nihilo* of a peculiarly American writer. Emerson in his writing life recapitulated the situation of the Founders, facing the problem of how to begin afresh, as if from an absolute newness, how to lay a foundation, so to speak, in midair. "In England," Emerson remarked in his later travels, "every man you meet is some man's son; in America, he may be some man's father.[16] As Emerson experienced it, the condition of being American was one of continuous beginning, of necessary founding and refounding.

It was when Emerson returned from his European travels following the tragically early death of his first wife that he discovered his way in an acceptance of his own unique access to revelation, however sporadic:

> As the law of light is fits of easy transmission & reflexion such is also the soul's law. She is only superior at intervals to pain, to fear, to temptation, only in raptures unites herself to God and Wordsworth truly said:
> Tis the most difficult of tasks to keep
> Heights which the soul is competent to gain.[17]

It is these heightened moments of vision, raptures which by their nature are discontinuous, that account for the decentralizing, aphoristic intensities in Emerson's *Essays*. And it is his complete acceptance, his almost-affirmation, of the discontinuity which Wordsworth's lines lament between vision and material life that made Emerson the latter-day American Founder and the first in a tradition of a distinctive American literature.

The Constitution, too, is a text in which the individual parts have an independent existence in a way that is emphasized in relation to the larger design or form of the work. In the case of the Constitution, each clause had been inserted to answer one demand or another of the interests engaged in the creation of the United States, and thus it may seem that this fragmented condition is merely an aspect of its legal language, every phrase modulated in accordance with the weight of various interpretive strategies. This is true, but such a textual quality is also a result of the very nature of so collaborative a composition, and of the task the delegates had taken on, namely, the need to construct, as if brick by brick, a new political reality. Behind Emerson's fragmentary, discontinuous composition there is, however strange it may seem, a similar kind of conflictual collaboration and from-the-ground-up construction. In his case, the collaborators, though they, too, had to struggle to find a pathway to union, were all named Emerson, and what they likewise constructed, as if brick by brick, was what Emerson in the guise of an "Orphic Poet" had chanted in "Prospects," the concluding section of *Nature,* his first book: "Every spirit builds itself a house; and beyond its house a world; and beyond its world, a heaven."[18] Unlike the solid political building demanded by the communal Constitution, however, Emerson's—guided by whim—was a profoundly "frolic architecture."[19] Yet it is emphatically an "architecture," or as Sir Philip Sidney once called the aim of poetic composition, an "architectonic."

This frolic composition is closely related to the inevitability of self-contradictions in any text powered by a dynamic of paradox. Most strikingly, in the passage that follows the point in *Self Reliance* where Emerson enjoins upon himself the commandment to whim, he pauses to question the very basis of his own idea: "I hope it is somewhat better than whim at last, but we cannot spend the day in explanation."[20] And more dramatically still, having sounded the tocsin for self-reliance repeatedly through the first half of the essay, he suddenly throws his whole operation into reverse and all but retracts the very idea:

> Life only avails, not the having lived. Power ceases in the instant of repose; it resides in the moment of transition from a past to a new state, in the shooting of the gulf, in the darting to an aim . . . Why, then, do we prate of self-reliance? Inasmuch as the soul is present, there will be power not confident but agent. To talk of reliance is a poor external way of speaking. Speak rather of that which relies, because it works and is.[21]

Here the very idea of a self in all its whim-directed integrity is itself dismissed as too composed, too static; the independence Emerson is championing must itself be free from its very dependence on the self. As he expresses it in his Journal, "*Becoming somewhat else* is the whole game of nature, & death the penalty of standing still."[22] And this is true of thought as well as of life: "I cannot conceive of any good in a thought which confines & stagnates. Liberty means the power to flow. To continue is to flow. Life is unceasing parturition."[23] Again—to cite one more instance in place of many others—this from the Journal: "Everything teaches transition, transference, metamorphosis: therein is human power, in transference, not in creation; & therein is human destiny, not in longevity but in removal. We dive & reappear in new places."[24]

This restless, not to say ruthless, metamorphosing gave offense in

Emerson's time and gives offense in ours. A. Bartlett Giamatti, in an address to the Yale Class of 1991, found this thoroughgoing commitment to change and transition sufficient grounds for characterizing Emerson's thoughts as "those of a brazen adolescent."[25] "Adolescent" does refer to growth and is thus far perfectly justifiable, although Giamatti meant, of course, lacking the maturity and seriousness of the fully grown. (It is amusing to try to imagine what Emerson may have noted to himself in his Journal at the thought of such an epithet coming from a scholar on the verge of resigning the presidency of Yale in order to become the commissioner of baseball.) About the predictable opposition to this forever diving and reappearing, we know Emerson was perfectly clear: "This one fact the world hates, that the soul *becomes;* for that for ever degrades the past, turns all riches to poverty, all reputation to a shame, confounds the saint with the rogue, shoves Jesus and Judas equally aside."

Emerson's extreme commitment to motion and change was in part, no doubt, a response to emerging material conditions of mid-nineteenth-century America. Tocqueville is certainly clear in the second volume of *Democracy in America* that from a European point of view one of the striking characteristics of such a democratic society is both the expectation and the acceptance of change. In a chapter on the idea of the perfectibility of man, he tells of an encounter with "an uneducated man":

> I once met an American sailor and asked him why his country's ships are made so that they will not last long. He answered offhand that the art of navigation was making such quick progress that even the best of boats would be almost useless if it lasted more than a few years.[26]

More explicitly still, in his chapter delineating the effects of this new democracy on language, Tocqueville describes this state of continual transition as deeply internalized, explaining how "in a continually changing situation [the Americans] are never obliged by unchanging circumstances to stick to any view once held ... they never know whether what they say today will fit the facts of tomorrow."[27]

But it is Emerson's persistent conviction that "the aim of the true teacher ... [is] to teach the doctrine of perpetual revelation," and this is the deepest spring of his frolic compositional impulse.[28] Indeed, the last half century's scholarly editing of Emerson's unpublished writing has yielded an increased awareness of his highly idiosyncratic literary method, most dramatically in revealing the extent to which he used what his editors have taken to calling "parallel passages." This term refers to Emerson's reuse of sentences, even whole paragraphs, that had been written earlier, in some other context, whether from talks, lectures, letters, or most especially from what for convenience is referred to as Emerson's Journal. This Journal is actually a miscellaneous collection of diaries, commonplace books, and various other sorts of notebooks—some two hundred of them—first made available in a bowdlerized edition published by his son in the early part of the century, and since 1982 in a complete and carefully edited scholarly edition. The term *parallel* is a bit of a misnomer, since these are for the most part not merely analogous passages but verbatim repetitions. Emerson himself called his private journals a "Savings Bank," as if they served the conscious purpose of a repository of insights, where his accumulated riches could be safely stored to await their useful deployment. The editors of the *Journals and Miscellaneous Notebooks* have noted that Emerson tended to make a single vertical mark (a "use mark") through any passage he retrieved in his essays. Not infrequently, he would use a passage more than once. Thus, although there is nothing explicit in the text to alert the reader to the fact, as Joseph Slater has put it in his introduction to the volume of the *Essays First Series* in the current *Collected Works*, every Emerson essay is, in fact, "a collage, a chrestomathy, a mosaic of Byzantine intricacy."[29] This practice is only compounded by the fact that Emerson's journals are themselves filled with passages he copied from whatever "lusters" he uncovered in his wide and rambling reading.

In order to convey some sense of how extensive and peculiar Emerson's practice of assembling "some single cord out of my thousand and one strands of every color & texture that lie raveled around me in old snarls" (as he wrote to his friend Caroline Sturgis), Slater in his Introduction lays out the known sources behind the first ten paragraphs of "Circles," roughly a quarter of the entire essay.[30] "Circles" is often critically celebrated as one of Emerson's finest compositional achievements; Slater chose "Circles" for his demonstration precisely because of all the essays in the *First Series* it is probably the one least traceable to Emerson's notebook and journal entries and the only essay that had never been used, at least in part, for one of Emerson's lecture courses. Thus, the demonstration dramatically emphasizes all the more the sheer extent of these "parallel passages." Of the first ten paragraphs only three are actually new, having never appeared elsewhere. The first paragraph has a sentence from his Journal of 1835 and a further clause rewritten from another passage of 1839. The third paragraph uses sentences written in his Journal of 1836 and others from 1840. And again in the fourth, the first five sentences have their source in an earlier entry from that same year's Journal. Although the fifth paragraph is new, as is the seventh, the one between is based entirely on a talk he had delivered in Boston in 1837, along with a further entry from the Journal of 1840, a later Journal that likewise provided two other entries making up the bulk of paragraphs eight and nine. The tenth paragraph repeats almost in its entirety a Journal reflection from 1839, with the extraordinary penultimate statement, "I am God in nature; I am a weed by the wall" copied from a different journal entry, this one from May 1840.[31]

These fragments of his former writing and reading embedded in his essays are decentralizing, in that they exact a kind of attention that erodes the reader's perception of the single composition. The process by which Emerson produced his essay, his conjoining of those "infinitely repellent particles," amounts to a practice it is tempting to label discomposing. Emerson is the furthest from the kind of writer whose work one is to take by the fireside for repose. There is no settling down in his essays or into them. It is not merely that they are dialectical, since even that implies some sort of system, a regularity in balancing the one hand with the other; they are, rather, more meteorological, like gusts of wind blowing from what direction they will, from one moment to the next. If this suggests that Emerson's discomposing procedure engages in what in the next century would be called the aleatory—a conscious abandonment to the contingent and the random—then that is not entirely inappropriate. Emerson approvingly described Thoreau who, when talking of art "blotted a paper with ink, then doubled it over, & safely defied the artist to surpass his effect."[32] Revelation, however perpetual, came when it would. Just as the question arises in regard to an aleatory composition, Emerson's remarks make evident that the status of his artless artfulness, or his artful artlessness, was perplexing to Emerson himself.

In Chapter 2 I examined how the Constitutional Convention managed to create a text with a secular surface beneath which percolated the assurance of revelation by means of the severe secrecy of its proceedings and the elaborate misdirection of its authorship. Emerson, facing a similar need, composed his paradoxical essays through that very queer absence of what James meant by a style; Emerson, desiring to write an Essay, had no choice in the end but to cull those moments

of revelation from his daily work of journalizing and proceed to ag-
gregate them into the most perfect union he could manage. The "true
thoughts," the momentary revelations, were merely "fractions," as Emerson described them, "waiting to become integers."[33]

Again, in a way that parallels the Framers' predicament in constituting their union, needing as they did to remain always cognizant of
the diverse peoples and states, Emerson begins his essays with the fact
of his overwhelming experience of miscellany.

> Alas for America as I must so often say, the ungirt, the diffuse, the profuse,
> procumbent, one wide ground juniper, out of which no cedar, no oak will
> rear up a mast to the clouds! it all runs to leaves, to suckers, to tendril,
> to miscellany.[34]

The facts "on the ground" are consistent with this perception—the
threefold increase in Boston's population from the time of Emerson's
childhood to his middle age, a society Tocqueville observed as "practical, complicated, agitated, and active." Yet the apprehension of the
miscellaneous went deeper, something more properly described as
metaphysical. Thus Emerson writes in his Journal:

> Life
> If any of us knew what we were doing, or wither we were going!
> We are all dying of miscellany.[35]

It may well be that the apprehension of disunity, miscellany, even the
threat of incoherence, is a good index to the very need for union. Di-
derot in the previous century had sketched out in "Rameau's Nephew,"
a psychological portrait of the simple soul, the sincere or whole man,
a type that is shown as already beginning to fracture under the rising
pressure of modernity.[36] Emerson registers this change with his characteristic plain-style eloquence: "I am always insincere, as always
knowing there are other moods."[37] His thought derives in part from
the preceding age of Enlightenment, also known as the Age of the
Encyclopedia. The *Encyclopedia* was inevitably a collection of fragments, accepting the miscellaneous as a necessary aspect in its quest to
cover the widest variety of historical and intellectual topics.

Emerson's essays seek to bring together these fragments, his contending moods—("Our moods do not believe in each other")—to unite
these disparate states of mind.[38] Just as the Constitution asserts the
wholesale creation of an entire polity, so the essays are repeatedly given
to claims of completeness and expansive generality. Once again, this is
a trait common to the culture that Emerson dramatically exemplified,

so that there is a large consonance between the claim implied by one of Tocqueville's chapter headings—"Why the Americans Show More Aptitude and Taste for General Ideas than their English Forefathers"— and the very titles of Emerson's essays: "History," "Love," "Intellect," "Art," "Nature," "Experience"—none of these subjects so much as delimited by a Baconian "Of."

Consider, again, the figure of the circle which Emerson both accepts as the age-old sign of unity, totality, and completeness and at the same time denies. As in the case of the Constitution's union, its sovereign totality—the Union—somehow coexists with the sovereignty of its component parts—the separate states. This must be the case for any revelation that is at the same time a thing of secularity: the impulse to unity and totality is both asserted and continuously undermined. Emerson's circles, though remaining perfect, are at the same time forever being broken—that is the thrust of his essay. God's nature is "as a circle whose centre [is] everywhere, and its circumference nowhere," so "there is no outside, no enclosing wall, no circumference to us," and yet "around every circle another can be drawn." And so all of Emerson's essays, however inspired they are, are also merely the result of Waldo tacking things together at his study table. On the one hand there is the unity of revelation and on the other there is the miscellany of secularity, always one and always many: "The natural world may be conceived of as a system of concentric circles, and we now and then detect in nature slight dislocations, which apprize us that this surface on which we now stand is not fixed, but sliding."[39] The circle is perfect and eternal, yet likewise forever being "swallowed and forgotten."[40]

Emerson's rhetoric of wildness, its discomposing freedom, is exactly what was necessary in order to put all that was new and strange in the assumptions behind the United States into the work of verbal imagination. Emerson himself understood very well what kind of imaginative writing came naturally to him and just how contradictory it was: "I, who tack things strangely enough together, & consider my ease rather than my strength, & often write *on the other side,* yet am an adorer of the *One.*"[41]

This raises what at first appears to be a simple question of literary valuation: Is Emerson's achievement to be found in the *Essays,* or rather in his Journal (more accurately in his accumulated journals and notebooks)? Here, too, there is a parallel to the Constitution's secular revelation: what had been during the Ratification (though it sank quickly from sight afterward) the source of a lively political debate, namely, the relation between the "We the People" at the beginning of the Constitution and all those particular signatures at the end reappears reconfigured in this critical conflict assessing the relative value of Emerson's journals versus his essays. The source of revelation and the source of a secular text cannot be the same; yet, of course, in a secular revelation they must be. (Again, note Emerson's "I am part or particle of God:" what then—the question is—when that "I" speaks?) Some of Emerson's' most articulate critical champions—Harold Bloom most eloquently—indulge in the rhetorical claim that Emerson's real masterpiece is none of the texts he had published, but the multifarious Journal itself—and no mere selection from it either but the entire collection. It seems worth noting in this context that there is no modern reader's edition of these texts in publication and that the earlier, bowdlerized version has been out of print for well over half a century—in other words, throughout the entire period of the dramatic postwar expansion of American Studies.[42]

In 1988, Lawrence Rosenwald, took this position to its logical conclusion in a book whose contention is present in its title: *Emerson and the Art of the Diary.* Rosenwald argues from the fact that Emerson on occasion exchanged his journals with friends and relations, and even allowed a visiting stranger to read part of it through. Therefore, Rosenwald maintains, the diary aspect of the manuscript should be considered a work of art in its own right. But this perspective robs what is most peculiar about his prose of any interest or significance, and in any case flies in the face of Emerson's often alluded-to ambition, as most clearly articulated at the very beginning of his new postministerial career in 1835, namely, to write the very books he would go on to publish over the next twenty-odd years:

> When will you mend Montaigne? When will you take the hint of nature? Where are your Essays? Can you not express your one conviction that the moral laws hold? Have you not thoughts & illustrations that are your own; the parable of geometry & matter; the reason why the atmosphere is transparent; the power of Composition in nature & in man's thoughts; the use & uselessness of traveling; the law of Compensation: the transcendent excellence of truth in character, in rhetoric, in things; the sublimity of Self-reliance; and the rewards of perseverance in the best opinion? Have you not a testimony to give for Shakespear, for Milton? one sentence of real praise of Jesus is worth a century of legendary Christianity.[43]

It appears that we must simply accept the ambiguity of notions like primary and secondary in Emerson's essays. Most interestingly, if we were to inquire where in the universe of texts we can find a similar ambiguity, a case of secondariness compounded into a primary work, the clearest instance would be what has traditionally been revelation itself, none other than *the* Book, the Holy Bible.

Since his days at the Harvard Divinity School and the early years of his ministry, in large part through his brother William who had gone to study in Göttingen, Emerson had wrestled with the new higher criticism of the Bible. Throughout the eighteenth century, Enlightenment skepticism had eroded the textual integrity of the Bible, and by the end of the century scholars such as Johann Gottfried Eichhorn had begun to apply the scientific methods of critical analysis developed for the study of secular texts to the Holy Scripture. Whatever their religious motives were in investigating the seeming contradictions of the biblical texts, these scholars began to offer a new picture of revelation as a kind of anthology, or even patchwork, of various poems, legal codes, and other "Oriental" genres, both oral and written, oftentimes of strikingly diverse provenances one from the other. These critical studies, though often almost impossible for students of the Bible to resist, were in sum threatening to undermine the primary status of Scripture itself. The extent to which this scholarship had the effect of shaking Emerson's Christian faith and of being responsible for his ultimate resignation from the pulpit—as it did for his brother William—is of less interest in this context than what it says about Emerson's evolving understanding of what may account for the authority of the biblical text, or indeed of any text whatever.

Barbara Packer, writing on Emerson's response to the higher criticism, has traced what ultimately became Emerson's "admiration for [the] more radical form of source study that ends by exploding the identity of the author," as in his excited conviction that "from Wolf's attack upon the authenticity of the Homeric poems dates a new epoch of learning" (p. 90). Yet, as Packer asks by way of conclusion, "in demystifying the notion of origins, what has happened to the notion of authority . . . if the very notion of origin is exploded, and the text dissolved into a heap of fragments, by what right does the poet speak?"[44] Parker suggests that Emerson's answer to this question was "half psychological, half pragmatic" (p. 91) For the psychological half, she quotes Emerson explaining how previous texts, from a writer's perspective at least, lack any real substance in comparison to the writer's own thoughts: "the ministration of books and of other minds are a whiff of smoke to that most private reality with which he has conversed" (p. 91). For the pragmatic part of Emerson's response, Packer reminds us of his great admiration for the synthesizing genius of writers like Chaucer, Wordsworth, and Shakespeare, how they took from others in constructing their own words. Emerson cited even Jesus for praise as a borrower of the wisdom, in his case of the rabbis: "He picked out the grains of gold" (p. 92).

But Packer's explanation does not seem quite adequate an account, for Emerson after all engaged in a method of merging other texts, albeit largely his own, into a new primary text that resembled nothing so much as what he had learned about the accumulating composition of Scripture itself. Geoffrey Hartman in an attempt to arrive at a formal distinction between the prose narrative of Scripture and that of secular fiction, stresses the degree to which the composite aspect of the biblical text, "the redactional process"—and he is dealing primarily with the foundation stories of Hebrew Scripture—creates "a style in which every sentence is a jealously guarded deposit, as if language had to have authority, whatever uncertainties encompassed the reported event or act of naming it."[45] This seems to catch a quality not only of biblical storytelling, but of Emerson's prose as well, in which each assertion, no matter how immediately qualified or contradicted, has the distinctness and dignity of being chiseled in stone. "I would like to assert," Hartman writes further, "that Scripture can be distinguished from fiction by its frictionality." He acknowledges that a respect for such friction—the conflict between the fragments—exists in fictional or "literary" texts as well, but he insists that whereas in a novel, for instance, "the respect which shapes variant stories into narrative [reflects] only the aesthetic problem of blending them into a unified whole," by contrast Scripture "recalls, or should recall, the authority of traditions handed down, each with its truth claim."[46]

Of course, Emerson does not write stories; on the contrary, he is often described as having little interest even in reading them.[47] Barely a page of any kind of narrative is to be found in Emerson's writing, as if the temporal and psychological continuity that narrative entails simply held no interest for him. He writes only essays, that least formal of forms. In his description of Bacon, arguably the originator of the form in English, Emerson singles out precisely the necessary imperfection of the form: "Each of Shakespear's dramas is perfect, hath an immortal integrity. To make Bacon's work complete, he must live to the end of the world."[48] Bacon's essays "allowed," Emerson wrote, "of perpetual amendment and addition," as "every one of his works was a gradual growth."

This accretionary development of Bacon's essays, and the way that that development echoes, in a very general sense at least, the scriptural mode of composition is still more striking in the great original essayist, Montaigne. The diversity of "sources" in Montaigne's case is so extreme that modern editions of the *Essays* make use of some mark within the text, such as superscripts, in order, as Donald Frame explains in his complete English translation, "to distinguish the three certain strata [from] which the *Essays* were composed," roughly speaking fragments from 1580, from 1588, and anything added after that last date. Otherwise, as Frame puts it, "an attentive reader unaware of these strata is likely to find Montaigne puzzling and may write him off as irresponsibly inconsistent."[49]

Nothing could be more congenial to Emerson, who after all famously declared foolish consistency "the hobgoblin of little minds."[50] In many ways such inconsistency is the very appeal and purpose of the essay form. Montaigne claimed that he would never have written his *Essays* at all if he had ever managed to maintain a consistent perspective on anything: "If my mind could gain a firm footing, I should not speak tentatively, I would not make essays, I would make decisions."[51] He plays on the verb "to essay" (essayer) meaning "to attempt," as if the essay is not so much a form as merely an attempt at a form. "All contradictions are to be found in me," Montaigne writes; and "Even fixedness is nothing but a more sluggish motion."[52]

The essay, in its miscellaneous and wandering way, is the most secular of forms—often quotidian and peripatetic. For Emerson, Montaigne's books were "full of fun, poetry, business, divinity, philosophy, anecdote, smut . . . dealing of bone & marrow, or cornbarn & flour barrel, or wife, & friend, & valet, of things nearest & next."[53] And yet, it is precisely by the essay's wandering, by the discontinuous path of its digressions, that it reveals to the author what he knows that he did not necessarily know that he knew. The essay wanders, but with a true aim, so that what merely happens along the way becomes the very heart of the matter. This doubleness makes it a very fitting almost-form for the paradox of a secular revelation.

"I think nothing is of any value in books," Emerson writes in "The Poet," "excepting the transcendental and extraordinary." Emerson sought to "mend" his much beloved Montaigne by flooding the pragmatic of the essay with his vision of "the infinitude of the private man." Emerson noted in his Journal, "the remarkable trait in American character is the union not very infrequent of Yankee cleverness with spiritualism." By adopting and adapting the constitutional poetics that created American national identity, and making essays, each a speaking out of that paradoxical, self-contradictory claim to an ultimate authority deriving from no more than ordinary selfhood, Emerson set American literature on its self-regarding yet wildly ambitious course. As we shall see, in the case of both Whitman and Melville, their constitutional poetics also deformed the literary arts they practiced—the writing of lyric poems and of prose narrative—in the decided direction of the essayistic. Likewise it forced them into an embrace of self-contradiction, an inclination to the fragmentary, and a hyperactive oscillation between a revealed sense of cosmic, unifying totality and a doggedly secular miscellany of the intractably material.

CHAPTER ELEVEN

A Poetic Form for Straying

I teach straying from me, yet who can stray from me?
WALT WHITMAN, "SONG OF MYSELF," 1855

Walt Whitman wrote poetry on the assumption that American independence was best understood as a means of American union and that straying was a means of abiding by an American order: he is the poet par excellence of a constitutional poetics.

Whitman is said to have set the type himself for ten of the ninety-five pages of the first version of his one, ever revised, book of poetry, *Leaves of Grass* (1855). A printer's shop on Brooklyn's Fulton Street had produced almost eight hundred copies of the book, two hundred of which were bound in a green cover, the title stamped on the front in gold letters filigreed with entwining tendrils. Whitman sent a copy of this tall, thin quarto (8" × 12") to, among other notables, Ralph Waldo Emerson in the small New England village of Concord. Emerson's immediate response is one of the prime instances of what Melville, reading Hawthorne, had called "the shock of recognition": "Genius the world round stands hand in hand, and one shock of recognition unites them all."[1] The note Emerson sent in return evinced more enthusiasm for Whitman than he had for even the closest of his associates, like Thoreau, whose *Walden* was published the year before. Dazzled, Emerson admitted to Whitman: "I rubbed my eyes a little to see if this sunbeam were no illusion. . . ."[2] Reading Emerson's essay, "The Poet," now, a century and a half after *Leaves of Grass*, it is easy to fall into the mythic identification of Emerson's Annunciation, followed a decade later by Whitman's Arrival; *Leaves of Grass* is so much the great literary flowering of Emersonianism that it is especially gratifying to witness Emerson, against all the prejudices of class, region, and temperament, so unhesitatingly recognize the significance of Whitman's sudden appearance.

Nor was this a case of recognition alone, as valuable as that was; Emerson was, in fact, Whitman's first great critic. His remark meant in some ways to qualify his delight in Whitman's book—that it was a combination of "the *Baghavad Gita* and the *New York Tribune*"—is a judgment that has been elaborated upon, consciously or not, by nearly every writer on Whitman's poetry to this day. Not that there has ever been a secret of Emerson's relation to Whitman. The poet himself made sure of that the very next year in a second edition of *Leaves of Grass,* by stamping the spine of each book in gold print with the words: "I Greet You / at the / Beginning / of a Great / Career / R W Emerson." Whitman had immediately printed the whole of Emerson's private response as an advertisement in the *New York Tribune.* Whitman had the moral right of literary affiliation to quote Emerson's high praise, and the practical good sense not to ask first for the New Englander's permission. However distasteful Emerson may have found Whitman's self-promotion, he never retracted either the words or the judgment. Indeed, years later, he wrote recommending Whitman to Secretary of State Seward, saying of Whitman's poems that "they show extraordinary power, and are more deeply American, democratic, and in the interest of political liberty, than those of any other poet."[3]

Although Whitman himself could be critical of the later Emerson, he likewise maintained Emerson's centrality till the end. "Emerson never fails," he told Horace Traubel, his biographer and daily companion in his old age, "he can't be rejected; even when he falls on stony ground, he somehow eventuates in a harvest."[4] Even within their one moment of explicit disagreement over the open sexuality of the "Children of Adam" poems for the third edition of *Leaves of Grass* (1860), there remained a profound sympathy and understanding between the Boston Brahmin and the Broadway would-be B'hoy.[5] Whitman described to Traubel how the two had argued while walking the streets of Boston together,

[Emerson] did not urge [self-censorship] for my sake but for the sake of the people. He seemed to be arguing that I didn't need the people as much as the people needed me. I said: "You think that if I cut the book there would be a book left?" He said, "Yes." Then I asked, "But would there be as good a book left?" He looked grave; this seemed to disturb him a bit. Then he smiled at me and said, "I didn't not say as good a book—I said a good book." That's where we left it.[6]

Whitman's poetry is the clearest literary case of a secular revelation along the paradoxical lines of the Constitution. In fact the case is all but too clear. Whitman is so perfect an exemplar of the combination of forces I am describing that to look directly at the flux of the secular and the revealed in his poetry is to confront an unmediated mystery, rather like trying to stare at the sun. It is no accident that his followers felt the need to form a new religion in response to his work, nor it is an accident that they failed.[7]

The natural movement of Emerson's prose between philosophic abstraction and "the milk in the firken" differs from the movement of Whitman's poems only as village and rural life differ from the new environment of the city. Whitman's vision seems in many respects an Emersonianism from the perspective of New York's radically urban modernity. The restless rapidity of Whitman's transitions, and the miscellaneous multiplicity of the places and persons he describes, reflect the pulse and texture of city life. He darts without transition from vignettes, both public and private,

> The suicide sprawls on the bloody floor of the bedroom.
> It is so. . . . I witnessed the corpse . . . there the pistol had fallen.
>   (p. 33)[8]

> The heavy omnibus, the driver with his interrogating thumb, the
>   clank of shod horses on the granite floor,
> The carnival of sleighs, the clinking and shouted jokes and pelts of
>   snowballs. (p. 33)

to personal proclamations,

> And I know I am deathless,
> I know this orbit of mine cannot be swept by a carpenter's
>   compass,
> I know I shall not pass like a child's carlacue cut with a burnt stick
>   at night. (p. 46)

> I cock my hat as I please indoors or out. (p. 45)

to still moments of reflection and insight:

> Urge and urge and urge,
> Always the procreant urge of the world. (p. 28)

> And to glance with an eye or show a bean in its pod confounds the
>   learning of all times. (p. 85)

It is this urban environment as well that partially accounts for the political aspect of Whitman's imagination being so much more developed—or at least far more explicitly so—than Emerson's. All his adult life Whitman strongly supported the political cause of union, while Emerson's interest in the notion of union, never wholly detached from its political repercussions, nevertheless expressed itself overwhelmingly in the realm of personal integrity and nature. Not only did Whitman work as a newspaperman in an era when American newspapers were openly partisan and political, but he himself wrote pamphlets, engaged in popular political oratory, and even after his metamorphosis into a poet (and any glance at his earlier attempts at verse confirms the justice of so mythic a term as "metamorphosis"), questions of the union always touched his deepest, life-long political commitments. Both Allen Grossman and Kerry Larson have, in different ways, examined Whitman's "poetics of union," or "drama of consensus," for the way in which the poet inflected his political preoccupations in his 1855 *Leaves of Grass*, and later in his Civil War poems and beyond.[9]

The idea of a union is as much a literary as it is a political idea. An essay, or a poem, or any work of literary art, must possess its own unity, marking it out as an artifact, a work of *poesis*, however it wishes to be a part of nature as well. Amid all the revisions of Whitman's one ever-growing book of poetry, he never had any thought of changing the title: it remained *Leaves of Grass* that he continued to write, from the first edition of 1855 until the version he left upon his death in 1892. One man, one book: all the individual poems forever reintegrated into the whole. For this overarching unity Whitman makes use of that most common phenomenon of nature—the very ground upon which we stand—because it captures so perfectly the paradox inherent in his entire poetic enterprise. The title plays not merely on leaves as pages of a book, but more significantly still, upon the all but hidden ambiguity between leaves of *grass*, or *leaves* of grass—what a grammarian would distinguish as an objective and a subjective genitive. In other words, are these grass's leaves—one plant of grass, every blade a leaf of that plant; or are they leaves of grass—every leaf itself a separate plant? The single/collective grass is a very emblem for the oscillation in Whitman's poetry between, on the one hand, the meaning of a union or a unity, and on the other the meaning of the separate self—an echo of the very oscillation that sustains the vision of the Constitution.

Whereas Emerson repeatedly expressed his perplexity when confronting the disjointedness of his compositional technique, knowing himself committed, as he put it, to "the One," Whitman in his celebrated Introduction to the first edition of *Leaves of Grass* openly declared that "the United States themselves are essentially the greatest poem." This most peculiar and extreme statement of Whitman's constitutional poetics stretches the idea of a verbal artifact almost past the breaking point, and by insisting that these very states are, in fact, highly resistant to any kind of unity, he makes no attempt to ease the paradox:

> In the history of the earth hitherto the largest and most stirring appear tame and orderly to [the states'] ampler largeness and stir. Here at last is something in the doings of man that corresponds with the broadcast doings of the day and night. Here is not merely a nation but a teeming nation of nations. Here is action untied from strings necessarily blind to particulars and details magnificently moving in vast masses.

And when, in that same first edition, we reach the pages of poetry, we find that in fact of all these poems—and by their subsequent printing in later editions we know, if we doubted it, that there are twelve of them—none are individually titled, none are clearly demarcated from the others.[10] Beyond *Leaves of Grass* itself, there is not a single title in the book.

Not only are the poems untitled, but there is no stated author. All the first edition of *Leaves of Grass* offers by way of an indication of authorship is a frontispiece, a stippled engraving of a photograph of a young man in worker's clothing, an open-collared shirt, with one hand knuckled upon his hip, the other slipped into the pocket of his trousers, and his hat at a jaunty angle back from his forehead. Is this the Walter Whitman whose name is listed as possessor of the copyright, the "Walt Whitman, an American, one of the roughs, a kosmos" mentioned in the book's first poem? He does not, as the poem describes him, appear particularly "disorderly fleshy and sensual . . . eating drinking, breeding," nor "hankering, gross, mystical and nude."

Yet to describe the poetry simply as anonymous could hardly be more misleading, since the very person of the poet, from the unusual Introduction onward, is everywhere present.

> I celebrate myself
> And what I assume you shall assume
> For every atom belonging to me as good belongs to you. (p. 27)

The poetry begins with the author making it twice into the first line, as subject and object of the first brief sentence, and again into the second line, and the third, by which time the reader too (the "you") has appeared twice. What has not appeared, and page after page will not appear, is any semblance of the verbal patterning that in the middle of the nineteenth century all but defined the notion of a poem. Rhyme itself is dispensable; but meter as well, a photograph of a laborer, and poetry denuded of its distinctive rules and decorum—the whole odd-shaped volume shouts Democracy, both in its insistence on the commonal and the anonymous, and in its diametrically opposed insistence on the highly individual person.

Indeed, the very longest and the first of the untitled poems, known to us now by the title Whitman had assigned it by the time of the Deathbed edition of 1892, is none other than a "Song of Myself." While it is surely Whitman's single greatest poetic achievement, the critic Edwin Haviland Miller in his unusual edition of the poem refers to the generations-long "search for genre" and corresponding "search for structure" undertaken by its readers, with neither search having been particularly successful. Miller's "Mosaic of Interpretations" cites more than three hundred critics who have together offered various dozens of schemata without anything approaching a critical consensus. And yet unlike some of Whitman's early detractors, few now doubt the poem has a structure, however elusively protean it remains.

And notwithstanding what all agree is its superb lyricism, Whitman's 1855 "Song of Myself" has something distinctly essayistic about it, not merely in the indeterminacy of its genre and the openness of its form, but in the place that statement occupies in the poem. Like Emerson's essays, but more surprisingly in Whitman's poem, an informal discoursing will suddenly rise and dominate what had been lyrically or dramatically expressive. This impulse in Whitman toward the essayistic is a formal response to the antilogy—the tension of self-contradictoriness—underlying his very poetics, a poetics itself derived from the driving paradox beneath the nation's constitutional foundation. The essayistic permits a free oscillation between the two sides of the paradox; it maintains the self-contradiction as a dynamic motor. Emerson, modeling himself upon Montaigne, openly espoused such an essayistic on-the-one-hand and on-the-other-hand motion; for Whitman the essayistic amounted to a kind of imaginative inflation, a willed expansion of the freedom to move about, like an inner, poetic counterpart to the Western frontier within which self-contradiction could flourish without trespassing on the necessary boundaries demanded by any artistic form. Whitman could get everything into his poems, all the lyric intensities, and all the vast miscellany of the essayistic.

The union Whitman championed—political and literary—aspired to the adherence of not merely states and persons, but of perception and apperception, the visible and the invisible, the present and the absent, even the living and the dead. Above all Whitman celebrated a union between himself, his one book, and his reader. He advances toward his reader, while at the same time withdrawing, both a companion in the world and a revealer of the world—"in the game and out of the game." This is perhaps the most central of his many self-contradictory gestures toward union, one that goes to the heart of the kind of self Whitman both claimed and encouraged.

For what, after all, do those first three lines of "Song of Myself" proclaim if not the equality, indeed the almost-union, of the poet and the reader. The self-sharing poet is loafing in converse with his soul, observing, breathing, loving, undisguising himself, himself a song rising and meeting the sun, when without warning, the reader is accosted:

> Have you reckoned a thousand acres much? Have you reckoned the
> earth much?
> Have you practiced so long to learn to read?
> Have you felt so proud to get at the meaning of poems? (p. 28)

Is this mockery or condescension? Is it, in any case, a fitting address to the literate reader of a poem? The voice modulates at once to comforter, or at least to a comforting seducer:

> Stop this day and night with me and you shall possess the origin of
> all poems,
> You shall possess the good of the earth and sun . . . there are
> millions of suns left (p. 28)

Here is the promise of revelation, of insight with authority, offering origin and future. But no, he continues, the voice of the poet is not the source of revelation. That authoritative insight requires the active perception of the reader:

> You shall no longer take things at second or third hand . . . nor
> look through the eyes of the dead . . . nor feed on the spectres in
> books,
> You shall not look through my eyes either, nor take things from me,
> You shall listen to all sides and filter them from yourself. (p. 28)

The question is simple: who is in charge here? Who is the poet, and what claim, if any, is he making for himself? No authorship is claimed for *Leaves of Grass*—not because authorship is denied, but because authorship and its accompanying authority is evaded. The root of the word "authority" is to increase, presumably to increase the degree of order, so that an author brings an increase of order to the miscellany of experience and imagination, what we have been referring to as a composition. Robert Frost called it a "stay against confusion." Emerson struggled as an author with uniting the contending states of his mind into the composition of his essays, and constructed them with what he discerned as missing stairs, discovering himself first on one floor, then another, and accepting that thus it was. Whitman assumes a much greater degree of authorial control, but only by means of a near-complete mystification of his presence. He will reveal all the secrets to you because evidently you already know them. He is forcefully present in all his gross particularity—"Washes and razors for foofoos ... for me freckles and a bristling beard"—while he assures you that there is nothing of him that is not also of you.

The authorship of the great first edition of *Leaves of Grass* is not so much obscured as it is hopelessly entwined in misdirection, very much the way the Constitution makes use of its truthful fiction of "We the People." A persistent interest among critics of Whitman, particularly in recent years, has been what Tenney Nathanson's recent, very thorough discussion of it calls *Whitman's Presence*. What is Whitman's impulse to inject himself, and us his readers, so aggressively into his poems, such that they have, as Nathanson observes it "an uncanny quality that makes their very solicitude unsettling?"[11] Nor is this dismissed as a superficial stance. Nathanson rightly states that

> [a]t its best [Whitman's] work does bear on us with an immediacy not ordinarily associated with poetry: the figure who is said to rise up and appear to us in the poet's direct addresses to his audience seems to overflow the boundaries of the very work that conveys him to us, to shuck off his status as a fictive character, to extinguish a literary representation and impinge on us personally and directly.[12]

Indeed, to Nathanson this "unlikely sense of immediacy" is "one of Whitman's finest accomplishments."[13]

What need does Whitman's poetry address such that this strangely pressing intimacy should be one of its finest accomplishments, and does this bear on the claim here that it is the founding Constitution that is the filter through which Whitman, like Emerson before him, apprehended the possibility of order and authorship, of political union and literary composition? To return to the photograph across from the title page of *Leaves of Grass*, considered in this context it is best understood as an attempt to circumvent the mediating presence of language itself. There is a person here, nothing more, it says, and nothing less. Can a person exercise authority? I can, Whitman repeatedly explains, only to the extent that you can as well. The freedom of the verse, for all its intensities, refuses the conventional display of versifying talent and the hierarchical privileges of poetic form, in order thereby to invite the reader into an acceptance of his or her own authority.

Whitman as Everyman, as every man and woman and child? What could be a more preposterous claim to make about this prodigious personality? The poet does not merely reveal his charisma, willingly or no, he flaunts it, brandishes it like a beneficent weapon, a prehensile form of love. What are often referred to as Whitman's catalogues, the long stretches of lines given over to describing first one moment or scene, and then another, then another, another, and another, create in the reader an almost hypnotic passivity in the face of an endless procession of landscape and life. The poet's voice diffuses itself into a passive, passionate possession of others, not merely others, but their very worlds as well, indeed *the* world:

> My ties and ballasts leave me . . . I travel . . . I sail . . . my elbows
>   rest in the sea-gaps,
> I skirt the sierras . . . my palms cover continents,
> I am afoot with my vision. (p. 59)

> Looking in at the shop-windows in Broadway the whole forenoon
>   . . . pressing the flesh of my nose to the thick plate-glass,
> Wandering the same afternoon with my face turned up to the
>   clouds;
> My right and left arms round the sides of two friends and I in the
>   middle;
> Coming home with the bearded and dark-cheeked bush-boy . . .
>   riding behind him at the drape of the day;
> Far from the settlements studying the print of animals' feet, or the
>   moccasin print;
> By the cot in the hospital reaching lemonade to a feverish patient,
> By the coffined corpse when all is still, examining with a candle;
> Voyaging to every port to dicker and adventure;
> Hurrying with the modern crowd, as eager and fickle as any,
> Hot toward one I hate, ready in my madness to knife him;
> Solitary at midnight in my back yard, my thoughts gone from me a
>   long while (p. 62)

There are moments in "Song of Myself" when Whitman seems like no one so much as Bottom the Weaver, desperate to play all the parts:

> I am of old and young, of the foolish as much as the wise,
> Regardless of others, ever regardful of others,
> Maternal as well as paternal, a child as well as a man,
> Stuffed with the stuff that is coarse, and stuffed with the stuff that
>   is fine (p. 42)

> Comrade of raftsmen and coalmen—comrade of all who shake
>   hands and welcome to drink and meat;
> A learner with the simplest, a teacher of the thoughtfulest,
> A novice beginning experient of myriads of seasons,
> Of every hue and trade and rank, of every caste and religion,
> Not merely of the New World but of Africa Europe or Asia . . . a
>   wandering savage,
> A farmer, mechanic, or artist . . . a gentleman, sailor, lover or quaker,
> A prisoner, fancy-man, rowdy, lawyer, physician or priest.
> I resist anything better than my own diversity,
> And breathe the air and leave plenty after me,
> And am not stuck up, and am in my place. (p. 43)

Like Bottom, Whitman is easy to mock but full of poetry. His desire to ground his vision in the common earth—"If you would find me, look for me under your boot soles" (a quality that somewhat mitigated the austere Thoreau's intense admiration for "this most clear Democrat:" "It is as if the beasts speak"—likewise seems almost an echo of Bottom's transformation into an ass. Whitman's outrageousness, insisting to all that "the scent of my armpits is an aroma finer than prayer" is the expression of a man at peace with the animal of himself. Of course this Bottom is only a part of Whitman. Like many who make a fuss about being simple, the poet was a very complicated fellow.

John Jay Chapman, though a brilliant critic of Emerson, could say no more of Whitman than that he "has given utterance to the soul of a tramp":[14]

[Tramps] have always tried civilized life. Their early training, at least their early attitude of mind towards life, has generally been respectable. That they should be criminally inclined goes without saying, because their minds have been freed from the sanctions, which enforce law. But their general innocence is, under the circumstances, very remarkable, and distinguishes them from the criminal classes.[15]

Whitman is often all over the place and can sometimes barely stay in the same place, not to say in the same identity, for more than a few lines in a row. The theater, operatic and Shakespearean, set Whitman's imagination afire, and you can see in the series of photographs he had taken over the course of his life how comfortable he was with the idea of posing, playing the dandy, the tough, the prophet, the sage. In "Song of Myself" he became everyman by becoming everyone. Harold Bloom, in a brilliant piece of interpretation, described Whitman as not merely an autodidact but profoundly autoerotic.[16] This might sound like a very unlikely narrowness of experience for such a poet, but if you aspire to be everyone, onanism and orgy are not very far apart.

Are Whitman and Emerson not believably representative Americans, but in fact extra-ordinary men such that their relation to democracy is inherently problematic? Richard Poirier has addressed this consequential question in *The Renewal of Literature: Emersonian Reflections* under the rubric of "The Question of Genius." He describes Emerson as having "a tragic view of the disparity between desire and possibility, all the more so because the physical continent of America did sometimes seem like a bridge between the two."[17] For Emerson the significance of genius, including atavistic genius and the whole institution of literature, is that it "makes us feel our own wealth." Poirier quotes from Emerson's essay "The Over-Soul" on a "great poet:"

> His best communication to our mind is to teach us to despise all he has done. Shakespeare carries us to such a lofty strain of intelligent activity, as to suggest a wealth which beggars his own. . . . Why, then, should I make account of Hamlet and Lear, as if we had not the soul from which they fell as syllables from the tongue?[18]

Poirier concludes that "we are left with the peculiar prospect that works of 'genius' may enhance and create human life by the degree to which they make themselves inconspicuous."[19]

Perhaps Emerson may be said to make himself inconspicuous; he possesses a famously Olympian coldness. But Whitman? Yet it is Whitman who ends "Song of Myself" in the very process of disappearing: "I effuse my flesh in eddies and drift it in lacy jags. / I bequeath myself to the dirt to grow from the grass I love" (p. 88).[20]

Whether they are men of genius, or perhaps better called almost-prophets, what is it that they want from their readers? Their word is not, as the words of full-fledged prophets, "from the Lord," nor is it consistent, as the word of a prophet generally is, with a doctrine or a tradition. Emerson urges what he calls self-reliance, and Whitman expresses that demand in a way that could not be clearer or more self-contradictory: "I teach straying from me," he tells his reader, "but who can stray from me?" (p. 83). Following Emerson and Whitman is not to follow them. Just as the Constitution's secular mechanization of power is not to impinge upon the ineffable authority of its establishment, but to mind its business without recourse to the underlying mystery of an achieved union, so the Americans are to learn what Emerson and Whitman have to teach precisely by abandoning them as teachers. Emerson and Whitman highlight the degree to which the United States is founded in antifoundationalism, the established tradition to refuse what is handed down.

Whitman and Emerson encourage followers, even if they are highly paradoxical about how one may actually follow. For both, the future is always beginning, always open and thus they are most often referred to as optimists. They do not hasten after conclusions, or foolish consistency, and they hold out some promise that conflict, if it will not cease, will nevertheless allow further growth and not contraction. Neither of them writes narratives, in part because for neither of them does a story ever end.

From this perspective, the United States is not so much a nation of nations as it is a nation of strayers, or strays.[21] To be a stray is to be ownerless, masterless, free; but then it is also to be lonely, friendless, and isolated. To be a wanderer is not very far from being a vagrant. To stray is to escape but also to be abandoned. It is, in the end, a condition shot through with paradox. How, for instance, does one cultivate, or hand down, a sense of straying? Whitman and Emerson can teach freedom only by encouraging their students to abandon them. More to the point, how can one write a poem for strays and for straying? Whitman sometimes likened his poem to the nation itself: "I consider Leaves of Grass and its theory experimental as, in deepest sense, I consider our American republic itself to be, with its theory."[22] In 1857 Whitman made a note to himself on future plans of *Leaves of Grass:* "The Great Construction of the New Bible. Not to be diverted from the principal object—the main life work—the Three Hundred & Sixty five [poems].—it ought to be ready in 1859."[23] Whitman, the former carpenter and house-builder, in using the word "construction" for the writing of his "New Bible," echoes both the image and the conception of the Constitution's framing. The word "construction" is otherwise rather a peculiar word to describe what seems identified as a work of religious inspiration.

Is Whitman, then, a religious poet? Harold Bloom thinks so and claims that "part at least of [Whitman's] place as a center of the American canon is his still unacknowledged function and status as the national religious poet."[24] But there perhaps is no clear way to navigate these murky waters of the Ineffable. What is worth insisting upon in the context of this argument is that the revelational is not of necessity identical with the religious. However, both are assumed in contradiction to the realm of the purely secular.

It is important also to note that this modern idea of the "secular" is not, as the earlier idea was, merely the counterpart to the religious or the sacred. Such an older notion of the secular does not contradict so much as it complements the religious; the older sense of religious and secular exist alongside one another. The modern idea of the secular—modern in the sense that it is unclear whether and to what extent any persons held such a view before modernity—is of a realm that is effectively cut off from the religious or the supernatural. For our purposes here, the starkest condition of secularity is the absence of any effective authority independent of power or violence. As Hannah Arendt states in one of her superb historical essays, power and authority are radically different, even contradictory, ideas:

> Since authority always demands obedience, it is commonly mistaken for some form of power or violence. Yet authority precludes the use of external means; where force is used, authority has failed. Authority, on the other hand, is incompatible with persuasion, which presupposes equality and works through a process of argumentation. Where arguments are used, authority is left in abeyance.[25]

No clergy were present at the founding because when the nation got down to the serious business of creating itself, uniting the individual states and persons, no clergy were necessary. From the point of view of the Founders, no matter how personally religious some of them may or may not have been, the religious component of the political had become ceremonial, or primarily private and personal. The very notion of a political authority claiming independence from *secular* power would have been deemed a piece of tyrannous manipulation, a purposeful mystification.[26] This is yet another route to the same paradox—authority had to be independent of power; but there is no authority that can be independent of power. In other words, what was required for authority was the very thing for which the secular world had no place. What I have referred to as the "revealed," or "revelational" is actually, a contradiction of the incontestable secularity of all the arrangements of power the Constitution describes, yet one that does not raise any question of religious belief or practice. To revert to the image of the coin, it is the *other side,* what simply cannot be seen with the first side in view. This is a permanent offense to elementary logic—the very definition of a strong paradox.

Although Whitman refers to a New Bible, it is the case that his Bible is the most explicitly secular we can quite imagine. Whitman directly addresses the question of religious understanding, glossing in "Song of Myself" the key terms of religious thought and practice:

> And I have said that the soul is not more than the body
> I have said that the body is not more than the soul,
> And nothing, not God, is greater to one than one's self is . . .
>
> And I call to mankind, Be not curious about God,
> For I who am curious about each am not curious about God,
> No array of terms can say how much I am at peace about God and
>   about death. (p. 85)

It is not merely that this is unorthodox, or beyond conventional religious categories; at the same time that it asserts the reality of the soul, of the body, and of God, these lines uproot them from any context in which they may possess a sure and stable meaning or place. The category of religious is itself made irrelevant—indeed, it is invoked in order to be set aside, that we "be not curious" about it.

That Whitman's poetry so closely follows the constitutional impulse to a secular revelation does not make of the Constitution some kind of template for American writing. What Whitman does is invent a poetic form that gives a rebirth to the Constitution's mode, a founding text generated by a paradoxical identity of the secular and the revealed. He teaches independence as a means of union, straying as a way of following. The Founders suppressed, consciously and not so consciously, the paradox of self-constituting authority, while the anti-Federalists tried to force it out into the open, at least until the ratification succeeded, at which point they ceased and desisted. But Whitman proclaims the paradox—producing his ironically out-in-the-open elusiveness. Like the Constitution, "Song of Myself" finds a way to union without denying the full freedom of its own and its nation's anarchic impulses and experiences. Whitman's permanently strange work offers a literary expression of the Constitution's union of independent sovereignties. He adopted its jointly irreconcilable perspectives to create what his contemporaries called a lawless poetry, a lawlessness that, in fact, revealed a hidden higher order to the democratic miscellany of unabashedly secular life.

CHAPTER TWELVE

Clinging to Narrative

"Take the rope, sir—I give it into thy hands, Starbuck." Then arranging his person in the basket, he
gave the word for them to hoist him to his perch,
Starbuck being the one who secured the rope at last;
and afterwards stood near it. And thus, with one
hand clinging round the royal mast, Ahab gazed
abroad upon the sea for miles and miles,—ahead
astern, this side, and that,—within the wide expanded
circle commanded at so great a height.

MELVILLE, "THE HAT," *Moby-Dick, or
The Whale*, 1851

To claim that both the Constitution and *Moby-Dick* are paradoxes of
secular revelation, as also are Emerson's essays and Whitman's poems,
is not to imply that in all these texts the dynamic relation between the
two component parts of that paradox is identical. The Constitution in
large part functions by systematically ignoring the very fact of this
conflict between the secular and the revealed, and American culture
has largely followed its lead, turning away from any examination of
the text's conflicting assumptions of authority. Often as not, Whitman
and Emerson actively exult in the irresolvable enigma, slipping from
the secular side of the paradox to the revealed in a highly charged, self-
energizing alternating current.[1] But in the case of Melville and his most
distinctive and powerful novels, there is no frictionless transition available between the one realm and the other. Instead the reader is confronted by a palpably violent strife through which Melville's potent art
of narrative holds fast on its way.

A full thematic account of Herman Melville's single greatest work,
Moby-Dick, or The Whale—were such a thing possible—would need
to include the narrative's reflective engagement with the United States
Constitution, for the very figural ground of its fiction—the mythos of
ship, captain, and crew—refers not merely to the age-old image of the
ship of state but to an explicitly constitutional iconography. This is the
iconography that Longfellow drew upon in his long-famous poem "The

Building of the Ship": "Thou, too, sail on, O Ship of State! / Sail on, O Union, strong and great!" Carl Van Doren's narrative history of the Constitutional Convention appropriately concludes with an extended description of the several states' parades, each one focused on a different version of the symbolic ship of the Constitution. The grandest of them all, New York's, involved "a frigate of thirty two guns, twenty seven feet keel, and ten feet beam, with galleries and every thing complete and in proportion."[2]

Melville made explicit the *Pequod*'s allusion to the Constitution in referring to its crew as "an Anacharsis Clootz deputation from all the isles of the sea, and all the ends of the earth . . . federated along one keel."[3] And it was just at the mid-century mark, when Melville was engaged in writing *Moby-Dick,* that the sectional dispute had become so bitter that the very name of the nation, the "United States," seemed to be increasingly hypothetical. Nor should it be overlooked in this contest that *Moby-Dick* is, after all, the story of a shipwreck.

But the central literary force of the Constitution in Melville's great novel is not to be found in its explicit political allusions, even if the shipwreck is darkly prophetic of the catastrophe so many rightly feared. Rather, the Constitution's imaginative energy is betrayed by the very warping of its literary form. The process already described as it affected Emerson's discomposing essays and Whitman's formally straying poems operates as well through Melville's narration.

Emerson and Whitman both devoted a good portion of their imaginative energy to invocations of the United States as the vanguard of a new humanity, when, as Emerson put it in the rhapsody concluding his first book, man "shall enter without more wonder than the blind man feels who is gradually restored to perfect sight."[4] Melville did not fully share this enthusiastic embrace of the American experiment of self-constituting, although he was perfectly capable of seriously lamenting that Shakespeare had not lived to write amid the possibilities created by the emergence of the new American republic. Moreover, unlike either of these other writers, Melville wrote narratives—novels and stories—a mode in which statements, the "speaking in one's own voice," are formally less available than they are to poetry and essays. More to the point still, a constitutional poetics creates in and of itself distinctive difficulties for the making of any narrative art.

The Constitution itself, in marked contrast to the "Declaration of Independence," tells no story whatever. Whereas the Declaration offers, however indirectly, a fairly conventional narrative—the king did this and that, treated us in such and such a way, and now the bonds of loyalty have been severed and we are rightly independent—the Framers of the Constitution were only too anxiously aware that their work issued in no clear narrative, no "story," even in the most elementary sense of showing how the machinery would actually work should the nation set it into motion. The most the Framers had done—the most they could have done—was to lay out a detailed schematic, an elaborate blueprint for a building yet to be constructed. The very qualities that lie behind the Constitution's generating paradox—its contradictory perspectives, its fragmentary character, its aggressively secular assertion sharpened to a point by its assumption of sanctified authority—these all act as obstructions against any easy account of what might be called its narrative flow.

Indeed, the ultimate authority of the revealed, claiming as it does an immediate and direct access to the reality behind any mere appearances, would seem to burn through the petty contextual and contingent details that most often provide the very lifeblood of narration. Narratives unfold in time, whereas revelations assume a kind of atemporal self-sufficiency. The Constitution neither engages history nor expresses any anxiety about the future. It is utterly indifferent to anything whatever beyond itself, containing not a single reference to the Revolution, to the reigning Articles of Confederation, to the inherited rights of Englishmen or of Man.[5] Although it makes no explicit claim to timeless authority, its provision for amendment of its own law, however carefully qualified, actually incorporates the possibility of change itself. Thus, the world of the Constitution is fully circular, allowing no escape, itself determining even the course of its own possible transformation, and thereby incorporating the very idea of change as a structural support for its own stasis.

Yet one may well object that this is insisting on a far greater opposition between revelation and narrative than has, in fact, historically subsisted, and that whatever may be their conceptual conflict, the two have often been inextricably intertwined. Scripture itself, it could certainly be argued, is nearly incomprehensible without often very substantial narrative sections. Nevertheless, this ought not blind us to the fact that even in the case of biblical revelation, there has always been a powerful struggle between the narratives as narratives, and the doctrinally inspired interpretive restraints that the revelation exercises upon them. Bible stories must never be *mere* stories, never *simply* stories; they must express lessons, parables, allegories, and teachings. Indeed, they are most often formally mediated by an appended revelation, a range of authorized exegeses—the Talmud in the case of biblical narrative for the rabbis, the varied theologies and priesthoods in the case of the Christian churches.

Erich Auerbach's justly celebrated first chapter of *Mimesis*, presenting a comparative analysis of the Homeric story of the nurse's recognition of Odysseus and the biblical story of the binding of Isaac, can be read as a comparison between the kind of narrative that remains stubbornly framed as a work of narrative art, however much that art may be lauded and culturally central, as Homer's certainly was, and the kind of narrative, like the biblical almost-sacrifice of Isaac, that may well develop the authority of a revelation. Homer's story is highly externalized, precisely visualized, and articulated. Every moment is clearly and evenly illuminated. The Isaac story, by contrast, is often obscure, its very time and setting open to interpretation, its details seen as if for a moment only, in brief flashes of lightning—"the fire in his hand and a knife"; "a ram caught in the thicket by his horns." And as in the case of Abraham's silence in answer to Isaac's question—"But where is the lamb for a burnt offering?"—what is unexpressed is often the most crucial part of the story. The narrative's overall effect, as Auerbach describes it, is of "unrelieved suspense and directed toward a single goal."[6]

Returning to *Moby-Dick* with this distinction in mind, are Melville's descriptions of whales akin to the sunlit clarity of the *Odyssey*, or to the representations of reality in the obscure and mysterious story of Isaac on Mount Moriah? It seems that Melville's whales necessitate some combined representation of both types, and indeed of a type that seems neither the one nor the other.

In thematic terms, the sperm whale itself offered Melville a natural phenomenon both utterly quotidian and sublimely otherworldly. It was at one and the same time a common and economically significant article of trade, and a part of creation so massively strange that even today a *Field Guide to Whales* assures the nature tourist that "few people would have any difficulty identifying [it] if given a good look because it is one of the most distinctive and bizarre animals on earth."[7] Moreover, for a Bible-saturated nineteenth-century American reader, Melville's whale forced the association of the Book of Job's leviathan. Leviathan, it should be recalled, is the very creature that God adduces in order to dramatize for Job the awful disparity between His Own Nature and that of the merely human:

> Canst thou draw out leviathan with a hook?
> Or his tongue with a cord which thou lettest down?
> Canst thou put a hook into his nose?
>
> Canst thou fill his skin with barbed irons?
> Or his head with fish spears?[8]

One could say that the whole of *Moby-Dick* is a twofold response to this very question, answering with both a Yes and a No. It is as if these are two questions, not one, just as the novel itself actually offers two simultaneous, intertwined, but distinct stories, the one a narrative of process, the account of a whaling ship set off to fill its hold with oil—hunting sometime one species of whale, sometimes another, all merely anonymous prey; and the other story relating a mad captain's vengeful pursuit of one solitary creature, a white sperm whale known to sailors as Moby-Dick. The first story makes use of that Homeric form of representation, the second something like the biblical.

Representation itself is, of course, a vastly complex idea. In her seminal work, *The Concept of Representation,* Hanna Fenichel Pitkin helpfully simplifies matters by delineating two different kinds of "standing for" representation, naming them "descriptive representation" and "symbolic representation."[9] What is conventionally considered representative in the arts is akin to the descriptive "standing for": a painting of a bowl of apples, or a narrative account of a woman throwing herself in front of a train, are assumed to bear some kind of one-to-one, part-to-part correspondence between the thing represented and the representation, and the accuracy of such representations is a criterion of their value. A descriptive representation acts in some way as a substitute for that which it represents, and what is represented is knowable independent of its representation. By contrast, a symbolic representation functions as what the literary critic William York Tindall calls "a vehicle for [a] conception," and thus what is represented symbolically is not necessarily apprehendable without the symbol itself. Such representations are not in any ordinary sense verifiable. They reveal what we otherwise would not be capable of perceiving.

We can say, for instance, that we know Odysseus's scar and the way it stirs recognition in his ancient servant from our experience of some such phenomena as scars and persons in the world itself, whereas however we understand what is signified by the interceding angel, and the ram caught by its horns, we would not be able to apprehend it without some such symbolic representations themselves. Nor can we check on the accuracy of such biblical representation. Is that really the look of an angel? Is that really the way God would provide another sacrifice? Except to the most dogmatically childish intelligence, these are not themselves observable phenomena.

In *Moby-Dick,* the narrative of the crew's hunt for whales and their precious oil progresses through the use of descriptive representations. Indeed, there is very probably no other novel of comparable literary power that gives itself to such a nonjournalistic but detailed, and technical, representation of a working industry. The whale fishery in Melville's time was among the most economically significant in the United States.[10] Scarcely a single important aspect of the fishery goes unrepresented in the book, beginning with the financing and provisioning of the ships, and continuing with the whole vast array of its tools and mechanisms, including the organization of its diverse labors and the accumulated knowledge of its prey. The *Pequod* is a floating factory, and the reader follows step by step the processing of whales into the stuff of tapers, lamps, and candles, and the stays of umbrellas and hoop skirts. The whaler's workaday routine is, in fact, so accurately described in all its gritty novelty that Melville can direct his reader's attention—in a manner rather like William Burroughs claims for the narrative of *Naked Lunch*—to the otherwise hidden facts of their own immediate lives: "for God's sake, be economical with your lamps and candles! Not a gallon you burn, but at least one drop of man's blood was spilled for it."[11]

But in the other of the novel's narratives, the hunt for Moby-Dick himself, we have what could well serve as the *locus classicus* of symbolic representation. Captain Ahab himself, who has now devoted his life to finding and confronting the creature, is not exactly certain what it represents, however he refuses to doubt that what it represents is what he must destroy. It is the existence of the White Whale itself that opens Ahab's eyes to the tortured metaphysical obsessions for which he sacrifices both himself and his ship.

Ahab himself is well aware of the fact that the pursuit of the White Whale comes at the cost of the very business the crew has set out upon, and he broods upon the dangers of the crew arriving at a similar awareness: "They may scorn cash now;" he soliloquizes, "but let some months go by . . . this same quiescent cash all at once mutinying in them, this same cash would soon cashier Ahab."[12] Thus, descriptive representation is shown to be at war with symbolic representation, a conflict within a network of conflicts in *Moby-Dick:* between the ineffable and the hyperarticulate, the texture of poetry and that of prose, naturalistic observations and analogical speculations, sight and insight, the civilized and the savage, the worlds of land and of the sea.[13]

This conflict between the descriptive and the symbolic is a reverberation of a constitutional poetics, precisely parallel to the conflict between the secular and the revealed. The Constitution, by means of its ever active paradox, eludes this conflict, whereas Melville has neither the desire nor the capacity to do so. In the guise of conflicting kinds of representations, the conflict agitates Melville's narrative; whatever path the reader of *Moby-Dick* finds himself following, the path will soon enough experience a shunting turbulence. It is one of the peculiarities of the very concept of representation that it is as applicable to the arts as it is to politics. While *Moby-Dick* openly struggles with two different and conflicting, or contrary, kinds of "standing for" representation, the Constitution assumes both sorts of representation, without either explicitly articulating the rationale behind either of them or making any attempt to reconcile them with one another. For purposes of the larger body of the bicameral legislature, the persons of the People are descriptively represented as individuals whose numbers must be proportionately represented. Therefore, a national census every decade is instituted in order to ensure that this descriptive representation is accurate. But as for the other, smaller legislative body—and with it, indirectly, the presidency—to determine its symbolic representativeness requires no such careful counting. Two persons shall be elected to represent each of the separate states. That there are, of course, vast disparities in the populations of these states, in the actual numbers of persons whose views and interests will be represented, has no bearing on the legitimacy of this obviously symbolic representation. The larger legislative body stands descriptively for the citizens of the United States; the senators and the president stand symbolically for the abstract human collectivities known respectively as the states, separate and united, respectively.

During the secret proceedings of the Convention, the delegates arrived at the idea of combining these two conflicting forms of representation by the Great Compromise whereby the smaller states accepted proportional representation in the House in return for a guarantee of equality in the Senate, and indirectly in the Executive and the Judiciary as well. The one enduring qualification to the People's capacity to amend the Constitution that they themselves "ordained and established" is the explicit statement in Article VI that prohibits any amendment denying a state equal representation in the Senate unless that state agrees. But the Constitution says nothing of compromises, great or small: it merely assumes two competing and mutually exclusive sovereignties, the states and the Union of those states.

The Constitution appears, then, as a straightforward arithmetical formulation for a representative government, a logically ordered, self-evidently justifiable piece of electoral machinery, and yet from an equal and opposite perspective it reveals itself as a *vision*, a new nation with symbolically national institutions. That during the Ratification the Founders consistently refused any attempts at tinkering with the machinery reflects precisely this visionary aspect of the Constitution, for a vision, by its nature, does not allow tinkering and adjustment. And it remains the case, down to the present day, that when politicians, and even many historians, gaze at the Constitution they tend to treat it both as a mechanism, an intricate system of checks and balances, and as a grand conception. This is perfectly consistent with its dual function as a contractual compact, a mere legal starting point for the United States, yet at the same time the font of national origin.

While apparently much unlike *Moby-Dick,* the Constitution, with its discretely numbered sections and clauses, seems still and colorless; yet on closer examination it reveals a subsurface cauldron of potential conflicts. Indeed, many of its individual provisions actually delineate boundaries akin to battle lines between and among the three branches of the federal government, between the individual states and the Union, and in the subsequently appended Bill of Rights between the individual citizens of We the People and the duly constituted government itself. What appears static hides a powerful dynamic, the structure itself a controlled conflict, a restless exchange of energy among competing forces—a kind of energy that well describes the peculiar narrative pulse of *Moby-Dick.*

Both the authority of the Constitution and the authorship of *Moby-Dick* are instances of ordering, bringing union politically or aesthetically. It is worth repeating that both words—"authority" and "author"—derive from the same Latin root, *augere,* and meaning literarily "to increase." In the United States, what the sociologist Seymour Martin Lipset famously named "the first new nation," the consciousness of this analogy between political and literary construction, or composition, was sufficiently strong to permit Whitman's pronouncement that "the United States themselves are essentially the greatest poem."[14] Both a self-constituted union and a poem are acts of unifying, making a One from a many. Indeed, *Moby-Dick,* the Constitution, "Song of Myself," and *The American Scholar* can all be understood as unifying structures, each in part devoted to analyzing or diagnosing forms of representation, how the many are represented in and by the One.

But again, what I have here named a constitutional poetics creates difficulties specific to narrative and thus for Melville's work. The Constitution resembles other culturally central revelation-texts in actively discouraging literary imagination and most particularly works of narrative. An obvious example is the Hebrew Bible's place in early Rabbinic culture. In both the American and the Rabbinic cases, national identity hinged upon a canonized revelation, and in both cases that canonization tended to devalue all narrative not subservient to its own. For Rabbinic Jewry, literature that did not serve the communal life of the Torah seemed to serve barely any purpose at all, just as in the early American republic whatever did not serve the constitutional Union was considered, at best, a relatively trivial matter. Among the Jews storytelling itself became a kind of audacity, and the very activity retreated into the interstices of commentary and interpretation. In the early American Republic, the joint project of law and letters kept the idea of an American narrative art independent of political purposes very firmly in check. Indeed, the era's most powerful novels concerned themselves precisely with the dangers of storytelling's claim to truth.

James Wood has brilliantly demonstrated the extent to which Melville is a follower of the non-storytelling and endlessly digressive Sir Thomas Browne, who believed that by mining the endless riches of metaphor "there is all Africa and her prodigies in us."[15] "Melville had a way," Wood writes, "of following metaphor and seeing where it lead him," even to the point of his similes sometimes seeming "bizarrely elaborated" continuing on "over sentences and sentences."[16] But when Wood concludes that "in metaphor is the whole of the imaginative fictional process in one move" he seems to lose sight of *Moby-Dick* itself since, no matter its magnificently baroque troping and its metaphysical raptures, the novel never lets go of its elemental narrative. It is because of the elemental power of this narrative that filmmakers have always been drawn to what is, as any naïve reader discovers turning to the book itself, a vastly subtle and philosophical work. Continuously, amid lightning storms of revelatory digression, Melville always keeps an unrelenting grip on his narrative, on the what-happens-next of the *Pequod* and its crew.

Melville's divided attention, his double-consciousness, is in part, no doubt, a matter of temperament. Emerson and Melville were both drawn to intensities of feeling, to heightened states, but where Emerson cites with unhesitating approval Wordsworth's sentiment that "Tis the most difficult of tasks to keep/Heights which the soul is competent to gain," Melville is more likely to dissent. As a case in point, he alludes to Goethe's injunction to *"Live in the all"*—"You must often have felt it," he writes to Hawthorne, "lying on the grass on a warm summer's day. Your legs seem to send out shoots into the earth. Your hair feels like leaves upon your head. This is the *all* feeling." But then Melville feels immediately compelled to qualify this recognition, to testify to a contrary frame of mind, insisting that "what plays mischief with the truth is that men will insist upon the universal application of a temporary feeling or opinion."[17] Wood quotes this very passage of Melville's letter on Goethe, but significantly leaves unmentioned Melville's aphoristic dissent. Yet it is precisely this dissent that makes Melville neither an essayist nor a poet—however he nears the practices of both—but a storyteller. No matter how his love of language leads him away from the whale hunting and from the chase of the white whale— and Wood acutely describes the instances in which it does—Melville never ultimately jettisons the necessary ballast of his narrative voyage.

Nevertheless, the underlying paradox of a constitutional poetics, demanding revelation at the same time that it equally demands attention to the secular business at hand, does warp the nature of Melville's narrative in ways analogous to the way it dis-composes Emerson's essays and Whitman's poems. Just as from the first there have been readers who denied that Emerson's essays are really essays, or that Whitman's poems are legitimately poems, so many have suggested that Melville's novel is really not a novel at all. Nina Baym in a well known essay, argued that to approach *Moby-Dick* as a novel merely encourages a reader to reduce the book to a "third of [the] text to concentrate on the plot of Ahab and Ishmael."[18] According to Baym, Melville suffered from a "lifelong quarrel with fiction," and no matter that he dedicated *Moby-Dick* to Nathaniel Hawthorne, it is not Hawthorne the storyteller but Hawthorne the truth teller that he admired. By contrast, Northrop Frye, laboring in his *Anatomy of Criticism* "to think seriously of the novel, not as fiction but as a form of fiction," grants

Moby-Dick a place in its tradition, but along with writers like Peacock and Emily Bronte, only at its periphery.[19] Using a more informal but rather similar strategy, E. M. Forster, in *Aspects of the Novel* cites *Moby-Dick* as the prime instance of what he describes as the rarest sort of novel, a "prophetic novel." His understanding of such a form, however, is likewise opposed to Baym's, since to him it is a sign not of Melville's alienation from fiction in favor of truth telling, but merely of the peculiarity of the form of fiction Melville wrote:

> [The prophetic novelist's] theme is the universe, or something universal ... he is not necessarily going to 'say' anything about the universe; he proposes to sing, and the strangeness of song arising in the halls of fiction is bound to give us a shock ... the singer does not always have room for his gestures, the tables and chairs get broken, and the novel through which a bardic influence has passed often has a wrecked air like a drawing-room after an earthquake or a children's party.[20]

Richard Brodhead, writing of Melville as a student of "the School of Hawthorne," likewise refutes Baym's notion of narrative being peripheral to Melville's deepest concern and cites the "prophetical literary conception" as "*the* other literary self-conception, besides the domestic one, operative in American writing of the 1850's":

> It is the idea that released what, along with the new popular literature of domesticity, is the other authentic literary product of the American 1850's: that massively individuated, morally as well as formally innovative writing, unpurchased by the public but undaunted by its lack of public support, of which *Moby-Dick, Leaves of Grass,* and *Walden* are the three great examples.[21]

For if Brodhead Melville's prophetic form does not mitigate his commitment to narrative, it does diminish the narrative's effectiveness. For Hawthorne, according to Brodhead, incorporated and controlled the impulse to revelation and truth telling. In *The Scarlet Letter,* for instance, Hester is overcome by the recognition of the false, socially imposed values by which she has been stigmatized, and declares to her lover, "What we did had a consecration of its own"; and yet Hester willingly submits to wearing the emblem of her social shame. Thus, Hawthorne's fiction provides an aesthetic resolution of narrative and revelatory insight: "the energies [of prophecy] are fiercely contained." But Melville, according to Brodhead, refused his master's lesson that "prophecy is most productive as an artistic program when it does not quite believe it knows the whole, grand truth."[22]

Although this is helpful as a comparison between the two great narrative writers of the American Renaissance, it is also, from the larger perspective of American literary history, profoundly misleading. It focuses on the rhetoric of these writers, on the contrast between their narrative strategies, when what is more crucially at issue in Hawthorne and Melville both, and their relation to each other, is not strategy, not the how of literary creativity, but the what—not the *rhetoric,* the technique, of narrative, but its *poetics,* the question of what kind of thing a literary work aims to be.

For the writers of the American Renaissance, as for the Founders before them, the impulse to prophesy reflected their response to the predicament they shared: they all came at the beginning of a tradition—an oxymoronic condition, given that "tradition" means nothing other than a handing over of something already received. What they needed was somehow to transform their arbitrary beginning into a source of origin, whether that transformation was for the purpose of conjuring a national tradition, or developing a national literature befitting a "new order."

There is some justice in describing Hawthorne as engaged in an exemplary "artistic program." He is the most insistently historicist of novelists, the facts of history providing a kind of secular anchor to his play at prophecy, what the prophetic form itself always demands. (The biblical prophets were all neck deep in the impediments of the immediately secular history and consequently were often under assault by perfectly rational political enemies.) Although Hawthorne is in fact the most ambiguous figure of the American Renaissance, with one foot in the New World and the other in what he alone of all the major writers could comfortably call "Our Old Home," the traditions of England, he is also the writer most responsible for transforming the constitutional vision into narrative possibility. In his working theory of the Romance in opposition to the novel proper, he showed the way to an imagined narrative that could freely incorporate moments of revelation as a necessary part of its progression rather than a violation of that progression. Highly improbable events, like discontinuous moments of revelation, are made accessible to the cumulative art of narration, to the technique of representing actions in time. Events need not be causally prepared but can at any moment forcefully erupt into the otherwise predictable order of novelistic convention.

Such a Romance, Hawthorne writes, "though it sins unpardonably, so far as it may swerve aside from the truth of the human heart—has fairly a right to present the truth under circumstances to a great extent, of the writer's own choosing or creation."[23] Amid the Election Day multitude, the Reverend Mister Dimmesdale ascends the scaffold with Hester Prynne and his daughter Pearl, and as the final act of his life "tore away the ministerial band from before his breast" uncovering for all to see what Hawthorne tells his reader it would be "irreverent to describe," in the book's penultimate chapter entitled "The Revelation of the Scarlet Letter." It is a sign, a wonder, a vision, more or less, given its place in the somber historical tale without explanation or rationalization. The possibility of such a moment's arising not from a realm of doctrinal truth but from what Hawthorne calls "the truth of the human heart"—is this not, in its romantic way, a restatement of the very paradox of the origin of the American People, in which a moment of revelation, a "founding," arises from a humanly shared desire for union?

Hawthorne, always writing a kind of masque of history, remained within the decorum of Romance. *Moby-Dick,* on the other hand, though it contains aspects of Romance, is so protean that even Joel Porte who in *The Romance in America* insists upon the novel's centrality to that Hawthornian tradition, nevertheless justifies leaving the book out of his account on the grounds that "it is a romance *within* . . . an anatomy, to say nothing of Melville's excursions into dramatic and even operatic writing."[24] It could thus be argued, though somewhat tendentiously, that Hawthorne succeeded as a narrative writer in a way that Melville failed, and it is precisely such success that sets a limit to Hawthorne's fiction and such failure that heightens Melville's. Such a judgment is reminiscent of the form-breaking formalism maintained by one of the next century's American master-narrators, William Faulkner, who when asked to evaluate his contemporaries provocatively lauded the aspirations of Thomas Wolfe over the accomplished style of Ernest Hemingway on the grounds that Wolfe had failed better:

> I ranked Wolfe first because we had all failed but Wolfe had made the best failure because he had tried hardest to say the most. . . . My admiration for Wolfe is that he tried his best to get it all said; he was willing to throw away style, coherence, all the rules of preciseness, to try to put all the experience of the human heart on the head of a pin, as it were. He may have had the best talent of us; he may have been "the greatest American writer" if he had lived longer.[25]

It was Faulkner, after all, who said of *Moby-Dick* that it was the one American novel he most wished he had written:

> Moby-Dick is the book which I put down with the unqualified thought, "I wish I had written that" . . . a sort of Golgotha of the heart become immutable as bronze in the sonority of its plunging ruin. There's a death for a man, now.[26]

In a subtle and sophisticated analysis, the literary historian Lawrence Buell calls *Moby-Dick* something of a "sacred text," a piece of "literary scripturism."[27] The problem with what he himself describes as "an analogy and not a definition" is that after much intelligent discussion it leads him to the dubious conclusion that *Moby-Dick* "stands as a great pioneering work of comparative religion and as one of the most ambitious products of the religious imagination that American literature is likely to produce."[28] Compare this accolade of imaginative achievement with Hawthorne's famous description of Melville's visit to Liverpool five years after the completion of *Moby-Dick:*

> [Melville] informed me that he had "pretty much made up his mind to be annihilated;" but still he does not seem to rest in that anticipation; and, I think, will never rest until he gets hold of a definite belief. It is strange how he persists . . . in wandering to and fro over these deserts.

This is surely closer to the spirit of *Moby-Dick* than celebration of successfully ambitious religious imagination.

What is problematic about all these descriptions, insightful as many of them are, is that Baym's editing of the narrative down to one-third of the book, Brodhead's rhetorical criticism of Melville's insufficiently balanced literary program, and Buell's focusing on the work's subject tend to drain the churning tension between the secular and the revealed coursing through *Moby-Dick,* the very thing that raises the novel to its inimitable fever pitch.

It is the narrative of *Moby-Dick,* the temporal working out of the tensions in Melville's insights, that contains and controls that fever pitch. We are warned early on by "the prophet" of Chapter 19 that the comic tone of the novel's beginning is threatened by something darker and more mysterious, but it is not until the ship has been at sea and Ahab issues his highly unusual order that the crew be summoned for him to address them from the quarterdeck, that both the reader and the crew are fully exposed to the intensities that will dominate the voyage. It is then that Ahab first reveals his determination to seek revenge by pursuing Moby-Dick: "This is what ye have shipped for, men!" he tells them. "To chase that white whale." Ishmael, as he later acknowledges, is stirred to sympathy along with the rest of the crew. Only the First Mate, Starbuck, raises an objection: "Madness!" he responds. "To be enraged with a dumb thing." Ahab then explains, both to Starbuck and the crew:

> All visible objects, man, are but as pasteboard masks. But in each event—in the living act, the undoubted deed—there, some unknown but still reasoning thing puts forth the mouldings of its features from behind the unreasoning mask. If man will strike, strike through the mask! How can the prisoner reach outside except by thrusting through the wall? To me, the white whale is that wall, shoved near to me. Sometimes I think there's naught beyond. But 'tis enough. He tasks me; he heaps me; I see in him outrageous strength, with an inscrutable malice sinewing it. That inscrutable thing is chiefly what I hate; and be the white whale agent, or be the white whale principal, I will wreak that hate upon him.

The greatest threat here is not even the revelation of the white whale's malice, but that in the end there may be "naught beyond," nothing more than the simple fact of the creaturely whale—no access to a ground of meaning, no hidden significance behind the miscellaneous appearances of Nature. Against this threat Ahab insists that the whale's sheer, inexplicable power—"A dead whale or a stove boat," the crews sing out as they lower for the chase—is enough to suggest its malevolence and thus to justify Ahab's hatred.[29]

It is in the narrator's relation to the narrative, specifically in the voice and perspectival freedom of Ishmael, the novice whaleman, the survivor who tells the story, that the fever pitch is modulated, that the tone of the book's oscillating tension is given variety. He tells us from the start to call him by the name of Ishmael, that son of Father Abraham who was yet not the son of the Divine promise, a character thus at the heart of the narrative, and at the same time peripheral to it. From the point of view of narrative theory, Ishmael is an interesting problem in the book precisely because his narrative status is so ambiguous. Critics often treat him as though he were either an undigested bit of Melville's first draft of the novel or little more than a quasi-omniscient narrative crutch. He disappears and reappears. His voice dominates the beginning of the book, but once he sets out to sea it seems to become gradually dispersed, yielding to the voice not just of the captain but of the three mates, and at times to the whole of the thirty-man crew.

It is through Ishmael's perceptions, however, that Melville forces his two conflicting modes of representation directly against one another.

Throughout the voyage, Ishmael, like a naturalist hunter, seeks to understand the nature of his prey, but he finds that much about the whale is still obscure and that what has been claimed as knowledge is, in fact, inaccurate. Yet however close his own observations, he finds that some of the most obvious aspects of the whale seem to be inherently unknowable. In reviewing all current picturings of the creature, for instance, and after detailing their various inadequacies, he is forced to reflect on the sheer impossibility of its visual representation:

> The living whale, in his full majesty and significance, is only to be seen at sea in unfathomable waters; and afloat the vast bulk of him is out of sight, like a launched line-of-battle ship; and out of that element it is a thing eternally impossible for mortal man to hoist him bodily into the air, so as to preserve all his mighty swells and undulations. And, not to speak of the highly presumable difference of contour between a young sucking whale and a full-grown Platonian Leviathan; yet even in the case of one of those young sucking whales hoisted to a ship's deck, such is then the outlandish, eel-like, limbered, varying shape of him, that his precise expression the devil himself could not catch.[30]

Here is a form of representation that fits neither the Homeric nor the biblical model; it openly fails as descriptive representation, but neither does it offer a symbolic representation in its place.

Along the same lines, and more striking still, is Ishmael's frustrated attempt at what would seem the simplest and most direct apprehension, seeing the whale's face: "On your physiognomical voyage you sail round his vast head in your jolly-boat." There is nothing, he explains, that you can quite grasp: "For you see no one point precisely; not one distinct feature is revealed; no nose, eyes, ears, or mouth; no face; he has none, proper; nothing but that one broad firmament of a forehead, pleated with riddles." And in the end there is nothing for Ishmael to do but admit he has done all within his capacity: "I but put that brow before you. Read it if you can."[31]

Workaday reality presents the whale, a physical being with a body that can be hunted, butchered, and stowed away for sale, so that one ought to be able to describe its shape, to see it, as we say, face to face. Yet this is precisely what Ishmael insists one cannot do. It is all but a naturalized version of the explicit biblical prohibition against seeing the face of God, as when Moses himself is placed in the "clift of the rock" and told by the Lord "thou shalt see my back parts: but my face shall not be seen."[32] Similarly, the disparity in the scale of Nature between the whale and Ishmael that prevents his perceptual grasp of the creature's face echoes the incongruity between Leviathan and Job of which God's voice speaks from out of the whirlwind. But without a face, all is mystery, and what we think of as story becomes almost impossible. This is the parabolic force of Hawthorne's "The Minister's Black Veil" in which the minister forces the realm of the mysterious— all that is beyond appearances—upon his parishioners merely by veiling his face. Indeed, from the perspective of ordinary experience, the face offers the most dramatic and obvious example of what Michael Polanyi has named "tacit knowledge," the fact that we know more than we can say. As he explains, we apprehend the face as a totality, and though perfectly capable of recognizing one face "among a thousand, indeed among a million," we are most often unable to say what it is that gives us this knowledge.[33] The whale's face would seem, then, to be a kind of tacit ignorance, since Ishmael cannot know the whale's face but cannot find what exactly he does not know that keeps this knowledge from him. This in turn seems to violate the very assumption behind descriptive representation, namely, that what can be pointed to in the world can be described. Upon reflection, there is a counterpart to Ishmael's perplexity in the symbolic representation that is Moby-Dick. However real the white whale is, its significance as a symbolic representation is what drives Ahab and his monomaniacal hunt. But in the inner drama of Ahab's story, this vehicle of his conception is constantly under threat of being overwhelmed by the conception itself, so that it is only through Ahab's heroic will that he can remain devoted to its pursuit.

Moby-Dick, as a narrative aiming at secular revelation, attempts to give form to a conviction of the workaday reality of the world coexisting with the paradoxically equal conviction that that reality is nothing other than what is revealed to our sense of the numinous or the sublime. The attempt to give form to this paradox plays havoc with the relation between what Auerbach calls reality and its representation. The workaday reality is not, as it turns out, fully accessible to description, while what is revealed can only uncertainly find expression in a symbolic vehicle independent of any authoritative machinery of inherited mythology. It is such independence that is at the heart of the very newness of the American possibility. The final three days of the chase, ending with the side-to-side vibration of the white whale's "predestinating head" as he sends "a broadband of semicircular foam before him" and the final act, when Moby-Dick's "forehead smote the ship's starboard bow, till men and timbers reeled," represent Melville's own crashing through the paradox to a heroic self-assertion, akin to Ahab's own: "I have written an evil book," he wrote to Hawthorne, "and feel spotless as the lamb."[34]

Ishmael himself is drawn to project upon Moby-Dick thoughts analogous to Ahab's, though he entertains the thoughts rather than gives himself to them. It is these thoughts that are the subject of the central, brooding chapter on "The Whiteness of the Whale." "What the white whale was to Ahab had been hinted," Ishmael begins, "what, at times, he was to me"—and that "at times" is typical of Ishmael, no monomaniac he—"as yet remains unsaid." The final paragraph demands to be quoted in full:

> Is it that by its indefiniteness it shadows forth the heartless voids and immensities of the universe, and thus stabs us from behind with the thought of annihilation, when beholding the white depths of the milky way? Or is it, that as in essence whiteness is not so much a colour as the visible absence of colour; and at the same time the concrete of all colours; is it for these reasons that there is such a dumb blankness, full of meaning, in a wide landscape of snows—a colourless, all-colour of atheism from which we shrink? And when we consider that other theory of the natural philosophers, that all other earthly hues—every stately or lovely emblazoning—the sweet tinges of sunset skies and woods; yea, and the gilded velvets of butterflies, and the butterfly cheeks of young girls; all these are but subtle deceits, not actually inherent in substances, but only laid on from without; so that all deified Nature absolutely paints like the harlot, whose allurements cover nothing but the charnel-house within; and when we proceed further, and consider that the mystical cosmetic which produces every one of her hues, the great principle of light, for ever remains white or colourless in itself, and if operating without medium upon matter, would touch all objects, even tulips and roses, with its own blank tinge— pondering all this, the palsied universe lies before us a leper; and like willful travelers in Lapland, who refuse to wear coloured and colouring glasses upon their eyes, so the wretched infidel gazes himself blind at the monumental white shroud that wraps all the prospect around him. And of all these things the Albino whale was the symbol. Wonder ye then at the fiery hunt?[35]

This long, symphonic passage can be severely, if crudely, reduced to Ishmael's posing three possible explanations for Moby-Dick's place in his own imagination: (1) the white whale is a symbol of the vast, unimaginable immensity of the universe, and it is its sublimity that terrifies him; (2) the white whale is a symbol of our apprehension of the atheist's everything/nothing consciousness of the world, a place potentially full of meaning and absolutely blank, and it is such a consciousness itself that appalls him; and (3) the white whale dramatizes what natural science has demonstrated, that the varicolored phenomena of the world is nothing but fake front, that just beneath the surface is only the blinding colorlessness of Death. How, then, he asks in conclusion, could such a hunt whose object is a revelation of darkness, or what is perhaps even more horrifying, the absence of any revelation whatever, not be a fiery hunt?

In other words, there is no way around the terror of the questions Ahab forces upon Ishmael and the crew in his visionary pursuit of the white whale. A philosopher like Emerson, just as a lyric poet like Whitman, is able to articulate a persona that by the very persistence of a monologic voice, however protean and self-contradictory, evades the non-sense of naked paradox. But Moby-Dick is not a record of Ishmael's or any other character's thoughts—though it contains them—but a chronological record of what happens to the characters—their story. Consciousness can sustain the paradox's two sides of the coin by keeping it always spinning in air, never settling upon one side or the other; but a narrative must regularly come down to earth, so to speak. In a story there is no self, or persona, free of what Emerson called Nature—that is, free of everyone and everything outside of that self—so that the promise of maintaining freedom and integrity amidst all the flux of contradiction and the oscillations of perspective cannot but become a rather dubious business. How one is to exercise trust under such slippery conditions is the very question upon which Melville's fiction will come to founder.

CHAPTER THIRTEEN

Confidence and the Darkness of Revelation

"Then good night, good-night; and Providence have both of us in its good keeping."

"Be sure it will," eyeing the old man with sympathy, as for the moment he stood, money-belt in hand, and life-preserver under arm, "be sure it will sir, since in Providence, as in man, you and I equally put trust. But, bless me, we are being left in the dark here. Pah! What a smell, too."

MELVILLE, *The Confidence-Man*, 1857

The Constitution partakes both of a covenant and a contract. Written largely by lawyers, and since the time of its ratification the object of endless legal arguments, the Constitution's ultimate enforcement mechanism is dependent upon *trust*, the trust the Union's citizens have in one another. Confidence, with all its ambiguities, is the only guarantee the nation has for the Constitution's very authority.

To "trust thyself" is the summary demand of a self-reliance Emerson preached to his eager American audience, the "iron string" to which "all hearts vibrate."[1] Yet the demand to "trust thyself" possesses in itself an oracular, mysterious aura not unlike the explicitly Delphic "know thyself," for the very idea of trust denotes a contractual obligation invested in something or someone other than the self. Thus, to make the verb reflexive—to trust oneself—transforms the action into something at least approaching paradox. Indeed, it echoes America's national self-constituting, involving as it does the contortions of a self founding its own selfhood.[2] Is not Melville's Captain Ahab an extreme exemplar of this very doctrine? Driving his crew to destruction in pursuit of the White Whale, Ahab commands not by his rightful authority as the *Pequod*'s captain, but rather by means of a charisma arising from his very self-trust, by the sheer ferocity of his massive self-confidence.

That there is potential danger in such confidence Emerson himself makes a point of acknowledging early on, pausing in his secular sermon, the essay on *Self Reliance,* to give voice to a direct challenge of his own doctrine:

> On my saying, "What have I to do with the sacredness of traditions, if I live wholly from within?" my friend suggested,—"But these impulses may be from below, not from above." I replied, "They do not seem to me to be such; but if I am the Devil's child, I will live then from the Devil." No law can be sacred to me but that of my nature.[3]

This pointed moral challenge to the idea of self-reliance is given a still more central and powerful place in *Moby-Dick.* Early in the novel, before the *Pequod* and its crew even make an appearance, Ishmael visits the Seamen's Bethel to hear a sermon delivered by a former sailor, Father Mapple. Standing upon the prowed beak of a pulpit, amid chapel walls covered with memorials to the dead missing at sea—lost souls compounded by lost bodies—Father Mapple preaches upon the *Book of Jonah.* The Lord had commanded Jonah to prophesy an apocalypse, but rather than assume such a burden Jonah followed his own impulse and fled "as far by water as Jonah could possibly have sailed in those ancient days." Father Mapple draws a critical, self-denying moral: "If we obey God, we must disobey ourselves."

This is the very lesson that Emerson refutes with a seemingly insouciant insistence on his own integrity: "No law can be sacred to me but that of my nature." Ahab does not have Emerson's carefree confidence; when he asserts his own self reliance he does so with a self-justifying violence. The first mate, Starbuck, a decent man, shrinking from the evil he senses in his captain's resolve, questions such violence directed against a "dumb beast," to which Ahab angrily responds, "I'd strike the sun if it insulted me, for could the sun do that, then could I do the other."[4] And yet more directly, and with a still more profound violence, when Ahab witnesses the stark power of the Creator's divinity as a lightning storm sets corposants at the tips of the three masts—note *corpo santo* means literally holy body—he feels the heat and breathes it back: "I leap with thee; I burn with thee; would fain be welded with thee; defyingly I worship thee!" And in this defiance he accosts the power directly:

> Thou are but my fiery father . . . thou knowest not how came ye, hence callest thyself unbegotten; certainly knowest not thy beginning, hence callest thyself unbegun. I know that of me, which thou knowest not of thyself, oh, thou omnipotent.[5]

Ahab knows that of which this "fiery father" is ignorant; he knows his own beginning, as Americans knew their own, self-constituted beginning. Ahab is equal to anything he can face, more than equal, since he accepts his own self-authorization. It is the courage of this stance that inspires his crew, allowing him to pervert their aim from whales and wages to a symbolic doubloon and to the active pursuit of a beast that the sailors would naturally wish to avoid.

There is in a reader's response to Ahab a perplexity akin to a reader's response to Milton's Satan. For Milton, such self-origination seems inherently demonic, and there is much in Ahab's defiance reminiscent of Mammon's great speech in Book II of *Paradise Lost*, and Satan's exhortation as he commands his troops in Book V. There is, of course, the question made explicit since at least William Blake's comments, of how we are to judge such defiance. No one, however, has been happy at the observation that this Satanic self-reliance is somehow characteristic of a Protestant, Puritan, or English ideal. Yet Ahab does seem to give positive voice to an extreme version of American selfhood, a self-confidence that from this perspective does seem tantamount to self-deification. Such self-deification—if that is a fair term for it—is a posture that Harold Bloom, among others, has identified with the ancient, underground spiritual tradition of gnosticism. In its simplest sense, gnosticism is a conviction, a knowing, that the self is divine, in fact possessed of a divinity earlier than that of the creator-God, known as the demiurge who is responsible for the world we know of evil and white whales. Gnosticism thus represents—again to simplify mercilessly—a rather last-ditch hope for redemption in an unredeemable world, and consequently a heresy to every kind of normative religious faith. Ahab is a "God-like godless" man: by conventional standards, he is suffering from a highly intellectual form of madness. Melville has Ahab confront the paradox contained within the founding, a paradox Emerson and Whitman managed to maintain with a delicate and idiosyncratic balance, and in this confrontation he forces the full violence of its dynamic into a willful apocalypse of the human community— "all collapsed, and the great shroud of the sea rolled on as it rolled five thousand years ago."

Yet there is something more to Ahab, something other, than the courage and charisma of a towering self-trust. Ahab feels threatened. He is frightened. When he imagines striking the sun it is not for pleasure; it is not a bold expression of his power and fearlessness, but rather an act of elementary self-defense in keeping with the simple dignity of his person. Nor does the White Whale become his mortal enemy only for having "dismasted" him. The poet Charles Olson in his seminal essay on *Moby-Dick, Call Me Ishmael,* offers the crucial observation that it was "not the light of revelation, but the darkness of it" that engaged Melville's imagination; and it is this darkness that Ahab fears. It is this fear he articulates with such scarifying eloquence as to provoke and then to sharpen the very same fear among his men. It is this terror that Ishmael expresses in his meditation on the whiteness of the whale, that the great cosmic mystery may well be that there is no mystery, that there is no transcendent meaning of any sort, no Truth. The darkest revelation, darker even than the thought that Creation's "invisible spheres were formed in fright" is that there is not malevolence, but nothing whatever. It is against this fearful fantasy that Ahab voices an inspiring and fanatical opposition.

Melville himself, in one of the first of the series of super-heated speculative letters he wrote to Hawthorne while he worked on *Moby-Dick,* suggested as much:

> We think that into no recorded mind has the intense feeling of the visible truth ever entered more deeply than into this man's. By visible truth, we mean the apprehension of the absolute condition of present things as they strike the eye of the man who fears them not, though they do their worst to him. . . . He may perish; but so long as he exists he insists upon treating with all Powers upon an equal basis. If any of those other Powers choose to withhold certain secrets, let them; that does not impair my sovereignty in myself; that does not make me tributary. And perhaps, after all, there is *no* secret. We incline to think that the Problem of the Universe is like the Freemason's mighty secret, so terrible to all children. It turns out, at last, to consist in a triangle, a mallet, and an apron,—nothing more! We incline to think that God cannot explain His own secrets, and that He would like a little information upon certain points Himself.[6]

It is Ahab's self-trust alone that empowers him to bridge the gap between the silence of the "the visible truth" and what that truth reveals: "Sometimes I think there's naught beyond," he confesses for a moment. "But 'tis enough," he insists and continues. Such confidence or trust is all that can bridge the incommensurate gap between the secularity of machined will—knowledge, technique (including technology), common experience, and material certitude—and the profound ignorance of the purpose and meaning of human life without a transcendent warrant coming from somewhere—a church or cult or party, a king, a voice, God, tradition, or the mythic past—some kind of revealed knowledge.

The secular authority of Ahab's captaincy is amplified by the force of his prophetic conviction, so that his final voyage becomes a dark analogy to the nation's enlightened self-constituting. The crew trusts him, as the mates and Ishmael varyingly soliloquize, even more than they trust themselves. Ahab works over the crew to such a degree that he appears at times as a schemer, something like what Americans were learning to call a confidence man, although on a grand metaphysical scale, manipulating himself perhaps as much as he does his men.

In much of the fiction Melville wrote after *Moby-Dick*, the question of trust, self-trust, and confidence is often crucial. In his next novel, *Pierre, or the Ambiguities,* a character's courageous act of self-trust amounts perhaps to nothing more than self-delusion and ends in death and destruction. Melville's next work, the often curiously inert *Israel Potter,* tells of a young man who through his own familial declaration of independence gives himself to the American Revolution only to suffer the unintended consequence of a life-long exile in the former Mother Country. Likewise, a number of the varied *Piazza Tales* focus on characters whose self-confidence is a central issue. Such is the case in "Bartleby" whose lawyer–narrator suffers a profound subversion of his well-contented life by a perversely passive clerk; and in "Benito Cereno," the eponymous narrator relates a story of misplaced confidence and thereby dramatizes the precariousness of his reliance upon his own perceptions.

As the doubtfulness of self-trust and confidence deepens, the possibility of secular revelations becomes increasingly muted. The stories Melville tells are of characters who often cannot, as Ahab or Ishmael still can, engage in vigorous action; they are stymied or passive, as the novels containing them often are, certainly in comparison to the intensity of *Moby-Dick*. It is when Melville comes to publish his last novel that he attacks the question of confidence most directly. The result is a narrative that is barely story-like with only the shadow of a protagonist. If the action on the *Pequod* is a kind of reenactment of the Union's founding, the action, such as it is, of Melville's last novel, *The Confidence-Man,* diagnoses the nature of a society so founded. There is no drama of heroic self-trust, but rather an analysis of the routine workings of trust, how it is generated and sustained amid what he again refers to, through an allusion to the revolutionary Anacharsis Cloots, as a "congress of all kinds of that multiform pilgrim species, man."[7]

The term *confidence man* actually made its first appearance, in the 1850s in the United States. Among the earlier instances of its use there is a fascinating passage, presumably penned by Melville's literary associate, the well-known New York editor, Evert Duyckink:

> It is not the worst thing that can be said of a country that it gives birth to a confidence man. . . .
>
> It is a good thing, and speaks well for human nature, that, at this late day, in spite of all the hardening of civilization and all the warnings of newspapers, men can be *swindled*.
>
> The man who is always on his guard, always proof against appeal, who cannot be beguiled in the weakness of pity by *any* story . . . he lives coldly among his people—he walks an iceberg in the marts of trade and social life—and when he dies, may Heaven have that confidence in him when he had not in his fellow mortals![8]

Although it is now very difficult to know just how ironically this is meant to be read, it does reveal, at the very least, the extent to which some in the United States were fully aware of the degree to which their society, their social experiment, depended upon trust and little more than trust. Self-constituted as they were, without a source of higher authority other than what they themselves had constructed, the people of the United States must trust themselves to trust one another. Yet the occasion of Duyckink's passage is the "subject of a police fingering" so that this same crucial trust is, of course, the very ploy of swindlers and the faith of fools. Duyckink redoubles the contradiction by matter-of-factly identifying the pillars of American commercial and political life as themselves confidence men:

> Who is there that does not recollect, in the circle of his acquaintance, a smart young gentleman who, with his coat buttoned to the throat and hair pushed back, extends his arms at public meetings in a wordy harangue? This is the young confidence man of politics. In private life you remember perfectly well the middle-aged gentleman with well-developed person and white waistcoat, who lays down the law in reference to the state of the trade, sub-treasury, and the tariff—and who subscribes steadily to Hunt's excellent Magazine (which he never reads.) This is the confidence man of merchandise.[9]

The scene of Melville's novel is once again set upon the water, now no longer on the open ocean but along the inland waterway of the muddy Mississippi, the central artery of American commerce and expansion. This boat's crew are nowhere to be seen; all our attention is focused on the passengers, each pursuing a strictly personal interest. There is not merely a lack of hierarchy among them, but something resembling anarchy, a free-for-all among the "piebald parliament" of the crowd.

At every landing the boat receives "additional passengers in exchange for those that disembark; so that, though always full of strangers, she continually, in some degree, adds to, or replaces them with strangers still more strange." In place of a presiding authority in the person of a captain, we find only a series of imposters and masqueraders, all of whom, so we are led to believe, are ambiguously the work of one master confidence man who boards the boat on April Fool's Day in the most peculiar guise of a deaf and dumb evangelist in cream-colors with a white fur hat: "in the extremist sense of the word, a stranger."

As a crowd gathers about a poster warning of a "mysterious imposter" this strangest of strangers holds up a slate with words from St. Paul which he gradually amends in response to the hostility he arouses, each time with a new verse from First Corinthians. He begins with "Charity thinketh no evil," and he cycles through "Charity suffereth long, and is kind," "Charity endureth all things," "Charity believeth all things," ending at last with "Charity never faileth."[10] Immediately afterwards we witness the boat's barber beginning the day with the routine posting of his gilt pasteboard sign: "No Trust;" In marked contrast the barber's message does not "provoke any corresponding derision or surprise, much less indignation." And so begins *The Confidence-Man*'s repetitive conflict, between the suspicion demanded by a transient society of self-interested strangers and the need for what the King James Version here calls "charity"—a word the Revised Standard translates as "love"—for which Melville elsewhere substitutes the words "confidence," "faith" (the boat itself is named the *Fidèle*), and most common of all, as here, "trust." Indeed, the word "trust" in its different forms appears over one hundred and fifty times in the novel's forty-five chapters.[11]

The narrative of *The Confidence-Man*, if narrative it is, is too desultory even to be called episodic; it is constituted not so much by a beginning, a middle, and an end, as it is by beginnings only, a promising series of them, as if getting started leads nowhere but to getting started again. The book obsessively dramatizes the outrageous swindles pulled off by games of confidence at the same time that it argues, just as obsessively, for the absolute social and even moral necessity of confidence itself, and consequently reads like something of a nervous breakdown of a novel.

Melville pays no attention to the river itself or to the natural world through which the riverboat passes; instead, he focuses exclusively on the verbal interactions taking place on his ship of fools. In *Moby-Dick* the reader is confronted by the mystery of the whale, which evades each and every effort of a thorough apprehension; in *The Confidence-Man* the mystery circulates through the very narrative itself, making for what Elizabeth Renker has most clearly described as the text's radical "unreadability."[12] She does not attribute this obscurity to any diminishment in Melville's great narrative gift, arguing in fact that the book is "Melville's most fully controlled novel, the one in which he's most in command of his craft." Melville instead composed the text to be "aggressively resistant" not merely "to interpretation but also to even superficial comprehension."[13] The eponymous protagonist possesses an indeterminate number of identities, generally unnamed and as often as not distinguished only by some attribute or detail of costume—"the man with the weed"; "a gentleman with gold sleeve-buttons"; "the Cosmopolitan." The editor and biographer Herschel Parker understands *The Confidence-Man* as "a satiric allegory in which the Devil comes aboard the world-ship to swindle its passengers," aiming at two major targets: optimism and its fellow-traveling liberal theology.[14] Many critics have recognized the parodies of both Emerson and his student Thoreau in the minor characters Mark Winsome and Egbert. And yet the satire, if that is what it is, is too balanced in its argument and altogether too blunted for it to be anything but an inexplicably inept satiric performance.

Hopelessly entangled in its own narrative indirections, *The Confidence-Man* seems to offer a diagnosis of a bafflingly incoherent society, one that by constituting itself seems particularly susceptible to fraud. It seems that in every direction there is chicanery and greed. In place of the authentic eloquence of the mad authoritarian captain of the *Pequod*, language on the *Fidèle* has degenerated into democracy's bombast and hucksterism, or perhaps more fundamentally still, the ground from which such salesmanship arises, a cacophony of voices. The second chapter, following immediately upon the stranger with the slate dozing off on the deck, has as its title one of the central assumptions of a free, democratic polity, "Showing that Many Men have Many Minds." It begins with nothing but a page-long series of unattributed responses to the sleeping figure. In all their disunity, the People speak:

"Odd fish!"
"Poor fellow!"
"Who can he be?"
"Casper Hauser."

"Bless my soul!"
"Uncommon countenance."
"Green prophet from Utah."
"Humbug!"
"Singular innocence."
"Means something."
"Spirit-rapper."
"Moon-calf."
"Piteous."
"Trying to enlist interest."
"Beware of him."
"Fast asleep here, and, doubtless, pick-pockets on board."
"Kind of daylight Endymion."
"Escaped convict, worn out with dodging."
"Jacob dreaming at Luz."[15]

The *Fidèle* suffers from a condition that is almost an inverse varia-
tion of the *Pequod*'s. On the whaler the constituted balance is sub-
verted by the truth of the revealed, Ahab's fiery hunt overwhelming the
secular demand for the simple facts and verification, the demand that
that hunt should fully accommodate the business of filling the hold
with oil and safely returning to port. On the Mississippi riverboat, by
contrast, the spokesman for trust is a flimflam man, and any leap of
faith, any higher confidence, any attempt to transcend the plain secular facts of the matter in the interest of some more exalted perspective,
is a trap for dupes. It is as if Melville had come up against the ambiguity in the very notion of "truth" to which his literary ambition aspired.

Without venturing beyond the shallowest waters of philological reflection, it is clear enough that, in English at least, we may have two
different notions in mind when we refer to something as "true." In a
simple way, we can distinguish between these two meanings by the
phrases "true to" and "true of." The truth of "true to" is a truth of
covenant, of loyalty and dedication, the way we can be true to ideas,
or we can possess true friends. To claim something is "true of" is, on
the other hand, a truth of objective agreement, of what we ordinarily
call verification. In the terms we have been using, "true to" refers to a
kind of revealed truth, one akin to faith, to an inner conviction not
wholly or at times even partially susceptible to proof, whereas "true
of" in this sense is doggedly secular, the evidence of things seen. There
is no necessary conflict or confusion between these two kinds of truth;
but then there sometimes is. Just as in the larger interests of justice,

courts will often excuse those sharing bonds of presumed intimacy, spouses for instance, from testifying against one another in order to keep these two truths from open conflict, so the agents of discord and deceit will often force the conflict, or its facsimile, as Iago does in tormenting the suspicious and gullible Othello.

A nation and a people whose very existence is predicated upon a covenant are especially vulnerable to a manipulation of such conflict. Melville's confidence man in his various guises preaches trust, the need for people to be true to one another, even if that requires that they suffer some doubt about the precise truth of this particular, or that. Bringing these two notions of truth into conflict is all but a formulaic description of what a confidence game is. And is this not very close to what Emerson actually claims and Whitman celebrates in their radically democratic elitism? "To believe your own thought, to believe what is true for you in your private heart is true for all men—that," writes Emerson, "is genius."

Whether Emerson himself would have denied the very title of confidence man is not particularly clear, and if questioned about the consequent risks of fraud and double-dealing, he might well have explained that we cannot spend the day in self-defense, any more than we can spend it in explanation.[16] That this makes for a fertile environment in which to breed ever new varieties of shady cupidity, even what the country would learn to call "robber barons," seems an undeniable fact of the country's history and a consistent if crude charge against Emerson and all his admirers.

In the case of Melville's *Confidence-Man*, the reader can be forgiven for sometimes wondering whether and to what degree his game is actually focused on his own serious interests. In some of his encounters, the gains are so trivial—a haircut?—as to be hardly worth a fraction of the effort.

When, in fact, we reach the last page of this last great, and greatly puzzling, fiction of the American Renaissance, its affect, its emotional resonance, remains profoundly mysterious. Though not despairing, there seems no hint of hope.[17] The butt of its final joke, the last Confidence-Man's victim—if that's what he is—is an old man who, though devoted to a simple trust in both God and man, falls easy prey to a young huckster who sells him a sequence of technological fixes to fend off dangers from both God and man: a life preserver against Providence and a money belt against his fellow passengers. The Confidence-Man wishes him a safe sleep:

> "Then, good-night, good-night; and Providence have both of us in its good keeping."
>
> "Be sure it will," eyeing the old man with sympathy, as for the moment he stood, money-belt in hand, and life-preserver under arm, "be sure it will, sir, since in Providence, as in man, you and I equally put trust. But, bless me, we are being left in the dark here. Pah! What a smell, too."[18]

There's something strangely gentle, even touching, in this final send-off. Renker understands the book in the light of Melville's abandonment of prose; she maintains that, having failed "to penetrate the world of the material in order to attain a transcendent realm of truth," Melville had "given up this hope and turned his frustrations with the page on his reader."[19] Thus the circular, tautological titles he bestows on some of his chapters: "Worth the consideration of those to whom it may prove worth considering"; "Which may pass for whatever is may prove to be worth"; "In which the last three words of the last chapter are made the test of the discourse, which will be sure of receiving more or less attention from those readers who do not skip it."

But perhaps exhaustion even more than frustration describes the book's tone. Melville's narrative art ends in what appears to be a very secular apocalypse—an ending but one with nothing whatever absolute or final about it. The tension within the nation's founding paradox, both assuming and denying a transcendent authorizing of the strictly secular arrangements of communal life, what gives to classic American literature its peculiarly constituting character, runs down to a rather eerie indeterminacy. The mechanism of the Union's health, its belief in the Constitution's authorizing paradox, is running down under the wear of its tension and the demands it makes of a shared faith. The dynamic of that tension, the ceaseless oscillation of paradox suspended over time, loses its stability, whether that is imagined as a vertiginous speeding up, forcing something like a total dismemberment, or as a terrible slowing down like a satellite losing velocity and crashing to earth. Melville leaves the last two interlocutors aboard the *Fidèle* as if with nothing left to do but lean on one another "here in the dark," with a parting Shakespearean allusion to Yorick's skull and the stink of mortality itself. And in a manner reminiscent of Edgar Allan Poe, the spooky final sentence of Melville's final novel sounds a muted note of a similarly exhausted suspense: "Something further may follow of this Masquerade."[20]

The *Fidèle*, the ship of faith, carries with it a climate of deceit, for the reader a miasma of distrust so thick as to almost block the function of narrative itself. The style of that oscillation of incommensurate perspectives, which is so vigorously even if violently sustained in *Moby-Dick*, is coming apart at the seams. It is difficult to read this book now, from our later historical vantage point, and not to recall that at its publication the central American crisis of confidence, the all but apocalyptic breakdown of the truth of the constitutional covenant, a very war between the states, was just a few short years away.

The Literary Art of Uniting States

Discourse about the Constitution of the United States has been, at least since the Union victory in the Civil War, almost universally optimistic. Not that historians and critics have been blind to American injustice committed under that very Constitution, but as often as not the story has been one of injustice mitigated, of abuses partially corrected. Such self-congratulation is not altogether inappropriate: the Constitution has guided what is now the longest surviving government in the history of the world, and arguably the most stable. A very strong argument can also be made that it has fostered the most consistently free political system and the one most respectful of individual human rights. The most powerful argument of all in assuring its status perhaps is that it has promoted—or at the least has not seriously hindered—the development of the most prosperous economic system the world has ever witnessed. As the American adage accurately if none too elegantly puts it, there's no arguing with success.

However one understands the contribution made by the Constitution to these developments, none of them would be possible without some sense of a reliable underlying structure. There is an amusing story told, most recently by the physicist Stephen Hawking, of a protest lodged at a public lecture against an account of the Big Bang origin of the Universe. "None of that," cried the voice from the back of the room, "the world rests on the back of a turtle." And when the lecturer patiently asked upon what that turtle rested, the equally patient response was simply "another turtle." "But on what does that turtle rest?" asked the now exasperated physicist. "It's turtles," the protester explained, "it's turtles all the way down." The foundation (from Latin *fundus* meaning "bottom") on which the United States rests, though strictly historical unlike that mythic turtle, is the Constitution, and similarly, it is the Constitution all the way down. The Constitution has created the nation's constitution—its conditions and character, its form, fabric, temper, and tenor. Beyond any particular doctrines and tendencies— what we refer to by such shorthand as "balance of powers," "consent of the governed," "rights of individuals"—the Constitution provides a kind of procedural faith for Americans, something like a covenant-to-be-covenanted.

In a masterful book of over a decade ago, the literary critic Harold Bloom set himself the thankless task of becoming, at least temporarily, a religious critic. Not, it must be emphasized, as a normative theologian or as a critic of religion in the sense that the biologist Richard Dawkins has taken upon himself to critique the intelligence and coherence of religion in general, but in a manner analogous to the practice of literary criticism—to offer, in part, a description and an appreciation of particular religious phenomena. Bloom entitled his study *The American Religion,* the instances of which he examined being primarily the Southern Baptist Convention and the Mormon Church. What these native faiths commonly teach, in Bloom's view, is "a purely inner freedom." The primary point here is that for Bloom this freedom has been in a secret war precisely against the United States Constitution.[1]

Bloom himself openly regards this inner freedom as a spiritual triumph, but he sadly notes that it "seems always fated to make the believer, ultimately, a worse citizen." This is because, as he puts it, "authority, in the context of the American Religion . . . knows that it must replace the purely secular authority brought about by the American Revolution." Thus, according to his account, the political development and the religious development of the United States have long been hurtling toward potential collision, one which in the 1991 Coda to his book he sees as soon reaching its apocalyptic climax, with the Constitution seriously threatened by the increasing power of religious conservatives in their alliance and ultimate domination of the "Republican Party of Reagan and [the first George] Bush."[2] One cannot imagine that yet another George Bush has provided any detour from such a fearful trajectory.

My own argument has been that the secular authority established after the American Revolution had already depended upon a powerful sense of the revealed, suggesting that American literary culture has centrally shared in an impulse to secular revelation. The Constitution, as with a grandly blank façade, evades the distinction between secularity and the sanctified otherness of traditional revelation. Thus it is that historically both secularists and the religious—even those most accurately called Fundamentalists—have often understood themselves as looking to the Constitution for their security against one another. What Bloom characterizes as an ever-threatening conflict in the United States between the secular and the revealed, this book has treated as mature if imperfectly achieved oscillation, making for an American adherence to an unarticulated, largely unexamined paradoxy.

Perhaps in soberly honest retrospect all times are seen as dark times, but certainly some periods appear darker than others. The intense and rancorous politics of the present moment, amid the current commitment to what can be projected to be a generation-long world conflict, gives pause to anyone reflecting on the health of America's constitutionally inspired culture. Direct terrorist attacks on the United States are aimed at provoking a vast religious war, and it is not yet clear whether the Americans—beyond legitimately defending themselves—are going to rise to the provocation, though there are disturbing signs indicating that they may. Such a full-scale religious war would not bode well for the Constitution and the culture it has nurtured. The double-consciousness that the Constitution instituted, its spirit, and that of its Founders and ratifiers seem intended in part to forestall any such single-minded extremism, remaining strategically silent as it does on matters of deepest spiritual and personal commitments.

To argue, as I have, that the United States is founded upon a paradox is not to claim that this paradox often has risen to historical consciousness. On the contrary, the closest most Americans come to exposing the paradoxical basis of their national identity is in the distinctive quality of American humor, the joy it takes in linking the demotic to the sublime that has so often been pointed out.

It is instructive in this context to consider a famous Talmudic story that captures the ancient rabbis' attitude toward living with a definitive revelation.[3] Rabbi Eliezer, it is said, disagreed on a point of law with all the other rabbis, and in order to prove the correctness of his position successfully summoned a series of miraculous events. When the other rabbis rejected these as proof, Eliezer called for a voice from heaven, and indeed a heavenly voice confirmed that he was in the right. But still the rabbis overruled him, insisting that "the Torah is no longer in heaven," citing Scripture to prove that the decision is determined by the majority.

The paradox of majority interpretation taking precedence over the very Word of God once that Word has entered the human realm is underlined by the brief anecdote that immediately follows. Rabbi Nathan, the Talmud continues, once met Elijah and took advantage of the opportunity to ask the prophet about God's response to this rabbinic usurpation—if that is what it was. "God laughed," Elijah explained, "he laughed and said, 'My children have defeated me, my children have defeated me.' "

In the case of American political life and its Constitution, such profound wisdom, accepting paradox, the "laughter of God," as a necessary condition when interpreting an authoritative text, has not been universally adopted. Many in politics have instead claimed to adhere strictly to a single interpretation sanctioned by the equivalent of a heavenly voice in their reconstruction of the Founders' original intention. This is a procedure that, as we have seen, Madison himself rejected in the early years of constitutional government. Its proponents use their reconstructions to banish any interpretation of the Constitution with which they disagree. Unlike Lincoln, who argued for the sanctification of the revelation itself, the so-called originalists, opposing what they describe as "activist" justices, want to sanctify not the text of the Constitution, but *their own interpretations* of that text. Such a procedure radically flattens the paradox of a secular revelation—both authoritative and at the same time subject to our intervention—and thus removes it from living human agency. If given free reign, such an "originalism" would establish nothing less than a national system of church-like courts with the Constitution as its fundamentalist scripture. It would import notions of inerrancy and infallibility into our reading of a document we know to be the unembarassed product of intelligent human conflict and compromise.

The former colonists, demanding of themselves a national cohesion in order that something of sufficient strength and endurance should emerge from their idealistic and improvised revolution, acted on a bracing confidence in their capacity for self-invention. This confidence has led in due course to what the legal scholar Sanford Levinson has called a "Constitutional Faith." This book has been about the literary consequences of their leap of constitutional faith. Having inherited European, specifically English, traditions, literary among others, and having usurped the name of the continent, of the New World itself—

becoming simply, the Americans—they acted out a radical break with those traditions. Their Constitution's circular self-confidence, its firm midair footing with its implicit claim to provisional perfection, supplied the generating paradigm for an American poetics, making possible, even all but inevitable, the revelation-ambition of its writers. The desires, the aims, and the poetics of classic American literature seem different in kind from their antecedent British or European forms. The ambitious overreaching character of classic American literature may well strike a reader from those traditions as ridiculous, even if inspiring, but in either case as something set off at a peculiar tangent from the traditional poetic aims of instruction and pleasure.

Consider Melville as the classic American novelist of the sea in comparison to the great sea novelist of English literature, Joseph Conrad. Conrad could not, in fact, abide Melville's masterpiece, *Moby-Dick*. To him the whole seemed quite simply not credible: "It struck me," he wrote to Sir Humphrey Milford, "as a rather strained rhapsody with whaling for a subject and not a single sincere line in the 3 vols of it."[4] At the risk of a coarse comparison, where for Conrad, the one-time captain, the dramatization of life at sea provides a natural arena for examining the central issue of the individual's duty to a hierarchic social structure, for Melville, the former sailor "before the mast," what is central to the drama of men at sea is their facing the grandest philosophical and theological questions, the very largest perspectives on Nature, God, and the entire purpose of communal life. Even when Melville's central character is a captain, it is not his social position of command on which the story turns but, as has been shown, his strictly personal, charismatic authority in focusing the crew's shared anxiety. At the end of Conrad's *The Shadow Line,* Captain Giles, the man of experience, says to the newly matured narrator how "the truth is that one must not make too much of anything in life, good or bad." Such wisdom is almost diametrically opposed not merely to the tenor of Melville's fiction, but to the overriding tenor of Emerson's essays and Whitman's poetry as well.

The demands of constitutional poetics did not end with the mid-nineteenth-century renaissance, but they continued to haunt American literature. Emily Dickinson, for instance, an incomparably great and incomparably private poet, seems in many ways utterly unconnected to a public fact like the Constitution—her beloved father's career as an important lawyer notwithstanding—and yet some aspects of her poetry seem to be a response to those very self-constituting poetics. The way in which American reality, filtered through a constitutional vision, seems itself something constructed can be read even in one of her very brief and eerily charming poems of nature, when it recalls Virgil's fourth Georgic:

> To make a prairie it takes a clover, and one bee,—
> And revery
> The revery alone will do
> If bees are few.

The echoes of a constitutional poetics are still clearly audible some hundred years later in Wallace Stevens, for instance, who, when he writes of the larger function of poetry (as he often does), seems to be invoking, explicitly if unconsciously, the largely hidden, paradoxical status of the United States Constitution:

> The final belief is to believe in a fiction, which you know to be a fiction, there being nothing else. The exquisite truth is to know that it is a fiction and that you believe in it willingly.[5]

The desire to encompass everything, to make the local cosmic, is revealed in the very titles to which American writers are partial, titles whose distinctiveness is evident if a different nationality is substituted in, for instance, *An American Tragedy* or *The USA Trilogy*, in *The Fall of America*, *The American Dream*, *Angels in America* or *American Pastoral*. Philip Roth, author of the last of these works, once wrote that if America had a surname, it would be "Amnesia." An equally appropriate choice, and a closely related one, might be "Aspiration": lack of historical memory is a necessity if the way to begin anything is always to begin everything. It is, as it were, always required to invent the nation again, that nothing short of the whole will do as a subject.

But if American writers often imagine themselves in possession of a blank and open field of personal sovereignty and independence, there is also a sense in which that heady freedom can instead of an opportunity become a predicament, even a desperate one. So it is seen by a foreign observer like the Slovenian philosopher Slavoj Zizek who in commenting upon the internationally infamous American obsession with disaster films has contrasted an American perspective with that of older cultures:

> Unlike other peoples who have long-standing traditions and with whom there is a suspicion that if you scratch below the surface, you will discover the old traditions, [people] who face the problem of having to deal with

these traditions. The American vision is completely different—this is a vision in which order is not something with deep roots. It is instead superficial and fragile. Something is liable to happen at any moment; a small disaster might dismantle the social order.[6]

From this point of view, Emerson preaches self-reliance for the simple reason that in the United States there remains so little else to rely upon. It is as if within the most boastful American self-confidence one can hear a whisper of nihilism. Thus, Richard Poirier has described Stevens in the context of writers including Emerson, Frost, William James, and Gertrude Stein as "given to the oscillations between deprivation and creative ebullience."[7] It is a simplification to align this oscillation with that between the secular and the revealed, but it would not be altogether misleading.

Perhaps this very fear of fragility is the reason American identity has seemed such a perpetual obsession for Americans, this very book being but another instance in an innumerable catalogue of instances. Perhaps it is this fear of fragility that accounts as well for the degree to which the deeper cultural role of the United States Constitution has remained so strangely underexamined. In the case of the classic literature of the United States, an art of uniting contradictory states or conditions of existence, I have attempted to peer into the silent engine of constitutional paradox and freeze if only for a moment its perpetually alternating current, which seamlessly joins the transcendent exaltation of *We Are One* to the workaday demand to *Mind Your Business*. It makes for a delicate balance, easily slipping on the one side into airily optimistic abstractions and on the other into coarseness and righteous self-regard; but whether for good or for ill it is the condition in which a native literary art has been practiced, and continues to be practiced, often in unlikely and surprising ways.

Notes

Index

Notes

Introduction

1. Of course one of the most important of the methods by which the modern world has attempted to escape this perplexity is by means of some meta-narrative dictating the course of the future, such as many versions of Marxist progress. It is true that the strategy of mythologizing "history" bears some relation to what this study describes as the founding generation's creation of a "secular revelation," though it is fundamentally different in being usually conscious and philosophical, as opposed to what in the American case is more or less unconscious and what might be called pragmatic.
2. The often repeated phrase seems to have been derived from Alexander Hamilton's *Federalist No. 22.*
3. Article V reads: "The Congress, whenever two thirds of both houses shall deem it necessary, shall propose amendments to this Constitution, or, on the application of the legislatures of two thirds of the several states, shall call a convention for proposing amendments, which, in either case, shall be valid to all intents and purposes, as part of this Constitution, when ratified by the legislatures of three fourths of the several states, or by conventions in three fourths thereof, as the one or the other mode of ratification may be proposed by the Congress; *provided that no amendment which may be made prior to the year one thousand eight hundred and eight shall in any manner affect the first and fourth clauses in the ninth section of the first article; and that no state, without its consent, shall be deprived of its equal suffrage in the Senate"*(emphasis added).

   Two rare attempts at sustained criticism of the Constitution have recently been published—William Eskridge and Sanford Levinson, eds., *Constitutional Stupidities, Constitutional Tragedies* (New York: New York University Press, 1998), and *How Democratic Is the American Constitution?* (New

Haven, Conn.: Yale University Press, 2001) by political scientist Robert A. Dahl. Given the important and useful insights displayed in both these volumes, their critiques should have entered political discourse but not unexpectedly have not. The reason, as I will suggest, is that the Constitution founds far more than merely a governmental structure. Upon it rests the very identity of the nation, not a subject much open to discussion.

4. Carl Becker famously made the point that the American Revolution was as much about "who was to rule at home" as it was about "home rule." See Becker, *The History of Political Parties in the Province of New York, 1760–1776* (Madison: University of Wisconsin Press, 1909; reprt. 1960), p. 22.

5. See Yosef Hayim Yerushalmi, *Zakhor, Jewish History and Jewish Memory* (Seattle: University of Washington Press, 1982).

6. See Martin Flaherty, "John Marshall, McCulloch v Maryland and 'We the People,'" *William and Mary Law Review* 43 (2001), pp. 1339–1397. Flaherty examines recent attempts by the current Supreme Court to revise this interpretation favoring the states as against the united people, but the traditional view as definitively expressed by John Marshall still seems to prevail: "The government proceeds directly from the *people;* is 'ordained and established,' in the name of the *people;* and is declared to be ordained, 'in order to form a more perfect union, establish justice, insure domestic tranquility, and secure the blessings of liberty to themselves and to their posterity.' The assent of the states, in their sovereign capacity, is implied, in calling a convention, and thus submitting that instrument to the *people.* But the *people* were at perfect liberty to accept or reject it; and their act was final. It required not the affirmance, and could not be negatived, by the state governments. The constitution, when thus adopted, was of complete obligation, and bound the state sovereignties" (p. 134)

7. This is not to suggest that the Constitution has gone unmentioned in the context of literary study. But no one to my knowledge has argued for the Constitution as the primary form-shaping text for American literary tradition. Nor has anyone attempted to hypothesize a mechanism of a constitutional dynamic, one that I identify with a specific paradox. Michael Warner, for instance, in *The Letters of the Republic: Publication and the Public Sphere in Eighteenth Century America* (Cambridge, Mass.: Harvard University Press, 1990), presents a thoughtful and persuasive understanding of the Constitution as central to his subject, the way in which the earliest novels of the new republic (which he comes close to acknowledging as subliterary; see pp. 151–152) engaged in the construction of a crucially *written* "public sphere." As for the classic texts associated with achieving a distinctive American literature, they do not concern Warner, because in his view they are products of a "liberal aesthetic" that postdates the period he examines (p. 176). Christopher Gustafson, in *Representative Words: Politics, Literature, and the American Language, 1776–1865* (New York: Cambridge University Press, 1993), in the course of his substantial work, does mention that the "moral and political conflicts, inscribed in the text of the Consti-

tution" are ultimately "inscribed in the plots, as the stuff of American Renaissance literature" (p. 295). This is an interesting claim, but it is not the subject of his work, and he neither clarifies the point nor develops it. It seems in any case limited to what I would call literary thematics, and not formal literary properties. A few critics, notably Allen Grossman, "The Poetics of Union in Whitman and Lincoln: An Inquiry toward the Relationship of Art and Policy," in Walter Benn Michaels and Donald E. Pease, eds., *The American Renaissance Reconsidered* (Baltimore, Md.: Johns Hopkins University Press, 1985) and Kerry Larson, *Whitman's Drama of Consensus* (Chicago: University of Chicago Press, 1988), have offered insights into the specific way constitutional politics, and the issues of union and consensus, are manifested, or paralleled, in the formal poetics of Walt Whitman. Most often, however, when the Constitution is considered in American cultural contexts, it engages in the larger perspectives of language and interpretation, as in Christopher Looby's *Voicing America: Language, Literary Form, and the Origin of the United States* (Chicago: University of Chicago Press, 1996).

8. There has been some considerable work touching upon the Constitution in the area generally known as "law and literature." See, for instance, Brooks Thomas, *Cross-Examinations of Law and Literature: Cooper, Hawthorne, Stowe, and Melville* (New York: Cambridge University Press, 1987) and much of the commentary of Michael Rogin's *Subversive Genealogy: The Art and Politics of Herman Melville* (New York: Alfred A. Knopf, 1983). These often excellent volumes focus on the Constitution strictly in its legal and political interpretation and are of a piece with the largely political interpretation of American literary classics sponsored by the many works of Sacvan Bercovitch. See Bercovitch's most succinct summary, *The American Jeremiad* (Madison: University of Wisconsin Press, 1978), and his most recent collection of applications, *The Rites of Assent: Transformations in the Symbolic Constructions of America* (New York; Routledge, 1992). The major weakness of these works, notwithstanding their often considerable interpretative insight, is that they feel compelled to treat masters of literary expression as masters of political thought and so constantly elide the distinction between artistic achievement and political intelligence, not to say moral decency, most frequently by redefining the experience of such artistic achievement in purely cognitive and largely political terms.

9. Michael Kammen, *A Machine That Would Go of Itself: The Constitution in American Culture* (New York: Alfred A. Knopf, 1986), p. 11.

10. George Anastaplo, *The Constitution of 1787: A Commentary* (Baltimore, Md.: Johns Hopkins University Press, 1989), p. 3.

1. At The Beginning

1. Howard Mumford Jones, *O Strange New World: American Culture: The Formative Years* (London: Chatto & Windus, 1965), Chapter 1.

2. John Locke, *Treatise of Civil Government and A Letter Concerning Toleration,* ed. Charles L. Sherman (New York: Irvington Publications, 1979), p. 32

3. J. Hector St. John de Crèvecoeur, *Letters from an American Farmer and Sketches of Eighteenth Century Life,* ed. Albert E. Stone (New York: Penguin, 1981), p. 66; Harold Rosenberg, *The Tradition of the New* (New York: McGraw-Hill, 1960), p. 18.

4. Jon Butler, *Becoming America: The Revolution before 1776* (Cambridge, Mass.: Harvard University Press, 2000), pp. 2–3. "Distinctively modern" is the description of a tendency and direction, of course. As Butler himself writes, "two characteristics of modern society [urbanism, and rapid technological development] never appeared in the colonies."

5. Edward Said, *Beginnings; Intention & Method* (New York: Columbia University Press, 1985). See especially the first two chapters, which are full of suggestive remarks about the conditions necessary for making beginnings.

6. Thomas Mann, *Joseph and His Brothers,* trans. H. T. Lowe-Porter (New York: Alfred A. Knopf, 1948; reprt. 1978), p. 3.

7. Michael Kammen, *People of Paradox: An Inquiry Concerning the Origins of American Civilization* (New York: Alfred A. Knopf, 1972), p. 43.

8. The list is included in an appendix in Stephen L. Schechter, ed., *Roots of the Republic: American Founding Documents Interpreted* (Madison, Wis.: Madison House, 1990), pp. 449–454.

9. There is an argument about whether language's primacy is imagined as oral or written. For one side of the argument, see Christopher Looby, *Voicing America: Language, Literary Form and the Origins of the United States* (Chicago: University of Chicago Press, 1996), and Jay Fliegelman, *Declaring Independence: Jefferson, Natural Language and the Culture of Performance* (Stanford, Calif.: Stanford University Press, 1993). For the other side, see Michael Warner, *The Letters of the Republic: Publication and the Public Sphere in Eighteenth-Century America* (Cambridge, Mass.: Harvard University Press, 1990), and Larzer Ziff, *Writing in the New Nation: Prose, Print, and Politics in the Early United States* (New Haven, Conn.: Yale University Press, 1991). I have chosen to emphasize the written over the oral for the rather obvious reason that I am less interested in the more general questions of national foundation than I am in the consequences of that foundation for American writing.

10. See, for instance, the work on early Rabbinic Judaism and its relation to the ancient Greeks by Elias J. Bickerman, among others *The Jews in the Greek Age* (Cambridge, Mass.: Harvard University Press, 1988).

11. This is part of an often-stated larger claim, in recent decades associated especially with Sacvan Bercovitch, that the pattern of New England imagination had a determinative influence on the whole of what would become the United States. See specifically Bercovitch's *The Puritan Origins of the American Self* (New Haven, Conn.: Yale University Press, 1975), and *The American Jeremiad* (Madison: University of Wisconsin Press, 1978). This

claim has been vigorously contested by some historians such as Jack Greene in *Pursuits of Happiness: The Social Development of Early Modern British Colonies and the Formation of American Culture* (Chapel Hill: University of North Carolina Press, 1988), for whom the South is the more typical and representative region. It should be noted, for instance, that Ben Franklin, a child of New England, made his reputation in the middle colony of Pennsylvania and was as admired in Virginia as he was in Massachusetts. (Indeed the censorious, supreme New Englander John Adams could not abide the great man, while the Southern planter James Madison, in Philadelphia for the Constitutional Convention, was delighted to record Franklin's conversation in a notebook he dedicated to the purpose.)

12. Benjamin Franklin, *Writings,* ed. J. A. Leo Lemay (New York: Library of America, 1987), p. 91. This is the epitaph that more than half a century later he engraved upon his tombstone in Philadelphia, where it is still readable.

13. Ibid., p. 1307.

14. Thomas Paine, *Common Sense,* ed. Isaac Kramnick (New York: Penguin, 1982), p. 29.

15. Ibid.

16. Gordon Wood, "Disturbing the Peace," *New York Review of Books* 13 (June 8, 1995), p. 20.

17. Washington Irving, "Salmagundi No. vii, Sunday April 6, 1807," in *History, Tales, and Sketches,* ed. James W. Tuttleton (New York: Library of America, 1988), pp. 144–145.

18. Ibid., pp. 493–494.

19. Jacques Derrida, "Declarations of Independence," *New Political Science* 15 (Summer 1986), p. 8. The central concern of Derrida's little talk, which plays around the question of who signs such a founding act, "and with what so-called proper name," is far more applicable to the Constitution's "We the People" than it is to Jefferson's drafting of the Declaration.

20. Kenneth Silverman, *A Cultural History of the American Revolution: Painting, Music, Literature and the Theater in the Colonies and the United States from the Treaty of Paris to the Inauguration of George Washington, 1763–1789* (New York: Thomas Y. Crowell Company, 1976), p. 319.

21. What I hope will be clear by the end of this chapter is that the title of Maier's splendid book, *American Scripture: Making the Declaration of Independence* (New York: Alfred A. Knopf, 1997), uses the notion of "scripture" in rather a loose, general sense.

22. Edward Countryman, *The American Revolution* (New York: Hill and Wang, 1985), p. 125, puts the case succinctly: "In metaphorical terms, the colonials killed their king in 1776. In very real terms, they destroyed the whole ancient pattern of institutions, beliefs, habits and usages that had comprised the British Constitution in America."

23. Maier, *American Scripture,* pp. 154–160.

24. John M. Murrin, "A Roof without Walls: The Dilemma of American Na-

tional Identity," in *Beyond Confederation: Origins of the Constitution and American National Identity,* eds. Richard Beekman, Stephen Botein, and Edward C. Carter II (Chapel Hill: University of North Carolina Press, 1987), p. 334: "The sprawling American continent had taken a remarkably homogeneous people, the Indians, and divided them into hundreds of distinct societies over thousands of years. America was quite capable of doing the same to Europeans. The seventeenth century created, within English America alone, not one new civilization on this side of the Atlantic, but many distinct colonies that differed as dramatically from one another as any of them from England."

25. See the engaging study by David Hackett Fisher, *Albion's Seed: Four Folkways in British America* (New York: Oxford University Press, 1989).

26. These terms—Virginians, Pennsylvanians, New Yorkers—are themselves collectives, aggregates of social groups from more local regions. Virginians of the Tidewater plantations did not identify with Virginians of the backcountry. And we can continue in this vein to consider families, and then individuals, and in a more modern vein Nietzsche's "rendezvous of selves." It is nevertheless the case that every union, not only the Union, suppresses differences. The point here is that the colony, and then the state, was the largest entity that engendered loyalty and offered identity for most Americans.

27. The observation, and the citation to the letter to William Fleming, July 1, 1776 in *The Papers of Thomas Jefferson,* eds. Julian P. Boyd et al. (Princeton, n.g.: Princeton University Press, 1950–), vol. I, pp. 411–412, are to be found in Joseph Ellis, *Founding Brothers: The Revolutionary Generation* (New York: Alfred A. Knopf, 2001), p. 11.

28. This is by no means meant as a summary, even an inadequate one, of the "prodigals and pilgrims" of Fliegelman's richly rewarding study—*Prodigals and Pilgrims: The American Revolution Against Patriarchal Authority 1750–1800* (New York: Cambridge University Press, 1982), much of which is relevant to the tensions, both religious and legal, of imagining the movement from dependence to independence.

29. Fliegelman quotes in this context a starkly simple statement of this sentiment in the correspondence of John Adams: "The People is Clarissa." Ibid., p. 89. However, in Adams's letter from which the quotation comes—a letter Fliegelman himself supplies in a later chapter (p. 237)—Adams's point is not that the People prior to independence are being tyrannized by the king, who by rights should be a loving father, but rather that, at the time of the French Revolution, the People are being seduced by a Lovelace, viz. the "awful spirit of Democracy."

30. Tom Paine, *Collected Writings,* ed. Eric Foner (New York: Library of America, 1995) p. 83.

31. D. H. Lawrence, *Studies in Classic American Literature* (New York: Viking Press, 1923, reprt. 1961), p. 3.

32. King James II had ordered the creation of a New England Confederation in

the late 1680s uniting Massachusetts, Connecticut, Rhode Island, and Plymouth Colony, to which soon were added New York and New Jersey to form the Dominion of New England; but Confederation and Dominion together survived less than five years. The Congress held in the middle of the next century at Albany's City Hall, intended to pacify the Iroquois along with uniting the colonies, was primarily a Northern affair, though both Carolinas attended, and the plan was intended to encompass all the British mainland colonies except the frontiers of Georgia and Nova Scotia.

33. Murrin, "A Roof without Walls," p. 340.
34. Maier, *American Scripture,* p. xxi.
35. Adams expressed the view to Horatio Gates that the "popular Principles and Maxims" that would inevitably guide the creation of new state governments would be "abhorrent to the Inclinations of the Barons of the South, and the Proprietary Interests in the Middle Colonies." See Maier, *American Scripture,* p. 36.
36. Paine, *Common Sense,* ed. Kramnick, p. 24.

2. The Path to Union

1. Here is a description by a political scientist: "American constitutional interpretation takes for granted the elemental preposterousness of its subject, namely the presumption that a political world can be constructed and controlled by words." See William F. Harris II, "Bonding Word and Polity: The Logic of American Constitutionalism," *The American Political Science Review* 76 (1982), p. 34.
2. Jack Rakove, *Original Meanings: Politics and Ideas in the Making of the Constitution* (New York: Alfred A. Knopf, 1996), p. 342.
3. Gordon Wood, *The Creation of the American Republic, 1776–1787* (New York: W.W. Norton, 1972), p. 75. This paragraph to which this endnote is appended, and the next, directly, or indirectly, derive from Wood's work.
4. Wood thus summarizes the period: "By the mid 1780's gentlemen up and down the continent were shaking their heads in disbelief and anger at the 'private views and selfish principles' [these were Washington's words] of the men they saw in the state assemblies." Ibid., p. 76.
5. Rakove, *Original Meanings,* p. 377.
6. Max Farrand, *The Framing of the Constitution of the United Sates* (New Haven, Conn.: Yale University Press, 1913), p. 28, with additional ellipses added.
7. James Madison, *Writings,* ed. Jack N. Rakove (New York: Library of America, 1999), p. 62.
8. Farrand, *The Framing,* pp. 55–59. There were two breaks—a recess for the Fourth of July and ten days in August.
9. It was Benjamin Franklin who proposed this formulation as a compromise that would enable the Convention to conclude with something approaching unanimity, though according to Madison it had originated with Franklin's

Pennsylvania colleague, Gouveneur Morris, who hoped Franklin's prestige would carry the motion.

10. Edward Countryman, *The American Revolution* (New York: Hill and Wang, 1985), p. 134.

3. The People, Having Spoken, Speak

1. Needless to say, this is merely a gesture in the direction of a potted account of this vast historical debate. For the purposes of this argument, as I hope will become clear, the outcome of this debate is of no great relevance, since the form of the Constitution that is of interest in this context is not affected by it. Joseph Ellis in his recent popular account, *Founding Brothers: The Revolutionary Generation* (New York: Alfred A. Knopf, 2001), has commented on the persistence of this debate: "It is truly humbling, perhaps even dispiriting, to realize that the historical debate over the revolutionary era and the early republic merely recapitulates the ideological debate conducted at the time, the historians have essentially been fighting the same battles, over and over again, that the members of the revolutionary generation fought originally among themselves. Though many historians have taken a compromise of split-the-difference over the ensuing years, the basic choice has remained constant, as historians have declared themselves nationalists, liberals, or conservatives, then written accounts that favor one camp or the other, or that stigmatize one side by viewing it through the eyes of the other, just as the contestants did back then" (p. 15).
2. Hannah Arendt, *On Revolution* (New York: Penguin, 1963), p. 93. The quotation from Jefferson is from a letter to Madison, December 16, 1786.
3. Gordon Wood, *The Creation of the American Republic, 1776–1787* (New York: W. W. Norton, 1972), p. 562.
4. The details of the relative size of the legislature is from Edward Countryman, *The American Revolution* (New York: Hill and Wang, 1985), p. 200. The whole of his sixth chapter is a brief summary and masterful balancing of the many "reasons" behind the adoption of the Constitution, from large-scale economic tendencies to some ill-timed drinking among New Hampshire anti-Federalists.
5. Jack Rakove, *Original Meanings: Politics and Ideas in the Making of the Constitution* (New York: Alfred A. Knopf, 1996), p. 342.
6. Bernard Bailyn, ed., *The Debate on the Constitution: Federalist and Anti-federalist Speeches, Articles, and Letters during the Struggle over Ratification*, 2 vols. (New York: Library of America, 1993), I, p. 446.
7. Lance Banning, "Republican Ideology and the Triumph of the Constitution, 1789–1793," *William and Mary Quarterly* 31 (1974), p. 170.
8. Ibid.
9. Bailyn, ed., *Debate on the Constitution*, II, p. 596.
10. James Madison, *Notes of Debates in the Federal Convention of 1787,* ed. Adrienne Koch (New York: W. W. Norton, 1977), p. 655.

11. It is on this point, chief among others, that modern critics as well fault the Constitution for itself subverting popular sovereignty.

12. Stanley Elkins and Eric McKitrick, *The Age of Federalism: The Early American Republic, 1788–1800* (New York: Oxford University Press, 1993), p. 11.

4. Almost a Miracle

1. John Adams, *The Selected Writings of John and John Quincy Adams,* eds. Adrienne Koch and William Peden (New York: Alfred A. Knopf, 1946), p. 57.

2. Max Farrand, *The Framing of the Constitution of the United Sates* (New Haven, Conn.: Yale University Press, 1913), pp. 61–62.

3. Robert A. Ferguson, "The Forgotten Publius: John Jay and the Aesthetics of Ratification," *Early American Literature* 34 (1999); p. 233.

4. Sir Francis Bacon, *The Essayes or Counsels Civill and Morall,* ed. Michael Kiernan (New York: Oxford University Press, 2000), p. 164.

5. *The Debate on the Constitution: Federalist and Antifederalist Speeches, Articles, and Letters during the Struggle over Ratification,* ed. Bernard Bailyn, 2 vols. (New York: Library of America, 1993) II, p. 194.

6. Michael Kammen, *A Machine that Would Go of Itself: The Constitution in American Culture* (New York: Alfred A. Knopf, 1986), p. 45.

7. Farrand, *Framing of the Constitution,* pp. 206–207. Morris also suggests that "others have given [the Constitution] a less righteous origin"—in effect an anti-Federalist inversion of the same thought.

8. John M. Murrin, "A Roof without Walls: The Dilemma of American National Identity," in *Beyond Confederation: Origins of the Constitution and American National Identity,* eds. Richard Beekman, Stephen Botein, and Edward C. Carter II (Chapel Hill: University of North Carolina Press, 1987), p. 347. The image of a roof and walls is borrowed from Francis Hopkinson, composer, poet, and signer of the Declaration.

9. Kammen, *A Machine* (pp. 46–48) traces the question from the late nineteenth century, although he himself expresses some qualified reservations about the basis for the question. He sees skepticism about the perfection of the Constitution lingering into the early nineteenth century and receiving a fresh impetus with the increasing agitation over slavery. But the statements he cites all seem rather self-conscious dissents against what it is difficult not to see as a very rapidly achieved and exceedingly broad consensus.

10. Lance Banning, "Republican Ideology and the Triumph of the Constitution, 1789–1793," *William and Mary Quarterly* 31 (1974), pp. 167–168.

11. Stanley Elkins and Eric McKitrick, "The Founding Fathers: Young Men of the Revolution" in *The Reinterpretation of the American Revolution,* ed. Jack P. Greene (New York: Harper and Row, 1968): "In the end, of course, everyone "crossed over" [to the side of the Constitution]. The speed with which this occurred once the continental revolutionists had made their

point, and the ease with which the Constitution so soon became an object of universal veneration, still stands as one of the minor marvels of American history" (pp. 394–395).

12. Frontier settlers of western North Carolina had named their state "Franklin."

13. Farrand, *Framing of the Constitution,* p. 94.

14. Carl Van Doren, *The Great Rehearsal* (New York: Penguin, 1948), p. 100.

15. James Madison, *Notes of Debates in the Federal Convention of 1787,* ed. Adrienne Koch (New York: W. W. Norton, 1987), pp. 209–210.

16. Jared Sparks, *Life of Benjamin Franklin, A Continuation of Franklin's Autobiography* (www.ushistory.org, *The Electronic Franklin,* Chapter xiv). Here is the key passage of Franklin's now famous letter to Stiles, written the month before he died: "Here is my Creed. I believe in one God, Creator of the Universe. That he governs it by his Providence. That he ought to be worshipped. That the most acceptable Service we render him is doing good to his other Children. That the soul of Man is immortal, and will be treated with Justice in another Life respecting its Conduct in this. . . .
    As to Jesus of Nazareth . . . I think the System of Morals and his Religion, as he left them to us, the best the World ever saw or is likely to see; but I apprehend it has received various corrupting Changes, and I have, with most of the present Dissenters in England, some Doubts as to his Divinity; tho' it is a question I do not dogmatize upon, having never studied it. . . . *Writings,* ed. J. A. Leo Lemay (New York: Library of America, 1987), p. 1179.

17. Madison, *Notes,* p. 211.

18. "Religious Dimensions of the Early American State" in *Beyond Confederation: Origins of the Constitution and American National Identity,* eds. Richard Beeman, Stephen Botein, and Edward C. Carter II (Chapel Hill: University of North Carolina Press, 1987), p. 320.

19. Arthur O. Lovejoy, "The Theory of Human Nature in the American Constitution and the Method of Counterpoise" in *Reflections on Human Nature* (Baltimore, Md.: Johns Hopkins University Press, 1961), pp. 37–39, 46.

20. *The Debate on the Constitution,* ed. Bailyn II, p. 1138.

21. Benjamin Franklin, "A Comparison of the Conduct of the Ancient Jews and of the Anti-Federalists in the United States of America," *Writings,* ed. Lemay, p. 1147.

22. In this context see J. A. Leo Lemay's interesting suggestion, which may "at first seem far fetched," that Franklin's "sense of self can best be thought of as a species of mysticism." See "Benjamin Franklin" in *Major Writers of Early American Literature,* ed. Everett H. Emerson (Madison: University of Wisconsin Press, 1972) p. 228.

23. Sanford Levinson has pointed out that there are in fact two instances of a recognition of God—subtle and indirect as they may be—in the Constitution itself: (1) It must be assumed that the president did not work on Sunday, since that day is excluded in the ten-day period for issuing an executive veto; and (2) the Constitution dates itself as in "the year of our Lord 1787."

It is true, however, that both of these instances could be considered in the realm of convention or custom rather than of religion proper—akin to the way non-Christians will matter-of-factly refer to the last week of the year as the "Christmas holidays."

24. See Richard Beeman, Stephen Botein, and Edward C. Carter II, eds., *Beyond Confederation: Origins of the Constitution and American National Identity* (Chapel Hill: University of North Carolina Press, 1987), p. 329. The attempt reached its height during the Civil War and then sank without leaving so much as a memory in the popular mind.

25. Martin E. Marty, "Religion and the Constitution: The Triumph of Practical Politics," *The Christian Century* (March 23–30, 1994), pp. 316–318, 327.

5. The Paradox of Secular Revelation

1. Exodus 19:8. The other details also come from Exodus chapter 19.

2. Jack Rakove, *The Beginnings of National Politics: An Interpretive History of the Continental Congress* (New York: Alfred A. Knopf, 1979), p. 399.

3. Jefferson, complaining to Adams about the request to publish the two friends' private correspondence wrote, "These people think they have a right to everything however secret or sacred." The passage dates from August 10, 1815, and is quoted in the "Preface" to Lester J. Capon, *The Adams-Jefferson Letters: The Complete Correspondence between Thomas Jefferson and Abigail and John Adams* (New York: Simon and Schuster, 1971), p. xxv.

4. Quoted in Jack Rakove, *Original Meanings: Politics and Ideas in the Making of the Constitution* (New York: Alfred A. Knopf, 1996), p. 362.

5. The Latin tag *e pluribus unum* does not appear in the Constitution. It was borrowed for the design of the Great Seal in 1776 from the popular London monthly *Gentleman's Magazine* where it appeared on each of its annual issues, and has gradually become associated—for obvious reasons—with Union formed in 1787.

6. Michael Kammen, *A Machine that Would Go of Itself: The Constitution in American Culture* (New York: Alfred A. Knopf, 1986), pp. 17–19. The phrase in his title is from James Russell Lowell, who, however, gently warns his countrymen against the "complacency" of the image.

7. Gary Wills, *Explaining America: The Federalist* (New York: Penguin, 1982), p. 255.

8. Max Farrand, *The Framing of the Constitution of the United Sates* (New Haven, Conn.: Yale University Press, 1913), p. 203.

9. Ibid., p. 201.

10. Hannah Arendt, *On Revolution* (New York: Penguin, 1963), pp. 159–160.

11. Joseph Ellis, *Founding Brothers: The Revolutionary Generation* (New York: Alfred A. Knopf, 2001), p. 16.

12. Everywhere amid the founding, it seems, is the aged Ben Franklin. He seems to have been the author of the coin's design, known now as the Fugio, or Franklin, cent, as well.

6. Declarations of American Literary Independence

1. Robert E. Spiller, ed., *The American Literary Revolution* (New York: Doubleday, 1967), pp. 11–12.

2. This interest in a distinctive American literature is not to be confused with the impulse behind such pre-Revolutionary works like Brackenridge's and Freneau's "A Poem, on the Rising Glory of America" (1771) or similar works by writers such as Jonathan Trumbull and Timothy Dwight. Kenneth Silverman, *A Cultural History of the American Revolution: Painting, Music, Literature, and the Theater in the Colonies and the United Sates from the Treaty of Paris to the Inauguration of George Washington, 1763–1789* (New York: T. Y. Crowell, 1976), explains that these writers had shared a belief in "a transnational community existing apart from place and time, embracing in one ecumenical present the writers of Athens, Rome, London, and shortly . . . New Haven and Philadelphia. To break with this community in the name of some 'distinctly American' literature . . . would be not a cultural necessity but an admission of defeat" (p. 231).

3. Michael Warner, *The Letters of the Republic: Publication and the Public Sphere in Eighteenth-Century America* (Cambridge, Mass.: Harvard University Press, 1990), p. 151. See also Michael Gilmore, in *The Cambridge History of American Literature*, ed. Sacvan Bercovitch (Cambridge, Mass.: Cambridge University Press, 1997), vol. 1, p. 555, who contends that "this picture [of an unworthy earlier literature] has now been revised, as new interest in the writing of the early Republic has brought fuller appreciation of that writing's goals and character"; that these goals and character were republican and communal, and had not yet yielded to a nineteenth-century "aesthetic paradigm that was congruent with liberal ideology and economic individualism."

4. Spiller, ed., *The American Literary Revolution*, p. 19.

5. Ibid., p. 28.

6. Ralph Waldo Emerson, *Emerson in His Journals*, ed. Joel Porte (Cambridge, Mass.: Harvard University Press, 1982), p. 440. The state, it must be noted, is Massachusetts.

7. Gilmore, *Cambridge History*, ed. Bercovitch, p. 541. This is followed by an equally representative statement about the writers "whose works established the national canon [for whom] imaginative art was differentiated from religious, moral, and civic forms of discourse." Although as a comparison of the tendencies in attitude toward literature in the respective periods, this is unobjectionable, these unqualified statements seem to imply that the literary itself somehow suffers a deserved devaluation, or even loses its identity, by revealing its historical contingency. This is hardly necessary and has a tendency to turn literary scholarship in the direction of polemics against literature's own highest achievements for lacking a putative transcendent, ahistorical basis. See also Cathy N. Davidson's methodological summary in the introduction to her study of early American novels, *Revolution and the*

Word: The Rise of the Novel in America (New York: Oxford University Press, 1986), p. 6: "*seemingly* nonliterary considerations still suggest the scope and nature of a particular work's use and appeal, the interpretive community to which the work appealed, how its appeal illuminated the sociological context in which it takes place, and all of these factors together can contribute to a history of texts, an archaeology of reading" [emphasis added]. That qualifying "seemingly" manages to evade the question of specifically literary value while seeming to address it. One suspects that much of this sophistical indirection is motivated by a needless anxiety to attribute the status of the "literary" to objects of minor literary interest, however much they may possess other, equally real, interests and appeals.

8. Warner, *Letters of the Republic,* pp. 151–152.

9. Ibid., p. 151, 176. This is to leave unquestioned Warner's assumption that the novel is "by nature divorced from the public sphere, designed as an occasion for a specially private kind of subjectivity." On the face of it, this would seem far truer of lyric poetry, for instance, than of almost any form of prose fiction.

10. Robert Ferguson, *Law and Letters in American Culture* (Cambridge, Mass.: Harvard University Press, 1984), pp. 4–5.

11. Ibid., p. 81.

12. Alexis de Tocqueville, *Democracy in America,* ed. J. P. Mayer, trans. George Lawrence (New York: Doubleday, 1969), p. 164.

13. Ferguson, *Law and Letters,* p. 93.

14. Ibid., pp. 230.

15. Charles Brockden Brown, *Wieland and Memoirs of Carwin the Bibloquist,* ed. Jay Fliegelman (New York: Penguin, 1991), p. xxxix.

16. Herman Melville, "Hawthorne and His Mosses," in *The Shock of Recognition,* ed. Edmund Wilson (New York: Farrar, Straus, Cudahy, 1955), p. 195.

17. Henry Wadsworth Longfellow, *The Poetry of Longfellow,* ed. J. D. Mc-Clatchy (New York: Library of America, 2000), pp. 754–756.

7. Preserving the Revelation

1. After writing this chapter, I found that Paul W. Kahn's work on constitutional theory, *Legitimacy and History: Self-Government in American Constitutional Theory* (New Haven, Conn.: Yale University Press, 1992), assigns much the same role to Lincoln's Address to the Young Men's Lyceum of Springfield, describing it from his perspective as illustrating "the dimensions of the problem of changing from a constitutionalism of making to one of maintenance" (p. 32).

2. Abraham Lincoln, "Address to the Young Men's Lyceum of Springfield, Illinois, January 27, 1838," in *Speeches and Writings 1832–1858: Speeches, Letters, and Miscellaneous Writings: The Lincoln-Douglas debates.* ed. Don E. Fehrenbacher (New York: Library of America, 1989), vol. I, p. 33.

3. Daniel Webster, "First Bunker Hill Address" in *Daniel Webster: "The Completest" Man,* ed. Kenneth Shewmaker (Hanover, N.H.: University Press of New England, 1990), p. 104.

4. Robert Ferguson, *Law and Letters in American Culture* (Cambridge, Mass.: Harvard University Press, 1984), p. 313.

5. Deut. 6: 6–7. The "schema" encompasses the whole of Deut. 6:4–9.

6. David Donald, *Lincoln* (New York: Simon and Schuster, 1995), p. 81.

7. Lincoln, "Address to the Young Men's Lyceum," p. 34. Edmund Wilson, *Patriotic Gore: Studies in the Literature of the American Civil War* (New York: Oxford University Press, 1962), pp. 99–130.

8. Lincoln, "Address to the Young Men's Lyceum," p. 34.

9. Lester J. Capon, *The Adams-Jefferson Letters: The Complete Correspondence between Thomas Jefferson and Abigail and John Adams* (New York: Simon and Schuster, 1971), p. 678.

10. Thomas Jefferson in *Writings,* ed. Merrill D. Peterson (New York: Library of America, 1984), p. 959.

11. Herbert Sloan, "The Earth Belongs in Usufruct to the Living," in *Jeffersonian Legacies,* ed. Peter S. Onuf (Charlottesville: University of Virginia Press, 1993), p. 281.

12. Hannah Arendt, *On Revolution* (New York: Penguin, 1963), p. 232.

13. William Wordsworth, *The Prelude, 1799, 1805, 1950,* ed. Jonathan Wordsworth, M. H. Abrams, and Stephen Gill (New York: W. W Norton, 1979), p. 323 (9:198–199, 1850 ed.)

14. Ibid., p. 397 (11:108–112, 1850 ed.).

15. Jefferson, *Writings* p. 1401.

16. Ibid., p. 1402.

17. As with all such categorical statements, there are always exceptions. However unlikely its influence, note, for instance, the recent political pamphlet of a book, *The Velvet Coup: The Constitution, the Supreme Court, and the Decline of American Democracy* (New York: Verso, 2001) in which Daniel Lazare, in the light of George W. Bush's Supreme Court-assisted election, presents a powerful argument for the complete abandonment of what the great wit and provocateur Gore Vidal refers to as "our rotted constitution." And see the still more recent volume, by a long-term critic of the Constitution, Robert A. Dahl, *How Democratic Is the American Constitution?* (New Haven, Conn.: Yale University Press, 2001), referred to in Chapter 1.

18. Lincoln, "Address to the Young Men's Lyceum," pp. 31–32.

19. Donald, *Lincoln,* p. 82.

20. Ibid., pp. 63–64.

21. *New York World,* November 27, 1863, cited in Donald, *Lincoln,* p. 465.

22. Gary Wills, *Lincoln at Gettysburg: The Words that Remade America* (New York: Simon and Schuster, 1992), p. 144.

23. Pauline Maier, *American Scripture: Making the Declaration of Independence* (New York: Alfred A. Knopf, 1997), p. xx. Indeed, it would appear that Roy P. Basler attributes to the 1838 Lyceum Address itself Lincoln's having

reasoned out "how American political institutions may be preserved and yet modified by the people to rectify errors in the structure of justice." See *Abraham Lincoln: His Speeches anhd Writings,* Roy P. Basler, ed. (New York: World Publishing Company, 1946), p. 85.

24. Horace Mann, *Dedication of Antioch College and Inaugural Address of Its President* (Boston: Crosby and Nichols, 1854), p. 4.

25. That this tacit dialectic remains in practice is evidenced by the unending argument between constitutional originalists, or so-called strict constructionists, and those who advocate a "living constitution." Neither side carries the day for very long, and the underlying principles of constitutional interpretation remain an active battlefield.

8. Preserving the Paradox

1. Ralph Waldo Emerson, *The Journals and Miscellaneous* Notebooks, ed. William H. Gilman et al. (Cambridge, Mass.: Harvard University Press, 1960–1982), Vol. 5, p. 333.

2. Ralph Waldo Emerson, "The American Scholar," *Essays and Lectures,* ed. Joel Porte (New York: Library of America, 1985), p. 53.

3. Although his speech did not give offense, if it had, such offense would not have been altogether free of material consequences. The next year, after his Address to the Harvard Divinity School, the criticism he faced was so severe that three decades passed before he received his next invitation to speak at Harvard.

4. Emerson, "The Poet," *Essays,* p. 450.

5. J. L. Austin, *How to Do Things with Words,* 2nd ed. (Cambridge, Mass.: Harvard University Press, 1975), p. 104.

6. Emerson, "The American Scholar," *Essays,* p. 53.

7. Ibid., p. 57.

8. Emerson, "The Divinity School Address," *Essays,* p. 83.

9. Emerson, "The American Scholar," *Essays,* p. 68.

10. And once one becomes conscious of it, it is startling to find how often the words "constitution" and "constitutional" come up in Emerson's prose.

11. Emerson, "The American Scholar," *Essays,* p. 63.

12. Ibid., pp. 66–67.

13. Emerson, "Nature," *Essays,* p. 7.

14. Emerson, "The American Scholar," *Essays,* p. 63.

15. Ralph L. Rusk, *The Life of Ralph Waldo Emerson* (New York: Charles Scribner's Sons, 1949), p. 251.

16. Stanley Cavell, *The Senses of Walden: An Expanded Edition* (San Francisco: North Point Press, 1981), pp. 141–160.

9. The Literary Renaissance of Secular Revelation

1. Ralph Waldo Emerson, "The American Scholar," in *Essays and Lectures,* ed. Joel Porte (New York: Library of America, 1985), p. 71.

2. Emerson, "Self Reliance," in *Essays,* p. 262.

3. Emerson, "Circles," in *Essays,* p. 403.

4. It was to these five years that F. O. Matthiessen devoted his book, *American Renaissance* (New York: Oxford University Press, 1941). As he summarizes the facts: "The half-decade of 1850–1855 saw the appearance of *Representative Men* (1850), *The Scarlet Letter* (1850), *The House of Seven Gables* (1851), *Moby-Dick* (1851), *Walden* (1854), and *Leaves of Grass* (1855). You might search all the rest of American literature without being able to collect a group of books equal to these in imaginative vitality" (p. vii)

5. Matthiessen, *American Renaissance,* p. vii.

6. Perhaps the paradox which that anarchy permitted reminded Matthiessen of the seventeenth-century metaphysical poets of the English Renaissance, one of the central literary interests of the New Criticism then dominant, and this in part accounts for the name coming to mind. (Matthiessen does have a chapter on "the metaphysical strain" in which he asserts the importance of this literature to his authors, though he nowhere makes the connection between this strain and the appropriateness of the book's title.) In addition, the very notion of a renaissance, a period of roiling tension, when the new rushes in over all that is established, often creating a kind of rip tide of change, might have appealed to Matthiessen as appropriate to the United States of the 1850s. Nor—to be still more speculative—may it be coincidence alone that both the English Renaissance and what Matthiessen named the American Renaissance came to their more or less decisive ends with the cataclysm of prolonged Civil War.

7. Quoted by Jay Fliegelman in his Introduction to Charles Brockden Brown, *Wieland* (New York: Penguin, 1991), p. xxxvi.

8. John Jay Chapman, *Selected Writings,* ed. Jacques Barzun (New York: Farrar, Straus and Cudahy, 1957), p. 144.

9. David Reynolds, *Beneath the American Renaissance* (Cambridge, Mass.: Harvard University Press, 1988) warns us against taking Whitman's "indolent loafing persona [as being in] direct opposition to an increasingly capitalistic American culture" because Reynolds's diligent research revealed "a whole class of so-called loafers ... mainly young working-class men and women who had been impelled by hard times to reject normal capitalist pursuits" (p. 64). How Whitman's voluntary identification with this "loaferdom" invalidates the characterization is not clear to me.

10. Paul Zweig, *Walt Whitman: The Making of the Poet* (New York: Basic Books, 1984), p. 82. These descriptions are as much a matter of image as reality: Whitman worked as a carpenter as well and was not always so physically inactive.

11. Herschel Parker, *Herman Melville: A Biography Volume 1, 1819–1851* (Baltimore, Md.: Johns Hopkins University Press, 1996), p. 165.

12. Ibid.

13. Newton Arvin, *Herman Melville* (New York: William Sloane Associates, 1950), p. 78. As one instance of this amateur mentality, Melville explicitly

asked his publisher not to advertise his third novel, *Mardi*, as by the best-selling author of *Typee* and *Omoo*. See Parker, *Herman Melville*, p. 615.

14. The word "pontification" is not meant as derogatory but alludes to the "bridge-building"—the etymological root of pontificate—described in Kenneth Burke's "Aye, Eye, I in Emerson," in *Language as Symbolic Action: Essays on Life, Literature and Method* (Berkeley: University of California Press, 1966).

15. Deut. 6:4–9.

16. Stanley Cavell, *The Senses of Walden: An Expanded Edition* (San Francisco: North Point Press, 1981), pp. 153–154.

17. Ralph Waldo Emerson, *The Journals and Miscellaneous Notebooks*, ed. William H. Gilman et al. (Cambridge, Mass.: Harvard University Press, 1960–1982), vol. IV, p. 274.

18. The anti-Federalists tried to point this out without much success. Theirs was not the last experience in the history of revolutions where political opposition is fatally weakened by having to assume the rhetorical burden of opposing "the People."

10. Essays in Time

1. Henry James, "*A Memoir of Ralph Waldo Emerson* by James Elliot Cabot" in *Literary Criticism* (New York: Library of America, 1984), p. 271.

2. Ibid., p. 270.

3. Ralph Waldo Emerson, "Intellect," in *Essays and Lectures*, ed. Joel Porte (New York: Library of America, 1985), p. 412.

4. Ibid., "Nature" in *Essays*, p. 550.

5. Ibid., "Nominalist and Realist," in *Essays*, p. 587.

6. Ibid., "Prudence," in *Essays*, p. 360.

7. Ibid., "Circles," in *Essays*, p. 412.

8. Ibid., "Spiritual Laws," in *Essays*, p. 316.

9. Ibid., "Compensation," in *Essays*, p. 289.

10. Ibid., "The Over Soul," in *Essays*, p. 391.

11. Ralph Waldo Emerson, *The Selected Letters of Ralph Waldo Emerson*, ed. Joel Myerson (New York: Columbia University Press, 1997), p. 177.

12. Ralph Waldo Emerson, *Letters*, eds. Ralph Rusk and Eleanor M. Tilton (New York: Columbia University Press, 1939; 1990–1995), vol. 2, 378.

13. Ralph Waldo Emerson, *Emerson in His Journals*, ed. Joel Porte, (Cambridge, Mass.: Harvard University Press, 1982), p. 378.

14. Ralph Waldo Emerson, *The Journals and Miscellaneous Notebooks*, ed. William H. Gilman et al. (Cambridge, Mass.: Harvard University Press, 1960–1982), 11:327.

15. Ibid., 8:106.

16. Ibid., 10:329.

17. Ibid., 4: 87.

18. Emerson, "Nature," *Essays*, p. 48.

19. Ralph Waldo Emerson, "The Snowstorm," in *Nineteenth Century Poetry,* ed. John Hollander (New York: Library of America, 1993), vol. 1, p. 174.
20. Emerson, "Self Reliance," *Essays,* p. 262.
21. Ibid., p. 271.
22. Emerson, *Emerson in His Journals,* p. 460.
23. Ibid.
24. Emerson, *Journals and Miscellaneous Notebooks,* 10:76.
25. *The Cambridge Companion to Ralph Waldo Emerson,* eds. Joel Porte and Saundra Morris (Cambridge, Mass.: Cambridge University Press, 1999), p. 8.
26. Alexis de Tocqueville, *Democracy in America,* ed. J. P. Mayer, trans. George Lawrence (New York: Doubleday, 1969), p. 453. This is a helpful reminder to those who believe that the attitudes of our current "computer revolution" represent something particularly recent or new. Anticipated obsolescence is a part of our ironic "American tradition."
27. Tocqueville, *Democracy in American,* p. 482.
28. Emerson, *Journals and Miscellaneous Notebooks,* 7:111.
29. Ralph Waldo Emerson, *Essays: Second Series,* in *The Collected Works of Ralph Waldo Emerson.* ed. Robert E. Spiller with an Introduction by Joseph Slater (Cambridge, Mass.: Harvard University Press, 1971–) p. xxiv.
30. Ibid., p. xxv.
31. Ibid., p. xxvi.
32. Emerson, *Journals and Miscellaneous Notebooks,* 10:151.
33. Ibid.
34. Ibid., 10:79.
35. Ibid., 8:420.
36. See Lionel Trilling, *Sincerity and Authenticity* (New York: Harcourt, Brace, Javanovitch, 1972).
37. Emerson, "Nominalist and Realist," in *Essays,* p. 587.
38. Emerson, "Circles," in *Essays,* p. 406.
39. Ibid., p. 409.
40. Ibid., p. 413.
41. Emerson, *Emerson in His Journals,* p. 466.
42. There is a very costly scholarly edition, with an elaborately exact apparatus meant to reproduce precisely every mark and gesture one might discern looking at the actual handwritten pages themselves, though many of these sixteen volumes have been out of print as well. The Library of America series has been promising such a reader's edition of the Journals more or less since its inception decades ago.
43. Emerson, *Journals and Miscellaneous Notebooks,* 5:40.
44. Barbara Packer, "Origin and Authority: Emerson and the Higher Criticism," *Reconstructing American Literary History* (Cambridge, Mass.: Harvard University Press, 1986), p. 91.
45. Geoffrey H. Hartman, "The Struggle for the Text," in *Midrash and Literature* (New Haven, Conn.: Yale University Press, 1986), p. 5.

46. Ibid., p. 13.
47. See, for instance, Alfred Kazin's picturesque description of Emerson in *American Procession* (New York: Alfred A. Knopf, 1984). It must be said, however, that from the facts of his biography Emerson's disapproval of novels was a principle more honored in the breach than the observance. Indeed in his Journals he complains of Thoreau's intolerance of the habit among young clerks: "You do us wrong, Henry T., in railing at the novel reading. The novel is that allowance & frolic their imagination gets. Everything else pins it down" (*Emerson in His Journals,* p. 369).
48. Joel Porte, *Representative Man: Ralph Waldo Emerson in His Time* (New York: Oxford University Press, 1979), p. xiii.
49. Michel de Montaigne, *The Complete Essays of Montaigne.* trans. Donald M. Frame (Stanford, Calif.: Stanford University Press, 1965), p. xvi.
50. Emerson, "Self Reliance" in *Essays,* p. 265.
51. Montaigne, "Of Repentance," in *The Complete Essays,* p. 611.
52. Ibid., p. 610.
53. Emerson, *Journals and Miscellaneous Notebooks,* 7:68.

11. A Poetic Form for Straying

1. Herman Melville, "Hawthorne and His Mosses," in *The Shock of Recognition: The Development of American Literature by the Men Who Made It,* ed. Edmund Wilson (New York: Doubleday, 1943), p. 199.
2. Ralph Waldo Emerson, *The Selected Letters of Ralph Waldo Emerson,* ed. Joel Myerson (New York: Columbia University Press, 1997), p. 384.
3. Robert D. Richardson Jr., *Emerson: The Mind on Fire* (Berkeley: University of California Press, 1995), p. 528.
4. Ibid., p. 530.
5. A "b'hoy," or Bowery b'hoy was New York slang for a young working-class man who played at upper-class life, frequenting Shakespeare plays and operas, but with a tough reputation, possessed of what we now call street smarts.
6. Richardson, *Emerson,* p. 529.
7. An impulse to see Whitman as a prophet rather than a poet began with his earliest disciples, Horace Traubel and William O'Connor, and probably reached its height with the work of R. M. Bucke's "cosmic consciousness."
8. Whitman, "Song of Myself," *Walt Whitman: Poetry and Prose,* ed. Justin Kaplan (New York: Library of America, 1982).
9. In his very inventive and suggestive critical essay, "The Poetics of Union in Whitman and Lincoln: An Inquiry toward the Relationship of Art and Policy," in The *American Renaissance Reconsidered,* ed. Walter Benn Michaels and Donald E. Pease (Baltimore, Md.: Johns Hopkins University Press, 1985), Allen Grossman has examined the "poetics of union" as found in the poetry of Whitman and the policy of Lincoln. In both he sees an antihierarchical valuing of the person, although he distinguishes Whitman

from Lincoln in the poet's reader needing to engage in a "continual critique." Although Grossman's formulations have had no part in this thesis, his determined and imaginative engagement with discerning a relation between the founding texts and the development of American poetry served as an inspiring confirmation of my own intuitions.

10. All twelve poems, in various revised versions, were republished in one or another of the subsequent editions of *Leaves of Grass,* with titles.

11. Tenny Nathanson, *Whitman's Presence: Body, Voice and Writing in Leaves of Grass* (New York: New York University Press, 1992), p. 179.

12. Ibid., p. 181.

13. Ibid., p. 180.

14. John Jay Chapman, "Walt Whitman," in *The Selected Writings of John Jay Chapman,* ed. Jacques Barzun (New York: Farrar, Straus and Cudahy, 1957), p. 145.

15. Ibid., p. 144.

16. Harold Bloom, "The Real Me," *The New York Review of Books* 31 (April 26, 1984).

17. Richard Poirier, *The Renewal of Literature: Emersonian Reflections* (New York: Random House, 1987), p. 70.

18. Ibid., pp. 68–69.

19. Ibid., p. 83.

20. Whitman, "Song of Myself."

21. This makes Chapman's remark about Whitman as a tramp a good deal more insightful than it first appears or than he fully expresses.

22. Quoted in Kerry Larson, *Whitman's Drama of Consensus* (Chicago: University of Chicago Press, 1988), p. xxii.

23. Jerome Loving, *Walt Whitman: The Song of Himself* (Berkeley: University of California Press, 1999), p. 234.

24. Harold Bloom, *The Western Canon: the Books and the School of the Ages* (New York: Harcourt Brace, 1994), p. 286.

25. Hannah Arendt, *Between Past and Future: Eight Exercises in Political Thought* (New York: Penguin Books, 1977), pp. 92–93.

26. It should be noted that many of the most prominent of the Founders, both those at the Convention and those not, were not—later-day pleading notwithstanding—traditionally pious men. See the admittedly argumentative, but devastating, account of their relative irreligion in Isaac Kramnick and R. Laurence Moore, *The Godless Constitution: The Case Against Religious Correctness* (New York: W. W. Norton, 1996).

12. Clinging to Narrative

1. Of course, these are only general characterizations of prodigious imaginative minds. Emerson, for instance—"Oh, you man without a handle" as Henry James Sr. said of him—was perfectly capable even in his early years of noting the seeming impossibility of connecting the two states between which he

makes his transitions: "The worst feature of this double consciousness is that the two lives, of the understanding and of the soul, which we lead really show very little relation to each other, never meet and measure each other: one prevails now, all buzz and din; and the other prevails then, all infinitude and paradise; and, with the progress of life, the two discover no greater disposition to reconcile themselves." Emerson, "The Transcendentalism," in *Essays and Lectures,* ed. Joel Porte (New York: Library of America, 1985), pp. 205–206.

2. Carl Van Doren, *The Great Rehearsal; The Story of the Making and Ratifying of the Constitution of the United States* (New York: Viking Press, 1948), pp. 239–240.

3. Herman Melville, *Redburn, White-Jacket, Moby-Dick,* ed. G. Thomas Tanselle (New York: Library of America, 1983), p. 921 (Chapter 27). The reference is to Baron Jean Baptiste de Cloots, a Prussian supporter of the French Revolution who led a delegation to the French National Assembly composed of representatives of the whole of the "human race" (1755–1794). See Alan Heimert's 1963 essay, "*Moby-Dick* and American Political Symbolism," *American Quarterly* 15 (Winter 1963), pp. 498–534. Also see Michael Paul Rogin's much celebrated political allegory of Melville's work, *Subversive Genealogy: The Politics and Art of Herman Melville* (New York: Alfred A. Knopf, 1983). For some, including this reader, Rogin's book is a learned and ingenious *reductio ad absurdum*—a genuine achievement of interpretation but misleading, at best, as literary criticism.

4. Emerson, "Nature," *Essays,* p. 48.

5. The one qualification to this statement is found in the words "a more perfect union." This is the only concession, subtle as it is, that something existed before the Constitution itself.

6. Erich Auerbach, *Mimesis: The Representation of Reality in Western Literature* (Princeton, N.J.: Princeton University Press, 1953), p. 20.

7. Steven V. Katona, Valerie Rough, and David T. Richardson, *A Field Guide to Whales, Porpoises and Seals from Cape Cod to Newfoundland* (Washington, D.C.: Smithsonian Institution Press, 1993), p. 140.

8. Job 41:1–2; 7.

9. Hanna Fenichel Pitkin, *The Concept of Representation* (Berkeley, University of California Press, 1967, pp. 92–143.

10. Charles Olson, *Call Me Ishmael: A Study of Melville* (New York: Grove Press, 1947), p. 19: "of 900 whaling vessels of all nations in 1846, 735 were American." There are, of course, some other novelistic candidates for emphatic descriptions of industry, including works by Frank Norris and Emile Zola.

11. *Moby-Dick,* p. 1012 (Chapter 45).

12. Ibid., 1019–1020 (Chapter 46).

13. One of Melville's finest critics of an earlier generation, Newton Arvin, put it with admirable succinctness: "to speak of *Moby-Dick*'s structure and texture . . . is to embark upon a series of paradoxes that are soberly truthful

and precise." Newton Arvin, *Herman Melville* (New York: William Sloane Associates, 1950), p. 151.

14. Whitman, *Complete Poetry and Collected Prose,* ed. Justin Kaplan (New York: Library of America, 1982), p. 5.

15. James Wood, "The All and the If: God and Metaphor in Melville," *The Broken Estate: Essays on Literature and Belief* (New York: Random House, 1999), p. 34.

16. Ibid., pp. 34–35.

17. Ralph Waldo Emerson, *The Journals and Miscellaneous Notebooks,* eds. William H. Gilman et al. (Cambridge, Mass.: Harvard University Press, 1960–1982), vol. 4, p. 87. Herman Melville, *The Letters of Herman Melville,* eds. Merrell R. Davis and William H. Gilman (New Haven, Conn.: Yale University Press, 1960), pp. 130–131.

18. Nina Baym, "Melville's Quarrel with Fiction," *PMLA: Publications of the Modern Language Association of America* 94 (1979), p. 912.

19. Northrop Frye, *An Anatomy of Criticism* (New York: Athenaeum, 1968), p. 304.

20. E. M. Forster, *Aspects of the Novel* (New York: Harcourt Brace Jovanovich, 1955; originally 1927), p. 125.

21. Richard Brodhead, *The School of Hawthorne* (New York: Oxford University Press 1986), p. 41.

22. Ibid., p. 44.

23. Nathaniel Hawthorne, *Novels,* ed. Millicent Bell (New York: Library of America, 1983), p. 351.

24. Joel Porte, *The Romance in America: Studies in Cooper, Poe, Hawthorne, Melville and James* (Middletown, Conn.: Wesleyan University Press, 1969), p. xi.

25. Herman Melville, *Moby-Dick,* eds. Herschel Parker and Harrison Hayford (New York: W. W. Norton, 2001), p. 640.

26. Melville, *Moby-Dick,* ed. Parker, p. 640.

27. Lawrence Buell, "*Moby-Dick* as Sacred Text," *New Essays on Moby-Dick,* ed. Richard H. Brodhead (New York: Cambridge University Press, 1986), p. 53.

28. Ibid., p. 69.

29. See Robert Frost's poem, "Design of Darkness," a miniaturized revision of Melville's vision, as if looking with the novelist's eye through the wrong end of a telescope.

30. *Moby-Dick,* ed. Tanselle, p. 1076 (Chapter 55).

31. Ibid., p. 1165 (Chapter 79).

32. Exodus 2:33:21–23.

33. Michael Polanyi, *The Tacit Dimension* (New York: Doubleday and Co., 1966), p. 4.

34. Melville, *Letters,* p. 142.

35. *Moby-Dick,* ed. Tanselle, p. 1001 (Chapter 42).

13. Confidence and the Darkness of Revelation

1. Emerson, "Self Reliance" in *Essays and Lectures,* ed. Joel Porte (New York: Library of America, 1985), p. 260.

2. It is rather as if Napoleon, instead of taking the imperial crown from the Pope and putting it upon his own head, were to have performed the whole ceremony singlehandedly, offering the crown himself and leaping across to an opposite position in order to receive it.

3. Emerson, "Self Reliance," *Essays,* p. 262.

4. Melville, *Redburn, White-Jacket, Moby-Dick,* ed. G. Thomas Tanselle (New York: Library of America, 1983), p. 967 (Chapter 36).

5. Melville, *Moby-Dick,* p. 1334 (Chapter 119).

6. Herman Melville, *The Letters of Herman Melville,* eds. Merrell R. Davis and William H. Gilman (New Haven, Conn.: Yale University Press, 1960), p. 125.

7. Herman Melville, *Pierre, Israel Potter, The Piazza Tales, The Confidence Man, Billy Budd,* ed. Harrison Hayford ((New York: Library of America, 1983), p. 848 (Chapter 2).

8. Herman Melville, *The Confidence-Man,* ed. Herschel Parker (New York: W. W. Norton, 1971), pp. 227–228.

9. Ibid.

10. Although all the standard annotations (e.g., Hershel Parker's Norton edition) describe these as citations from 1 Corinthians, they are not, in fact, exact quotations but very slight adaptations, taking the phrases out of a series and making independent statements of them: "Charity suffereth long, *and* is kind; charity envieth not; charity vaunteth not itself, is not puffed up, doth not behave itself unseemly, seeketh not her own, is not easily provoked, thinketh no evil; rejoiceth not in iniquity, but rejoiceth in the truth; beareth all things, believeth all things, hopeth all things, endureth all things" (1 Corinthians 13:4–7).

11. For those who are curious, in *Moby-Dick,* which is over twice the length of *The Confidence-Man,* "trust" in its various forms shows up a scant fifteen times.

12. Elizabeth Renker, " 'A———!': Unreadability in *The Confidence-Man,*" *The Cambridge Companion to Herman Melville,* ed. Robert S. Levine (Cambridge: Cambridge University Press, 1998), pp. 114–134.

13. Ibid., p. 114.

14. Melville, *The Confidence-Man,* ed. Parker, p. ix.

15. Melville, *The Confidence-Man,* ed. Hayford, p. 846 (Chapter 2).

16. Emerson, "Self Reliance," *Essays,* p. 262.

17. It is the last great fiction, unless one reserves this honor for Hawthorne's *Marble Faun.*

18. Melville, *The Confidence-Man,* p. 1112 (Chapter 45).

19. Renker, "A———!" p. 132.

20. Melville, *The Confidence-Man,* p. 1112 (Chapter 45).

Conclusion: The Literary Art of Uniting States

1. Harold Bloom, *The American Religion: The Emergence of the Post-Christian Nation* (New York: Simon and Schuster, 1992).
2. Ibid., pp. 266–271.
3. This story can be found in the Babylonian Talmud, Tractate *BAVA MET21A*, Chapter 4, 59A–59B.
4. Joseph Conrad, *The Collected Letters of Joseph Conrad Vol. 3 1903–1907*, eds. Frederick R. Karl and Laurence Davies (New York: Cambridge University Press 1988), p. 409.
5. Wallace Stevens, *Collected Poetry and Prose*, eds. Frank Kermode and Joan Richardson (New York: Library of America, 1997), p. 903.
6. Noam Yuran, "Philosopher and cultural gadfly Slavoj Zizek, on a mini-lecture tour, talks to Ha'aretz" Ha'aretz, January 15, 2003 (English edition: www.haaretz.co.il) The somewhat garbled syntax is evidently a result of the interview source of the comments.
7. The judgment is found in one of his important books on the peculiarities of American literary culture, *Pragmatism and Poetry* (Cambridge, Mass.: Harvard University Press, 1992), p. 158.

Index